Women of Color and the Reproductive Rights Movement

Women of Color
and the Reproductive
Rights Movement

Jennifer Nelson

NEW YORK UNIVERSITY PRESS
New York and London

NEW YORK UNIVERSITY PRESS
New York and London
www.nyupress.org

Library of Congress Cataloging-in Publication Data
Nelson, Jennifer, 1967–
Women of color and the reproductive rights movement /
Jennifer Nelson.
p. cm.
Includes bibliographical references.
ISBN 0–8147–5821–5 (cloth : alk. paper) —
ISBN 0–8147–5827–4 (pbk : alk. paper)
1. Birth control—United States—History—20th century.
2. Abortion—United States—History—20th century.   3. Minority
women—United States—History—20th century.   4. Sterilization
(Birth control)—United States—History—20th century.
5. Women's rights—United States—History—20th century.
6. Feminism—United States—History—20th century.   I. title.
HQ766.5.U5N45   2003
363. 46—dc21   2003008028

New York University Press books are printed on acid-free paper,
and their binding materials are chosen for strength and durability.

Manufactured in the United States of America

10 9 8 7 6 5 4

This book is dedicated to
Jane Nelson and Nicholas Pierre.

Contents

Acknowledgments

I could never have completed the dissertation that served as the basis for this book without the invaluable help of Alice Kessler-Harris, my dissertation advisor. She encouraged me when I wasn't sure I could get all the pieces of the story to fit together in a coherent manner, and she sent me back to the computer screen when she believed I could do better. I also received very useful comments and advice from the other members of my dissertation committee: Dee Garrison, Cynthia Daniels, and James Reed. Portions of the manuscript were read and commented on at various stages by other Rutgers history department faculty: Nancy Newitt, Virginia Yans, Phyllis Mack, and Jackson Lears. I also received support and encouragement during my coursework at Rutgers, particularly from Professors Jennifer Jones and Deborah White. I thank these people for all their help and for the lively women's history community they have created at Rutgers. Several of my graduate student peers, including Jennifer Milligan, Beatrix Hoffman, Amy Forbes, Rebecca Hartman, and Rebecca Gershenson, gave of their time in reading and critiquing chapters and provided much needed friendship and companionship. Rutgers departmental fellowships assisted me with financial support to complete my research and writing. A Rockefeller Archive Center Research Grant and an American Historical Association Albert J. Beveridge Research Grant helped fund valuable research trips.

My readers at NYU Press, including Rickie Solinger and Loretta Ross, supplied excellent suggestions for revisions as I completed the arduous task of turning a Ph.D. dissertation into a book manuscript. Jennifer Hammer, editor at NYU Press, read and reread the manuscript with a keen eye for detail in the final stages of revision.

Grateful acknowledgment is given to Indiana University Press for permission to reprint my chapter on abortion and the Young Lords that originally appeared in the *Journal of Women's History* 13, no. 1 (2001).

Of course, this book could not have been written without the help I received from the women who spoke with me about their experiences in the women's liberation and reproductive rights movement. I thank them for their commitment to getting their stories told.

I also want to thank Michael Harper of the Creative Writing Department at Brown University for recognizing my potential as a student and a scholar and for stressing the importance of history.

Finally, I thank my father, Jerold Nelson, for always encouraging me in every worthwhile endeavor I undertake.

Women of Color and the
Reproductive Rights Movement

Introduction

From Abortion to Reproductive Rights

In 1973, Guadalupe Acosta, a poor Mexican woman living in Los Angeles, gave birth at the University of Southern California-Los Angeles County Medical Center to an encephalic child who died shortly after delivery.[1] After her labor Acosta's obstetrician sterilized her without her consent. At a postnatal check-up, Acosta requested the pill; her doctor chose that moment to inform her that she no longer had any need for contraception because she could no longer conceive. The doctor insisted that her husband had signed a consent form authorizing her sterilization. Acosta's husband denied the charge, adding that he would never consent to a termination of his wife's reproductive capacity. Acosta, along with 10 other Los Angeles Chicanas with similar experiences, brought a lawsuit against Los Angeles County Hospital, the anonymous doctors who performed their sterilizations, the state of California, and the U.S. Department of Health, Education, and Welfare. Maria Hustado, another woman involved in the case, told of her sterilization: "I do not remember the doctor telling me anything about tubalization. All that I remember is after the doctor injected my dorsal, spinal cord, he told me, 'Mama sign here. No more babies. Sign here.'"[2]

Acosta and Hustado's stories are emblematic of how many poor women of color lost their ability to bear children through involuntary sterilization, but, in 1973, few mainstream feminists viewed ending sterilization abuse as an important demand in the fight for women's reproductive freedom. For most white women involved in women's liberation, reproductive freedom meant access to safe legal abortion and contraception. Yet, by the late 1970s, many white feminists had expanded their definition of reproductive freedom beyond abortion rights. In response to arguments made by women of color that legal abortion was not synonymous with reproductive freedom, reproductive rights feminists came to maintain that the right to bear children was as important to reproductive freedom as the legal right to terminate a pregnancy.

Most people believe that the movement to secure voluntary reproductive control for women centered on abortion rights. This perspective is understandable given that most of the writing concerning this movement focuses on the fight for legal abortion. It is essential, however, that we understand that for some women, abortion was not the only, or even primary, focus. For poor women and women of color, the right to bear healthy children and to raise them out of poverty was equally important. Women of color challenged the white middle-class feminist movement to recognize that the abortion rights movement needed to encompass "bread and butter" issues such as health care for the poor, child-care, and welfare rights in addition to anti–sterilization abuse efforts. By examining the larger movement for reproductive rights, rather than abortion rights, we begin to appreciate the importance of the contributions women of color made to the political movement to achieve reproductive autonomy—broadly defined—for all women regardless of race or economic class. This book tells the story of the feminist struggle for legal abortion and reproductive rights in the 1960s, 1970s, and early 1980s. It argues that feminism was central to the development of a reproductive rights discourse that began with the drive to legalize abortion and culminated in a broad-based grassroots movement to make reproductive control—including the right to bear children—a reality for all women regardless of economic status, race, or sexual identity.

In telling the story of the reproductive rights movement, this book also revisits the volatile debates that raged at the time—between second wave feminists, women of color, and Black and Puerto Rican Nationalists—around the controversial idea that fertility control among people of color equaled genocide. These debates brought popular public attention to the differences between coercive forms of national population control policy and personal autonomy over fertility. Individuals within all of these groups argued that population control rhetoric, although distinct from feminism, had tainted mainstream feminists' advocacy of individual fertility control for people of color and the poor. Criticism of population control rhetoric by black and Latino men and women ultimately led second wave feminists to rethink their abortion politics in order to create an inclusive movement for reproductive rights that took into account the particular reproductive experiences of poor women and women of color. As a result, problems of sterilization abuse, pre- and postnatal health care, and child-care became mainstays of a new feminist reproductive rights movement by the late 1970s and early 1980s.

Initially, many white middle-class feminists viewed the campaign for legal abortion as the most important goal in a struggle for women's reproductive autonomy. According to Susan Brownmiller, a member of New York City's radical feminist group Redstockings, founded in 1968, and author of the influential and controversial book *Against Our Will* about rape in the United States, abortion "made" second wave feminism in the late 1960s. The first of the second wave feminists, referred to as women's liberationists by those involved in the movement, met in small consciousness-raising groups to discuss what they saw as the primary problems contributing to unequal power relationships between men and women.[3] The demand for safe and legal abortion surfaced again and again in these discussions as one of the most pressing issues for women's liberation. After all, the women asserted, access to abortion and reproductive freedom was a matter of life and death.[4]

Feminists viewed abortion as central to their lives because so many of them had personally encountered the terror of an unwanted pregnancy and/or an illegal abortion. Ellen Willis, another Redstocking and well-known feminist journalist, agreed with Brownmiller that abortion dominated the agenda of second wave feminism in the late 1960s because it was a "concrete practical issue." She recalled that everybody knew somebody who had had an illegal abortion. Willis herself aided an acquaintance who suffered a botched illegal abortion. Bleeding profusely, the woman was rushed to the hospital and nearly died. Willis described the "enormous anguish that came with pregnancy scares," and the frustration associated with the search for a way to terminate an unwanted pregnancy. She also criticized those who dismissed the abortion rights movement by claiming that white and middle-class women always had access to safe abortion, as long as they had money. She countered that many white and middle-class women experienced tremendous difficulty finding an abortionist, particularly if they were young or unmarried. Furthermore, she argued, no woman should have to demean herself by begging and borrowing for an abortion when she had decided she wanted to terminate a pregnancy. Willis boldly declared, abortion rights was about "asserting autonomy and subjecthood; it was about the right to have sex, play God, to bring life into the world. This freaked people out."[5]

Yet women of color and poor women told a different story about their lack of reproductive control in the pre-*Roe v. Wade* period. While women of color and poor women lacked access to abortion and contraception, they also encountered reproductive abuses such as forced or coerced sterilization. Twentieth-century reproductive coercion among African-American women dates to the 1930s when southern states created publicly funded birth control clinics to lower the black birth rate.[6] The problem of sterilization abuse first came to popular public attention as members of Black Nationalist groups—including the Nation of Islam and the Black Panther Party—pointed out that poor women of color were often sterilized without their knowledge. Indeed, physicians in many states used eugenic sterilization laws, passed in the first two decades of the twentieth century, to justify the sterilization of poor and often very young women of color. In the late 1960s, as federal birth control programs were expanded under the Johnson administration, Black Nationalists argued that any birth control rhetoric that suggested population reduction would help alleviate poverty was not in the interest of people of color and termed these "population control" efforts genocidal. The 1973 sterilization of Minnie Lee Relf, an African American teenager who was sterilized without her knowledge or consent at a federally funded health clinic in Montgomery, Alabama, demonstrated when it became a public scandal that contraceptive providers judged women of color "incompetent" to make decisions about their reproductive lives.[7]

Women of color agreed with Black Nationalists that coerced fertility control was racist and abusive. For the most part, however, they wanted to control their fertility voluntarily, and they were willing to look to the state for contraceptive support. But the state needed to provide more than contraception. Women of color insisted that reproductive control meant having access to legal abortion and contraception, as well as access to the economic means to bear and raise healthy wanted children. They separated themselves from nationalist men of color on this issue, and they also separated themselves from white and mainstream feminists who made legal abortion the highest priority in the feminist movement. Women of color pushed for a more complex reproductive rights discourse: one that acknowledged that different women had varying reproductive experiences, in part, depending on their race and class position. These particular experiences constituted the need for different demands in a reproductive rights movement. Certainly, if you didn't have the means to have a child, if you were sterilized against your will or without your knowledge because a health care provider believed your race or your economic class made you incompetent to make decisions over your own fertility, legal abortion was not the most important issue for you. Women of color argued that if members of the feminist movement were to live up to their claim that they represented all women, they needed to create a reproductive rights agenda that put the needs of women of color, working women, and poor women at the center. This meant coupling demands for legal abortion and contraception with demands for an end to forced or coerced sterilization and economic guarantees that even poor women could bear the children they wanted.[8]

While they shared beliefs with mainstream and white feminists, feminists of color did not make easy alliances with white women and were skeptical that white women understood the particular experiences of women of color. For example, some mainstream white feminists of the early 1970s wanted to make access to sterilization into an issue of reproductive choice. Physicians often rejected white middle-class women for sterilization if they were young and had no children. It was assumed these women would change their minds and want children later in life. Because of these experiences, white middle-class women were not supportive of the initial suggestion by women of color that sterilization regulations needed to be more stringent; the Committee to End Sterilization Abuse (CESA), a group that formed in 1974 to regulate female sterilization in New York City, proposed a 30-day mandatory waiting period before a woman could become sterilized. Some white feminists argued that a waiting period further restricted a woman's choice to limit her fertility. Women of color, however, understood that sterilization was often not a matter of choice—that women of color had been sterilized without their knowledge or consent.

Depending on their feminist framework, feminist groups had very different perspectives on the meaning of abortion and reproductive rights. In this book, I focus on the radical feminist organization Redstockings in New York City, founded in 1967, women of color organizations prominent in the 1970s, and the socialist feminist group, the Committee for Abortion Rights and Against Sterilization Abuse (CARASA), also based in New York City and founded in 1976. I focus on Redstockings for several reasons. First, Redstockings activists made abortion and reproductive rights central to their feminist philosophy. While local affiliates of the liberal feminist organization, the National Organization for Women (NOW), including NOW New York City, were committed to the abortion rights movement, National NOW members were ambivalent about abortion rights at their 1966 formation. Furthermore, equality feminists, including NOW members, were more focused on political issues that concerned women's "public" condition in the workplace, in education, and in government than on "personal" issues of sexuality or reproduction. Radical feminists, like Redstockings, tended to focus on women's "personal" experiences of oppression in heterosexual sexual relations, the nuclear family structure, experiences of reproduction, and gender roles. They believed that to concentrate on women's personal oppression was to get at the origin of women's subjugation. Rather than turn to the courts or the legislature to promote women's equality like NOW, radical feminists formed small-unstructured "consciousness-raising" groups and developed their own feminist theory from their personal experiences. From their consciousness-raising, groups of radical feminists planned actions that would disseminate their new theoretical understanding.[9]

Both Redstockings and CARASA are central to my argument because both are part of the history of the feminist redefinition of the meaning of abortion. Redstockings made abortion into an issue of women's autonomy in the years immediately preceding the 1973 Supreme Court decision legalizing abortion, *Roe v. Wade*. They were some of the first feminists to demonstrate that abortion concerned women's bodies and, therefore, should be controlled by women, not male doctors, lawyers, judges, or legislators. Several years after legal abortion had been achieved with *Roe v. Wade*, CARASA, a socialist feminist organization, redefined abortion rights yet again by placing it within an economic context of linked demands that were necessary to guarantee even the poorest women reproductive autonomy. As a group that grew out of protest against the Hyde Amendment that ended federal Medicaid payments for abortion in 1976, they were particularly attuned to the reproductive demands being made by women of color and the poor in the 1970s. CARASA activists believed that by ending federal support for abortion, and by continuing funding for sterilization, the U.S. government promoted permanent methods of population control for poor women and women of color, while making nonpermanent methods of fertility control such as abortion less available.

CARASA members also argued that the state had an obligation to provide all women with the concrete means to bear as many children as they wanted; this guarantee required affordable and legal abortion and contraception, an end to sterilization abuse, and affordable access to prenatal care, child-care, and health care for both women and their children. These demands became the staple of a broadly constructed reproductive rights discourse, intended to improve access to reproductive control for poor and minority women who had the least reproductive autonomy. Reproductive rights feminists active after 1973 believed that while white and middle-class women may have secured a measure of power over their own reproduction with *Roe v. Wade*, no woman could claim true reproductive control until all women lived it.

The organizations of women of color I discuss are of two sorts. Some women of color addressed reproductive politics from within nationalist organizations that grew out of the civil rights movement after it shifted to Black Power such as the Black Panther Party, initially founded in Oakland, California, in 1966 to fight police brutality against African Americans, and the Young Lords Party, a Puerto Rican Nationalist group founded in New York City in 1970 and modeled on the Black Panthers. Women in both of these groups voiced their opposition to the belief, often adopted by nationalist groups as a whole, that all contraceptive use by women of color equaled genocide. They argued that people of color needed to distinguish between reproductive abuses such as coerced or forced sterilization and the choice to limit fertility voluntarily. By giving voice to these sentiments, women of color pushed both the Black Panthers and the Young Lords from within their nationalist organizations to embrace voluntary reproductive control.

Other women of color created their own feminist organizations autonomous from men of color. The women in these organizations—including the Black Women's Liberation Group of Mount Vernon, the Black Women's Liberation Committee (which grew out of SNCC), the Third World Women's Alliance, and the National Welfare Rights Organization (NWRO), a group primarily consisting of poor African-American women—were also critical of Black Nationalists, who equated any form of birth control used by women of color with genocide.

A History of Abortion Rights

To understand the feminist movement for abortion and reproductive rights, we need to place it within the larger historical context of abortion rights in the twentieth century. Abortion until "quickening"—when the mother felt the fetus move—was legal as a matter of common law in the United States until the middle of the nineteenth century. Nineteenth-century campaigners against abortion partially justified their opposition to abortion on grounds that it was more dangerous to women than pregnancy. By the beginning of the twentieth century, the anti-abortion campaign had succeeded in making abortion illegal in all states, but anti-abortion laws did not prevent women from choosing to abort unwanted pregnancies. Historian Leslie Reagan notes that early twentieth-century women had abortions in large numbers. She suggests that at least a tacit acceptance of abortion existed among most Americans despite its illegality, as is evidenced by the large numbers of women who were able to secure safe, illegal abortions from physicians and midwives during this period. By the 1930s, although the number of abortions increased, the practice of abortion had begun to shift from midwives and the private practices of physicians to hospitals. This transformation ushered in a new era of abortion provision and state regulation in the 1940s.[10]

In the 1940s, hospitals established therapeutic abortion committees to regulate the number of abortions performed. They operated according to a narrow interpretation of state laws that allowed termination of a pregnancy that threatened a woman's life—the "medical exception." Their goal was to protect themselves from charges of immorality associated with abortion provision and potential prosecution for performing abortions that were not "necessary" to save the pregnant woman. In the first three decades of the century, private physicians and midwives provided abortions liberally by broadly interpreting the "medical exception" to the anti-abortion laws, particularly during the economically challenging years of the Great Depression, when protecting life could mean preventing the birth of a costly child. In the newly conservative 1940s, however, hospital committees approved only a handful of therapeutic "legal" abortions each year. By bestowing access to abortion on "deserving" patients, doctors could ensure that pregnant women did not become masters over their own fertility. Some physicians even required that a woman be sterilized after her hospital abortion, punishing her for her transgression—engaging in sex without wanting a child—by eliminating her right to motherhood.[11]

Hospital committees operated under severe limits during this period. A hospital could acquire a reputation as an abortion mill if it approved too many. Committees therefore maintained arbitrary quotas and many hospital administrators proudly published the low incidence of abortion at their institutions. Typically, a hospital committee developed a system that limited abortions to a few each month. White and middle-class women accounted for the vast majority of therapeutic abortion cases and there is evidence that physicians and hospital committees were willing to bend the rules and interpret therapeutic abortion more liberally for white middle-class women. Furthermore, low-income patients were more likely to be forcibly sterilized after a therapeutic abortion than their white middle-class equivalents. Given these circumstances, the abortion committee system actually decreased the availability of abortion for indigent women or those without connections. By making a few approved therapeutic abortions legal, hospital committees helped make all other abortions illegal (and more difficult to procure), even those provided by physicians outside of the hospital committee system. Additionally, abortion committees protected hospitals from attack by the Roman Catholic hierarchy. Before the 1970s, the Catholic Church represented the only organized opposition to abortion.[12]

Some women confronted with the dilemma of unwanted pregnancy during this period sought out illegal abortionists, risking their lives by trusting an anonymous individual with no official accreditation to recommend him. It is important to acknowledge, however, that many women did obtain safe abortions, even during the illegal period. There were physicians and skilled lay practitioners who continued to provide safe abortions despite the crackdown on all but hospital-approved procedures. Whether they obtained their abortion at the hands of a physician, a layperson, or in a hospital, almost all women had difficulty obtaining an abortion during this period. Some traveled long distances—to Puerto Rico, Mexico, England, Sweden, or Japan—to acquire an abortion. Many of these women followed the advice of friends, or friends of friends, who had had successful abortions and could suggest an abortionist. Despite the reassurance that many women survived the procedure, some women died at the hands of illegal abortionists. Others died at their own hands.[13]

Poor and young women usually had no informal network to lead them to an abortionist. Young, poor, and minority women either gave birth or chose to abort themselves when they could find no other alternative. Common strategies for self-abortion included throwing oneself down a long flight of stairs, pounding on one's belly, ingesting a concoction of toxic substances, or inserting toxic or sharp instruments into the uterus. Some of these women arrived at the hospital emergency room bleeding profusely hoping that a physician would complete the procedure. Hospital staff could hardly allow a woman to bleed to death on the emergency room floor. All these methods of self-abortion resulted in injury; sometimes they caused sterilization, or, worse yet, death.[14]

Before *Roe v. Wade* in 1973, women of color and poor women risked mutilation and death from illegal and self-abortion in far higher numbers than their white and middle-class counterparts by patronizing the most dangerous and inexpensive illegal abortionists. Women of color died from abortion-related complications nearly four times as often as white women. This disparity was directly related to a lack of access to quality health care experienced by women of color. Most legal therapeutic hospital abortions cost far too much for a poor woman—$600 to $800. Finally, few poor and minority women had the connections to locate physicians willing to perform safe illegal abortions.[15]

In the mid-1950s through the 1960s, many white male professionals, particularly psychiatrists, doctors, lawyers, and clergy, recognized the disastrous circumstances that the abortion statutes had created for women of reproductive age. They began to apply pressure to change the abortion laws. Each group had distinct reasons for campaigning for the reform of the abortion laws. Psychiatrists, who were often relied upon to diagnose severe depression in women requesting therapeutic abortions, were the first to criticize the hospital abortion system. Both psychiatrists and physicians believed that the committee system turned doctors who performed abortions into borderline criminals and removed medical practice from their control. Most of the doctors who joined the campaign for abortion law reform viewed abortion as a medical procedure that needed to be controlled and regulated by medical doctors, not by hospital administrators. Some physicians had witnessed the damage caused by illegal abortion and wanted to make the procedure legal and safe by providing more therapeutic abortions. Others, who had performed illegal abortions or who had referred women to abortionists, had a keen understanding of the powerful demand for reproductive control.

Similarly, abortion reform lawyers, who witnessed the blatant disregard of the anti-abortion laws, argued that the laws had become obsolete. They pointed out that anti-abortion legislation had been passed in the nineteenth century to protect women from dangerous surgery. As the medical danger of abortion declined in the twentieth century, abortion laws became increasingly anachronistic. Civil liberties lawyers, several of whom were associated with the American Civil Liberties Union (ACLU), believed that the anti-abortion laws violated a number of constitutional rights, including both the right to privacy and equal protection under the law.

Protestant clergy members, such as the Reverend Howard Moody of the Judson Memorial Church in New York City and head of the Clergy

Consultation Service, became involved in the movement for legal abortion by helping women to acquire safe, illegal abortions. Many clergy felt drawn to this role because they viewed abortion as a moral life-and-death issue that individuals had a right to control as it affected their own lives. They hoped that by helping to repeal the abortion laws they could alleviate suffering among women who would abort regardless of the law. Clergy also reconfigured abortion as a social problem rather than strictly a medical problem.[16]

In 1965, several doctors and lawyers formed the Association for the Study of Abortion (ASA) in New York City. They believed the existing abortion laws were ineffective, because women continued to have illegal abortions, and harmful, because women regularly died from illegal abortions. The ASA included prominent New York City professionals such as Dr. Robert Hall, the president of the group and then associate professor of obstetrics at Columbia University, Dr. Alan Guttmacher, president of the Planned Parenthood Federation, and Harriet Pilpel, a lawyer (who, with a team of lawyers, argued the landmark contraceptive case *Griswold v. Connecticut* in front of the Supreme Court in 1965) and advocate for liberalized abortion laws. These activists used the panic around the drug Thalidomide to spotlight their reform efforts, part of which focused on the right of the medical profession to perform abortions under the existing laws.

Thalidomide was used frequently by women in Europe and America as a sleeping pill and to prevent morning sickness until 1961, when an Australian physician first linked the drug to severe birth defects in the fetus. Although evidence existed suggesting that a woman who had taken Thalidomide would likely give birth to a deformed child, an abortion under these circumstances would still have to be approved by a hospital committee.[17]

In 1962, Sherri Finkbine, a 29-year-old mother of four children, who hosted a children's television program in Phoenix, Arizona, chose to abort her fetus because she had taken Thalidomide early in her pregnancy. Finkbine believed that the chances her baby would be deformed were high, so she consulted her physician about an abortion. He agreed to perform it after approval by a hospital committee. At first, the committee seemed ready to grant the abortion. Subsequently, however, hospital administrators denied Finkbine's abortion when her lawyers failed to win a suit of declaratory judgment, allowing the surgeon to perform the abortion without violating Arizona state law. That decision, along with intense national publicity, made hospital administrators afraid of prosecution by the state of Arizona. After pursuing several dead ends, Finkbine flew to Stockholm, Sweden for a legal abortion. Finkbine's case revealed to a riveted nation the agonies a middle-class white woman might have to go through to obtain a therapeutic abortion.[18]

As a result of these events, the ASA began to push for the American Law Institute's (ALI) Model Penal Code of an abortion law, drafted in 1959. The ALI proposal would allow abortion in the event that there was "substantial risk" that the pregnancy would cause the woman's death; that the pregnancy would seriously impair the physical or mental health of the mother; that the child would be born with severe defects; or, if the pregnancy had been a result of rape or incest.[19] The Code also suggested that a licensed physician with the written referral of two additional physicians perform the abortion. Ultimately, the ALI law would have made abortion legal in cases already accepted by many hospitals. If passed, however, a state would no longer be able to deny an abortion to a woman in a situation similar to Sherri Finkbine's. At the same time, many women would not have access to abortion because their circumstances fell outside of the ALI's narrow stipulations.[20]

In 1967, as an alternative to the ALI reforms, the National Association for the Repeal of Abortion Laws (NARAL) advocated the repeal of all abortion laws and developed two related strategies designed to remove abortion laws from the books entirely. Those who championed this position included Dr. Lawrence Lader, cofounder of NARAL, several prominent New York City civil liberties lawyers, such as Professor Cyril Means of New York University Law School, Harriet Pilpel, and Aryeh Neier, executive director of the ACLU, and a group of pro-abortion clergy members, including Reverend Howard Moody, Reverend Jesse Lyons of the Riverside Church, and Reverend Finlay Schaef of the Washington Square Methodist Church.[21] The first strategy entailed setting up referral agencies through the Clergy Consultation Service (CCS), founded in 1967 by 21 clergy, to direct women to safe *illegal* abortions. The second strategy attempted to challenge the New York State law by establishing a test case that would be appealed to the Supreme Court, hopefully invalidating all anti-abortion laws in the United States.[22] By referring women for illegal abortions through CCS, civil libertarian lawyers and other abortion law repealers sought an appropriate case to challenge the constitutionality of the New York State law.[23]

By 1969, as feminists began to claim abortion rights as central to women's liberation, activists such as Lader and the Reverends Moody, Lyons, and Schaef agreed that the abortion rights movement would be most effectively led by women. In 1972, Lader argued that feminist intervention in the abortion rights movement was central to its success:

> Women themselves must bear the special responsibility of rallying opinion behind [abortion] reform, standing up and making their demands for justice known throughout the country. Nothing is stronger than the moral power of an idea once it has come of age. And the moral power of legalized abortion will surely prevail when women have directed their anger against the superstitions of centuries, and cried out for the final freedom of procreative choice.[24]

Lader summarized what had become the feminist demand that women needed to be involved centrally in all pro-abortion politics.[25]

The earliest feminist campaign for abortion rights began in San Francisco, California in 1961. In that year Patricia Maginnis, a medical technician, initiated a woman-centered (women's liberation had not yet emerged on the political scene) drive for abortion rights by collecting petitions for reform of the California anti-abortion law. Quickly becoming fed up with abortion law reform efforts, Maginnis founded her own organization, the Society for Human Abortion (SHA), in 1962. SHA members rejected reform in favor of the repeal of all state anti-abortion laws. They demanded that abortion should be unregulated like any other medical procedure. SHA members were also some of the first to argue that abortion was a woman's right and should be affordable and accessible to all women. In the mid-1960s SHA expanded their challenge to the existing laws by helping women obtain safe illegal abortions. During the same period, a group of Chicago women activists organized "Jane"—an illegal abortion provision service. Both SHA and Jane proved that women could take the matter of abortion into their own hands and procure safe, illegal abortions if need be.[26]

Beginning in 1968, feminists mounted the popular nationwide campaign for abortion rights and began to rally for "Free Abortions on Demand" and the total repeal of all abortion laws. They distinguished themselves from earlier professional abortion rights activists in that they believed that women should be central to abortion politics and have control over the abortion decision. Like the professionals, one of their strategies was to find a test case to challenge the constitutionality of the anti-abortion laws. Feminist lawyers in New York City and the abortion law repealers of NARAL and CCS joined forces and began the search for a case that had some similarities to two other cases that had challenged the constitutionality of abortion laws in California and Washington, D.C.

The first of these previous cases concerned Dr. Leon Belous of California. In 1967, Belous had been convicted of criminal abortion and conspiracy to commit abortion based on evidence that he had referred a teenage girl to a Los Angeles physician who performed abortions. The girl had threatened to go to Mexico for a dangerous termination if Belous refused to help her. Belous argued that the girl might have died if she had had a Mexican abortion. Therefore, he asserted, he had conformed to the California law that allowed abortion to preserve the life of the pregnant woman. In their ruling, which overturned the Belous conviction, the California Supreme Court judged that the abortion law was unconstitutionally vague, explaining that it forced a doctor to make a life or death choice that could result in a criminal sentence.[27]

The other previous landmark case involved Dr. Milan Vuitch, a physician convicted for criminal abortion in 1968. Dr. Vuitch had allowed the D.C. police to arrest him for performing an abortion. He hoped that abortion rights supporters could use his arrest to topple the vulnerable D.C. law. The District of Columbia, unlike most states including New York and California, allowed abortion to preserve the life *and* the health of the pregnant woman. Vuitch recognized that this law could be broadly interpreted to include non-life threatening and psychological justifications for requiring a legal abortion. On November 10, 1969, Judge Gerhard Arnold Gesell, of the U.S. District Court of the District of Columbia, handed down his decision on the *Vuitch* case; he interpreted the D.C. law broadly as giving physicians the power to perform abortions using their own medical discretion.

On appeal, the United States Supreme Court upheld the original interpretation of the D.C. law, reversing Judge Gesell's decision. In his majority opinion, however, Justice Hugo Black ruled that the state must prove that an abortion was not necessary to protect the life or health of the mother. By placing the burden of proof on the state, the Court made it easier for physicians to expand the meaning of the health proviso. On the other hand, by refusing to find the D.C. law unconstitutional, the Court frustrated the hopes of abortion rights activists who wanted all abortion laws overturned. Still, activists such as Lader and others involved in NARAL, lauded the Vuitch and Belous decisions as victories that would pave the way for similar decisions in other states.[28]

Feminist abortion rights activists, however, like those who joined New York City's Redstockings and those who became plaintiffs in *Abromowicz v. Lefkowitz*—the first feminist legal challenge to the New York State law—sharply criticized abortion rights activists who might rest on their laurels, assuming that legal abortion had been won for women in the District of Columbia or California. As long as only doctors performed abortions, the radical feminists argued, they would remain prohibitively expensive and inaccessible to indigent or young women. Furthermore, they pointed out that both the definition of legal abortion and the procedure itself still lay in the hands of men; as before, abortion would be granted to women when men deemed the circumstances appropriate. This radical feminist critique of abortion law reform became more popular in the last years of the 1960s and in the early 1970s, as feminists increased their numbers. Radical feminists argued that abortion was a woman's right and needed to be available on demand.

For most of the 1960s, the abortion rights movement remained the domain of a relatively small number of professionals concentrated in New York and California who fought their battle in the state court systems.[29] It would take the feminist movement to make abortion rights a popular national issue. Because feminists were the first to hold rallies, marches, and direct actions for abortion rights, they placed the issue directly before the public for the first time in the twentieth century. Feminists consciously decided to make their demands for abortion rights attractive to the media in order to gain the attention of a general audience. This strategy succeeded in making feminist arguments for abortion rights a central aspect of the national opinion on abortion.

Part of the radical feminist message offered by groups such as Redstockings was that abortion concerned all women equally. They maintained that every woman needed to get involved in challenging anti-abortion laws, because without the fundamental right to control reproduction in every instance, women remained subject to men. Redstockings asserted this position when they disrupted the first New York State legislative hearings on abortion law reform, which included expert witness testimony from 13 men and one woman—a nun. Redstockings insisted that women needed to be central to any discussion of abortion laws. They also organized a public speakout to encourage people to listen to women tell of their experiences with illegal abortion and unwanted pregnancy. Finally, New York feminists mounted a legal challenge to the New York State anti-abortion law in *Abromowicz v. Lefkowitz*. In this case, feminists forged a legal strategy that allowed women to tell their personal abortion stories to the court. They hoped that these stories would provide the impetus for a nullification of the New York State anti-abortion law.

In the late 1960s, feminist abortion rights advocates were primarily concerned with acquiring personal fertility control for American women through the use of abortion and birth control. They were largely unconcerned about a parallel movement for national and international population control that had been developing since the beginning of the decade. In the early 1960s, cold war concerns about communist insurrection and rebellion by people of color became national fears and fed anxiety about overpopulation. By 1965, demographers working for the Population Council, founded by John D. Rockefeller III in 1952, regularly studied the relationship between population growth and economic development abroad. The United States Association for International Development (USAID) received marked increases in federal appropriations for international population control programs between 1967 and 1969—$35 million in 1967 and $50 million in 1969. Planned Parenthood began to use the federal Organization of Economic Opportunity (OEO) funds for domestic welfare programs concerning fertility in 1964. In 1967, the Social Security Act stipulated that no less than 6 percent of funds for maternal and child-health services would be spent on family planning. In 1973, with the sterilization of Minnie Lee Relf, it came out that women of color had been sterilized without their consent in these federal programs. There was also considerable evidence that the Nixon administration could have prevented some of these sterilizations by distributing guidelines to federal clinics. By this time, all these programs had come under the scrutiny of Black and Latino Nationalists and women of color concerned with the abuse of fertility control among racial minorities. As will be discussed more fully, these critiques pressured white feminists to rethink their reproductive rights politics in the 1970s.[30]

From Abortion Rights to Reproductive Freedom

By the early 1980s, a decade after *Roe v. Wade*, American feminists had fundamentally reshaped notions of fertility control. After achieving legal abortion, they had transformed the movement for the legalization of abortion into a movement for reproductive rights to address the broad health care needs of all women, and particularly the need of women of color and poor women to be free from reproductive abuses. A historical account of the feminist movement in New York City from the middle of the 1960s until the middle of the 1980s illuminates contemporary understandings of reproductive rights. While I recognize the limitations of focusing on a small segment of a nationwide feminist movement, New York feminists contributed disproportionately to the creation of a reproductive rights discourse in the 1970s and 1980s. Further study of abortion rights and reproductive rights activism in other regions will increase our understanding of both feminism and the ideas underpinning the development of a contemporary reproductive rights politics.

Despite much discussion of the subject of abortion in recent years, very little has been written on the most recent history of the abortion or reproductive rights movements. Remarkably, too, historians have only begun to explore the story of second wave feminism in the United States, and the debates among feminists, Black Nationalists, and Puerto Rican Nationalists around abortion, population control, and genocide have never been explored comprehensively. This book presents a first look at the history of a volatile conversation that helped shape two of the most controversial and debated subjects of our time—abortion rights and feminism.

The first chapter discusses how radical feminists in the abortion rights movement transformed popular opinions about abortion, convincing the public that a woman had a right to control her individual reproduction and terminate a pregnancy regardless of circumstances. Radical feminists claimed that abortion should no longer remain in the hands of doctors, lawyers, or legislators because it is a woman's body that gets pregnant. Redstockings activist Ellen Willis articulated this point of view when she declared that "these phony experts [doctors, lawyers, and legislators] have no right to control our bodies and our lives. Forced childbearing is slavery. We want total repeal of the [anti-abortion] law and free abortion clinics."[31] The notion that abortion was a woman's concern undergirded much of the debate leading up to the Supreme Court's 1973 *Roe v. Wade* decision and helped make abortion rights into a popular political movement closely linked to the feminist movement. The chapter draws on the Redstockings' disruption of the New York State legislative hearings, the speakout on abortion, and the legal challenge to the New

York State abortion law in *Abromowicz v. Lefkowitz* to illustrate these points.

Redstockings and other feminists active in abortion rights, however, alienated black and Latino men and women from the feminist abortion rights movement by limiting their political goals to the legalization of abortion. The Redstockings viewed their personal lack of access to legal abortion and contraception as the primary barrier to their attainment of reproductive control. But black women and Latinas had a very different perspective on fertility control. They remained wary of both feminism and abortion rights because of feminists' singular focus on abortion as the ticket to reproductive control. They accused feminists of giving little consideration to the women who wanted children and discovered they couldn't have them, because they lacked economic resources or they had been sterilized involuntarily. In short, the problems of women of color would not be solved by legalized abortion.

Chapter 2 explores these criticisms of the feminist abortion rights movement by reconstructing the perspectives of black women, some organized in feminist groups and others involved in Black Nationalist organizations. Despite their differences, all these women championed the notion that black Americans required the means to bear children, which included the prevention of forced or coerced sterilization. They also argued that public support for child-care would help poor women have all the children they wanted. Finally, they insisted that poverty should not present a barrier to reproduction. At the same time, many black women believed that black liberation could not occur without access to fertility control, in the form of voluntary contraception and abortion. The Black Power revolution needed the support of black women; black women argued that they needed to control their fertility in order to fight a revolution. African-American women were, thus, the first to articulate an agenda for an inclusive reproductive rights.

During the late 1960s and early 1970s, members of both the Black Panther Party and the Nation of Islam, Black Muslim followers of the Honorable Elijah Muhammad, believed that abortion among black Americans constituted genocide. Black Nationalists feared methods of state-sponsored repression; the wholesale rejection of birth control and abortion as genocidal represented the paranoia generated by these fears. These two organizations published some of the most militant Black Nationalist criticism of the feminist abortion rights position. In chapter 3, I examine Black Nationalist rhetorical attempts to steer African-American women away from any sort of fertility prevention, contraceptive or abortive. I also discuss the debates around the meaning of black masculinity that fed these pronatalist beliefs. The Panthers and Black Muslims maintained that the path to a strong black nation lay in siring many children for the revolution. Black women could best support black men by staying healthy for childbearing and raising black militants. At the same time, the Panthers and the Nation of Islam spoke against the dangers of sterilization abuse and reported on several incidents wherein black, Latina, and Native American women experienced sterilization against their will and often without their knowledge. They joined black women in demanding the means to bear children regardless of race or income level.

Chapter 4 reconstructs the reproductive politics of the Young Lords, a group of Puerto Rican Nationalists based in New York City, who articulated a surprisingly feminist argument—considering their nationalist orientation and emulation of the Black Panthers—for reproductive rights in the early 1970s. Like the Black Panthers and the Black Muslims, the Young Lords iterated that people of color needed to combat reproductive genocide waged against them by population controllers. They also publicized the history of U.S. sponsored sterilization in Puerto Rico, arguing that this represented one of the negative effects of American colonization. They took a firm stand against forced sterilization in both Puerto Rico and in the mainland United States. Furthermore, they brought attention to Puerto Rico's role as the testing ground for the birth control pill, revealing its deadly consequences for several Puerto Rican women in the early 1960s. Finally, they pointed out that women of color sometimes risked their lives when entering a hospital for an abortion, even after *Roe v. Wade*, because public hospitals provided inadequate and, at times, dangerous service to poor and minority women. But they never equated the personal use of abortion with genocide. Rather, the Young Lords argued that women needed to have personal autonomy over their reproduction. And, like pro–fertility control black women, they demanded state-supported health care, prenatal care, and child-care.

By adopting some of the critiques made by African Americans and Puerto Ricans, the 1970s feminist group CARASA reformed the feminist abortion rights movement. CARASA coined the term "reproductive rights" to describe the goals of their new movement that became national in scope. Their major objective was to obtain safe and legal abortion access for all women, particularly poor women, and to end sterilization abuse. Additionally, feminists in the reproductive rights movement campaigned for government support for child-care, general health care and prenatal care for poor women, and work environments free of reproductive hazards. Chapter 5 narrates the activities of CARASA.

In my conclusion, I link the problem of sterilization abuse to contemporary violations of reproductive freedom, particularly among poor women of color. I also suggest what activists of the twenty-first century can learn from the reproductive rights movement of the 1970s and early 1980s.

Finally, I want to note what my book does not include. Absent from this study are the anti-abortion activities of the New Right. I believe that the anti-abortion movement significantly influenced the politics of abortion and reproductive rights groups. Certainly, many of the practical decisions as to strategy and political priority took shape in reaction to anti-abortion attacks in the 1970s and early 1980s. My chapter on CESA and CARASA begins to illustrate reproductive rights feminists' defensive posture in relation to the anti-abortion movement during this period. However, while I touch on the differences between anti-abortion proponents and feminists advocating reproductive rights, it is not my primary focus here. I leave this very complex history of the New Right and the anti-abortion movement to be written at a later date.

1

"Let's hear it from the real experts"
Feminism and the Early Abortion Rights Movement

On February 13, 1969, seven women from a radical feminist organization called Redstockings disrupted the first New York State legislative hearings on abortion law reform. The radical feminists were incensed to hear that 14 men but only one woman—a nun—were scheduled to testify before the legislative committee. During the disruption, Kathie Sarachild, one of the most provocative participants in the Redstockings' action and a founder of the group, shouted, "It is wrong for men of great age to decide this matter [abortion law reform]. And if we have to, we will force doctors at gun point, and we might even hijack airplanes to get this." Senator Seymour Thaler, a Queens Democrat, responded, "I would bet that all those ladies [the demonstrators] are mentally disturbed and shouldn't be allowed to have a baby." To which another radical feminist retorted, "The only way these people will listen to us is if we disrupt their meeting."[1]

On this point, the Redstockings were probably correct. The New York State legislators had no plans to include women in the abortion law debate. Redstockings, however, intended to challenge a cultural and political structure that excluded their voices and opinions, particularly on topics that concerned women centrally. Fortunately, for the Redstockings, the New York media and much of the nation was listening, some, with rapt curiosity at the oddity that radical feminism posed, others, with a mind to further build women's liberation nationwide. The disruption of the legislative hearings was just one feminist action among many that had grabbed media attention in recent months. By 1968, women's liberation had become part of the explosive political turmoil that had begun to sweep the nation and gather attention in major newspapers, magazines, and on television: the civil rights movement, the anti-war movement, Black Power, and the student protests all were transforming the way Americans thought about society and themselves.

I focus on Redstockings in this chapter because more than any other New York women's liberation organization they made the right to legal abortion central to their feminist struggle for women's autonomy. Why did Redstockings identify abortion rights as the key to women's emancipation? Certainly, other issues were important and were quickly taken up by other feminist groups: equality in the workplace, sexual harassment, sexism in educational institutions, and women's representation in the media, just to name a few important second wave topics. Part of the answer to this question can be found in a better understanding of Redstockings members' self-definition as radical feminists. They were not interested in fighting sexism through traditional political and institutional channels. They left these tasks to what feminist theorists refer to as liberal feminists, represented by organizations such the National Organization for Women (NOW). Redstockings members believed that women's most fundamental subordination occurred in what has often been conceived by women's historians as the private sphere. Redstockings argued that only by addressing women's oppression at its roots—in the family, in regards to women's bodies, and in regards to women's control over their reproduction—could feminists begin to eradicate sexism in the public sphere, the workplace, schools, the media, etc.[2]

The other part of the explanation for Redstockings' focus on abortion and body politics has to do with their decision to make a clean break from what they considered to be the sexist white male New Left. By leaving the New Left, the activists who would eventually constitute Redstockings, chose to make women's "personal" and "private" problems into political demands. They believed that women's liberation should focus singularly on women—not on the Vietnam War, not on civil rights, and not on student power. Issues that concerned the female body quickly moved to the center of this political agenda.[3]

Second wave feminists captured their commitment to making women's personal problems into public political issues in the banner phrase, "The personal is political." This contention is one of the most important legacies of women's liberation and second wave feminism. By making the personal political, women's liberation activists radically changed American political culture. Issues once confined to the domestic sphere or concerning the body were redefined as subjects for political discussion. Feminists not only brought the domestic into politics, but they also brought politics into the home. Challenging the sexual division of labor in the household or negotiating power in the bedroom was considered a feminist political act.

Defining the personal as political raised a question, however, that Redstockings and other women's liberation activists did not immediately address during the period from the late 1960s to the early 1970s. Whose personal problems should be elevated into political concerns? Because Redstockings and most other second wave feminist groups were almost all white and of middle-class background, the concerns of white middle-class women were most quickly addressed by the women's liberation movement. Redstockings took their personal experiences to represent the experiences of women, in general; they did not recognize that women of color and poor women had different experiences and, thus, different problems that needed to be addressed by another set of demands. This blind spot in women's liberation politics, and how women (and men) of color remedied it, is the subject of this book. It is also the subject of a vast body of feminist theory and debate. For more than three decades, feminists have been asking how feminism can represent the needs of all women, when women are so different from one another.

Redstockings referred to the female body when claiming the authority to define all women's reproductive rights demands. They adamantly contended that every woman must have complete control over her body's potential for reproduction through the use of legal abortion because only women experience pregnancy. Yet, while it is true that only women have the potential to become pregnant, Redstockings did not ask how different women experience their reproductive potential differently.

Despite their political blind spot around women's different perspectives on reproduction, Redstockings made essential contributions to the abortion rights movement of the 1960s. No one had yet put women at the center of a movement for reproductive empowerment, even though abortion rights had been a political issue of some importance since the early part of the decade. Women had been much more the objects of political discussion rather than primary subjects driving the movement for legal abortion. The idea that women needed to decide for themselves what to do with their reproductive bodies only gained preeminence in the abortion rights movement at the end of the 1960s as feminism and abortion rights became increasingly entwined. Soon thereafter, the Redstockings' vital claim to a woman's right to personal sovereignty over her body through the use of abortion became synonymous with a feminism that would forever change American women's perspectives on work, family, and childbearing.

Two related goals shaped Redstockings' determination to wrest authority over abortion and pregnancy from male legislators, who passed restrictive reform bills, and male doctors, who patronizingly handed out abortions to the most "deserving" women. First, they wanted to make legal abortion available to all women. They reasoned that the potential to become pregnant threatened to keep all women bound to traditional female social roles; thus, all women required access to legal abortion to free themselves from the confines of a sexist culture. Second, they criticized the "sexual revolution" as incomplete, as long as women lacked both reproductive control and social equality with men. The Redstockings maintained that the sexual revolution had given men easier access to heterosexual sex outside of marriage without forcing them to evaluate what that meant for the majority of women in a sexist society. Women had lost many of the traditional "guarantees" of commitment and economic security that accompanied a sexual relationship sanctioned by marriage. Yet, most women had not gained the economic autonomy that was necessary to free themselves from reliance on men and marriage. Redstockings feminists explained that women needed both economic power and access to reproductive control in order to begin to enjoy their sexuality fully.

Background

Redstockings evolved from New York Radical Women (NYRW), founded in 1967 by Pam Allen, who had been active in the civil rights movement with the Student Nonviolent Coordinating Committee (SNCC) and had subsequently established the San Francisco women's liberation group Sudsofloppen, and Shulamith Firestone, who wrote the germinal 1970 feminist tract *The Dialectic of Sex*. Many influential players in the radical feminist movement participated in NYRW. They included Kathie Sarachild, a Harvard peace activist and veteran of the civil rights movement, Anne Koedt, previously of Students for a Democratic Society (SDS), Kate Millett, author of the famous *Sexual Politics*, Robin Morgan, who gained her experience in the anti-war movement and with the Yippies and subsequently published her essays in the collection *Going Too Far*, and Ellen Willis, the well-known feminist journalist and rock critic for the *Village Voice*. All these women would go on to incorporate their experiences with feminism into their careers in journalism, academia, or as life-long activists.

Historian Alice Echols has described NYRW as a feminist organization with loose ties to the New Left. It was far more than that, however. Many of the members acquired their political education in the civil rights movement as opposed to anti-war or other New Left struggles. Both Allen and Sarachild gained their political experience during the 1964 Mississippi Summer Voter Registration Project organized by SNCC. Carol Hanisch, another prominent member of NYRW, traveled south from Iowa in 1965 to help the Southern Conference Education Fund (SCEF) with their civil rights organizing. As a result of their civil rights experiences in the South, women active in NYRW modeled their feminism on Black Power ideologies, arguing that women needed to organize around their own oppression—in their case sex and gender.[4] Like black activists who advocated Black Power, the NYRW believed that any truly effective movement would have to grow organically from the personal experiences of those involved. Another faction of women involved with NYRW, including Robin Morgan and Florika, who chained herself to a giant replica of Miss America dubbed the "Amerika Dollie" by feminists at NYRW's protest against the 1968 beauty pageant in Atlantic City, rejected the emphasis on personal oppression, opting instead for Yippie-inspired guerilla-type actions. A conflict emerged between these two groups, with the civil rights–trained women criticizing the guerilla theatre actions as elitist and frivolous.[5]

In November 1968, NYRW split into three groups for several reasons, including the organization's growing size, ideological differences among individuals, and personality conflicts within the group.[6] One of the factions to spin out of NYRW was Women's International Terrorist Conspiracy from Hell (WITCH), which included both Robin Morgan and Florika. The formation of WITCH from NYRW illustrates the ideological divide between feminists and politicos. This split occurred both among and within radical feminist organizations. The politicos relied heavily on the Marx-Engels supposition that women's oppression originated with private property and capitalism. By most accounts, NYRW fell into the feminist camp because they viewed women's oppression as separate from other political issues, and they saw sexism as the product of male dominance rather than as the direct result of capitalism. Yet, the lines between the factions tended to blur with people on both sides participating in NYRW. NYRW activists generally agreed that capitalism exacerbated women's oppression even if it did not cause it. They pinned the balance of responsibility, however, on the individual men who perpetuated sexism.[7]

In January 1969, some of the women who eventually formed Redstockings—Willis, Firestone, Irene Peslikis, Barbara Susan, and Rosalyn Baxandall, who had strong connections with the D.C. anti-war movement—participated in the now notorious counterinaugural demonstration in Washington D.C.[8] This demonstration was organized by the National Mobilization Committee to End the War in Vietnam (Mobe). The feminists decided to burn their voter-registration cards to symbolize that just as the draft was an affront to male political consciousness, so the franchise was inconsequential for women. Some women in the group suggested that men also burn their voter-registration cards to show their solidarity with women's liberation. The inspiration to "give back the vote" by burning voter-registration cards came from the anti-war protest of burning draft cards. The gesture illustrates how, despite their determination to distinguish themselves, NYRW and Redstockings often aligned themselves with the New Left. It is also possible that the idea for burning voter registration cards sprung from feminist identification with civil rights and Black Power and that movement's mid-1960s rejection of the vote as being ineffective toward empowering African Americans.[9]

Ultimately, events at the counterinaugural demonstration confirmed the suspicions of many feminists that a degree of political separation from the New Left would be necessary. During the demonstration a number of men in the audience shouted sexist epithets and heckled Marilyn Webb, then of D.C. Women's Liberation and formerly of SDS. Webb spoke about the link between capitalism and women's oppression—an analysis familiar to both men and women in the New Left at this point. Despite the cogency and familiarity of the argument, Webb had been added to the speakers list as an afterthought because most of the male organizers put the war and black liberation ahead of women's liberation. Willis has memorialized the infamous behavior of New Left men in response to Webb's speech: when Webb began her speech with a "moderate, pro-movement statement—men in the audience booed, laughed, catcalled and yelled enlightened remarks like 'Take her off the stage and fuck her.'" Such degrading treatment by supposed political "brothers" outraged feminists and forced many female activists to question the sanctity of movement solidarity.[10]

After this incident, Willis and Firestone founded Redstockings. They feared that organizing women in conjunction with the male left, particularly a male left that behaved "like rednecks," would hinder the development of a radical feminism truly committed to the liberation of women from domination by men.[11] Willis declared: "We have come to see women's liberation as an independent revolutionary movement, potentially representing half the population. We intend to make our own analysis of the system and put our interests first, whether or not it is convenient for the (male-dominated) left."[12]

Redstockings distinguished themselves among New York radical feminist organizations by using consciousness raising as a method for the development of feminist theory and by promoting their "pro-woman line." Both strategies emphasized a woman-centered and personal analysis of oppression. Consciousness raising gave each individual in a group of women a chance to speak on a specified topic with the hope that through this process the group would come to some general theoretical conclusions about women's position in patriarchal society. For example, the group might choose to discuss heterosexual sexual relationships in order to identify the primary problems contributing to women's oppression when women slept with men. Or they might discuss problems that arose when women lived with men, such as dividing housework and childcare.[13] Often they discussed fears of unwanted pregnancy, illegal abortion, and problems with contraception. With the pro-woman line, Redstockings feminists argued against the idea that women were brainwashed into acting in a feminine manner and thereby accepting their own oppression. Rather, women used their femininity to gain the only advantages allowed them by men.[14]

Through the consciousness-raising method, Redstockings brought second wave feminist attention to abortion. They found that as they discussed sexism in their small groups, problems of reproductive control recurred as fundamental issues contributing to these women's sense of oppression. As Willis recalled, almost everyone who had not herself had an illegal abortion knew someone who had had one.[15] The Redstockings predicted that without abortion as a tool to control their fertility, women would remain trapped in traditionally feminine roles, where their only resistance to male dominance was overtly feminine behavior. With the ability to terminate a pregnancy would come the freedom to transform traditional womanhood. After identifying abortion as fundamental to women's liberation, Redstockings began to formulate actions and strategies to make it legal.

The effectiveness of the consciousness-raising method is evident from the speed with which abortion moved to the core of second wave feminist politics. It was not without its drawbacks, however. One of the problems with consciousness raising was that it tended to universalize the experiences of the women in the small group. Consciousness raising encouraged the identification of similar experiences of oppression among women rather than focusing on their differences. This process reinforced the tendency for a mostly white middle-class group of women to believe they represented the political demands of all women. As a result, legal abortion became the focus rather than the reproductive demands (an end to sterilization abuse, for example) that would later come to the fore as women of color became involved in the movement.

"Let's hear it from the real experts": *Abortion Rights Become Feminist Politics*

In 1969, Redstockings adopted the repeal position—which advocated the eradication of all abortion laws—developed by Patricia Maginnis of the Society for Human Abortion (SHA). Lawrence Lader of the National Association to Repeal Abortion Laws (NARAL) developed these ideas further on the national level.[16] Redstockings, however, distinguished themselves with a rhetoric and style of their own. They argued that women should have the right to terminate a pregnancy at any point in a gestation and for any reason. The Redstockings also believed that only free abortion would guarantee the most oppressed woman control over her reproduction. Finally, Redstockings made explicit the connection between a liberated female sexuality and authority over female reproduction. They argued that the sexual revolution could not be completed until women gained control over their fertility.[17]

Redstockings criticized feminists in NOW for supporting abortion rights only half-heartedly. NOW added abortion to their "Bill of Rights for Women" in 1967, having almost left it off of their platform for fear of alienating Catholic women. National NOW remained ambivalent about abortion in the last years of the 1960s, leading radical feminists in Redstockings to see themselves as the only true champions of a woman's right to abortion. Some local affiliates of NOW, however, including New York City, took a strong stand for abortion law repeal. Lucinda Cisler, founder of New Yorkers for Abortion Law Repeal (NYALR) in 1969 and a vocal radical feminist campaigner for the repeal of all abortion laws, was also a very active and influential member of NOW-NYC. Eventually local chapters of NOW, including New York City, began to refer women to safe illegal abortionists with the help of the Clergy Consultation Service.[18]

Members of the New York State legislature had considered reform of the nearly 150-year-old abortion law, which allowed abortion only to preserve the life of a pregnant woman, for several years before the Redstockings' disruption of the legislative hearings.[19] In 1966, New York State Assemblyman Percy Sutton of Manhattan introduced the first bill that would have reformed the abortion law according to American Law Institute (ALI) guidelines, which, in addition to saving the life of the pregnant woman would allow abortion when there was a substantial risk to the physical or mental health of the woman, for congenital defects, and when the pregnancy resulted from rape or incest. The bill would have made abortion legal to save a woman's life or preserve her health, but it was killed in committee after it garnered much attention from the press. At the next legislative session, with the support of the Association for the Study of Abortion (ASA), Assemblyman Albert Blumenthal, Democrat of Manhattan, introduced another abortion reform bill that was also killed before it reached the Assembly floor for debate.[20] With the voices for absolute repeal of the state abortion laws becoming louder, Assemblywoman Constance Cook, a Republican from upstate, followed Blumenthal with a 1969 bill that would repeal the New York abortion statute entirely. The Redstockings supported the Cook repeal bill; they handed out an informational flyer pressing for its passage at their disruption of the legislative hearings.[21]

In 1969, the Joint Legislative Committee on the Problems of Public Health, chaired by State Senator Norman Lent (R-East Rockaway), bowed to pressure from feminists and other abortion rights supporters like Blumenthal and Cook to at least review the New York State abortion statute. The committee requested that experts on abortion testify at a series of hearings in New York City. Senator Lent recognized the need for reform of abortion laws because they were "widely disregarded and infrequently enforced."[22] The 13 experts who were invited to testify in front of the legislative committee had some professional knowledge about illegal abortion. They included a former judge, two psychiatrists, a former district attorney from Los Angeles, members of the Indiana State Senate and the Indiana House of Representatives, several medical doctors, and a nun who directed the Kennedy Child Study Center in New York City.[23] The legislators also heard testimony from Governor Nelson Rockefeller's Committee on Abortion Law Reform, chaired by Judge Charles W. Froessel, formerly of the State Court of Appeals. The Governor's Committee recommended that a reformed law allow legal abortions under certain restrictive circumstances in rough compliance with the ALI guidelines. In addition to these recommendations, Judge Froessel suggested that abortion be legalized for women with more than four children.[24]

The Redstockings believed that the "expert" recommendations to the legislature in 1969 might narrowly expand the number of women who could acquire a legal hospital abortion. But they discounted this reform as inadequate because they wanted all women to have access to abortion regardless of their personal circumstances. They also rejected any reforms that would allow physicians to maintain professional and medical control over women's reproduction.

On February 13, 1969, a group of about 30 women voiced their opposition to a reformist solution to the abortion question by picketing the legislative hearings on abortion law reform. Redstockings organized the demonstration with support from NYC-NOW and abortion repeal organizations such as NYALR. The protesters gathered on the street outside of the New York City Health Department where the Legislative Committee met. They passed out flyers that challenged both legislative and professional authority over abortion. The flyer declared: "The only real experts on abortion are women."[25]

At the same time, seven women from Redstockings, including Sarachild, Willis, Anne Forer, Helen Kritzler, Alex Kates Shulman, and Shulamith Firestone, entered the building and attended the hearings. These women sat quietly in the audience listening to the hearings until Judge Froessel, chair of the Governor's Committee, finished addressing the floor. At that point, Sarachild stood up and shouted, "Now let's hear from the real experts." Another woman demanded to know, "Why are 14 men and one woman on your list of speakers—and she a nun?" Sarachild cried out, "Repeal the abortion law, instead of wasting more time talking about these stupid reforms." A third woman complained, "We've waited and waited while you have held one hearing after another. Meanwhile, the baby I didn't want is 2 years old." In an effort to restore some order to the hearings, Senator Lent announced, "This meeting is designed not to measure public opinion of which we are already aware . . . but to gather information and evidence from experts." The Redstockings activists responded to this comment with shouts of: "What better experts are there on abortion than women?" And, "Do you have to be an expert to become pregnant?"[26]

Members of Redstockings protested that the "real" experts—women like themselves—had been excluded from the deliberations that concerned them most directly. They relied on their personal authority as women to bolster their demand for the total repeal of the New York State abortion law. As such, they reacted vehemently against the recommendations made by the Governor's Committee and rejected the 1967 reform bill proposed by Albert Blumenthal. They found any limitations placed on a woman's access to abortion unacceptable because only women could decide about their bodies. They argued that abortion needed to be available on demand, and that it should be performed in free clinics by trained paramedical staff rather than by doctors. Only with these provisions would abortion be accessible to women regardless of their financial position.[27]

The legislators at the hearings were divided as to the Redstockings' protest. Some argued that they had been trying to help the women by reforming the abortion laws and these women had no legitimate right to participate in the hearings. Judge Froessel warned Sarachild, "You're only hurting your own case." Despite some of his patronizing comments, Senator Seymour Thaler supported the Redstockings by telling those gathered in the room, "I am entirely in sympathy with these women, the law should be repealed, in my opinion. We have had enough hearings. You are quite right to be impatient." At the same time, Thaler admonished the demonstrators to remember that "this is the legislative procedure. We have to get on. Anarchy is no substitute for the orderly procedure of law."[28]

The Redstockings were eventually escorted out of the room and the hearings continued. Several of the protesters waited at the door of the resumed hearings with the hope that they would get a chance to speak again. Eventually, three of them, including Gale Greenwood and Barbara Susan, who each had had personal experiences with unwanted pregnancy, were allowed to address the committee. Both Greenwood and Susan had prepared testimony to be read in front of the committee. The speakers used the opportunity to demand "a public hearing that would be devoted entirely to the expert testimony of women."[29] (An event they would soon stage on their own.) Greenwood, a nursery school teacher who had become pregnant 10 years earlier, as a teenager, told the committee of her painful experience with illegal abortion. She used her own experience as evidence to justify what she viewed as a desperate need for the repeal of the archaic New York State abortion law. She also articulated the Redstockings' political stance on abortion—that abortion decisions belonged in the hands of women who were pregnant and wanted an abortion or who might find themselves in that predicament at some time in the future. Greenwood stated:

> Ten years ago, I had an illegal abortion at 17 years old. I'm not going into the gory details; it was an illegal thing. Today, I would not want a child, but if I were to become pregnant, I would not be covered by the law, and I wouldn't be covered by the reforms. I'm not insane, I'm not physically damaged. But I'm poor, I don't have the money, I would have to find a quack somewhere. Men have no right to decide these questions.[30]

Despite this heartfelt speech, the Redstockings viewed their limited opportunity to testify before the committee as an unsatisfying token. They argued that women should speak publicly and forcefully on issues of abortion en masse, not meekly address a committee in ones or twos. A public speakout would give large numbers of women an opportunity to act as experts on abortion, testifying in front of an audience as to their experiences with abortion and unwanted pregnancy.

On the day of the legislative hearings, the Redstockings distributed an informational flyer to passersby that explained their belief that women were the only legitimate experts on abortion law. The flyer read:

> Today a panel of clergymen, doctors and other professional "experts" is picking apart the abortion law. They will tell us, in their usual daddy-knows-best manner, just how much control over our reproductive processes we should be allowed to have.
>
> We say: The only real experts on abortion are women!
> Women who have known the pain, fear and socially-imposed guilt of an illegal abortion. Women who have seen their friends dead or in agony from a post-abortion infection. Women who have had children by the wrong man, at the wrong time, because no doctor would help them.

Any woman can tell you:
Abortion laws are *sexist* laws, made by men to punish women.
Let the experts testify.
Support Constance Cook's bill—repeal *all* abortion laws.[31]

In this flyer the Redstockings reiterated that women should have authority over abortion laws because only women have abortions. But the Redstockings did not merely believe that women who had abortions were qualified to act as experts; they held that *all* women have a privileged position in relation to laws that affect their reproductive bodies. The Redstockings directly connected their female bodies and their experiences as women to a new position of public authority and power over reproduction. What is particularly interesting about this rhetorical strategy is that the Redstockings elevated the reproducing function of their bodies—which is most often associated with traditional femininity, womanhood, and female subordination—to claim authority over legal and political decisions traditionally considered to be in the public realm of men. In fact, the Redstockings defined their position of power and authority over abortion and the reproductive body in stark opposition to the patriarchal power traditionally held by men.

The Redstockings also argued that the old abortion laws reinforced a sexual double standard that allowed men to walk away from an unwanted pregnancy, while women felt guilty about sex because they had to contend with the immediate and concrete consequences of their actions. Some women felt they deserved to die from an illegal abortion because they had had sex outside of marriage or without desiring a child. The anti-abortion laws reinforced the illusion that good girls had sex within the confines of a conjugal relationship and when they were prepared to give birth. The actress Polly Bergen confessed to having these feelings after her illegal abortion in the late 1940s: "The doctor said I was dying because I had lost a lot of blood by the time my roommate got me to see him. But you know, I'm sure there was a part of me that thought I was supposed to die. I had done this terrible thing—I had had sex and I'd gotten pregnant."[32]

On March 21, 1969, about three weeks after the disruption of the legislative hearings, the Redstockings held their own "public hearings" at Washington Square Methodist Church in Manhattan. The Redstockings had begun planning the event immediately after they had disrupted the legislative hearings. Their experience with the legislative hearings had convinced them that the only way to make their opinions known would be to orchestrate their own forum. They rented the church space from the Reverend Finley Schaef, who had been helping women acquire safe illegal abortions since 1967 with the Clergy Consultation Service (CCS).

As a counterpoint to the legislative hearings in which professional expertise had given the (mostly) male panelists their authority, the Redstockings speakout gave women an opportunity to testify publicly about their personal experiences with illegal abortion and unwanted pregnancy. To participate in the speakout as an expert a woman did not need to have any professional training; she only needed to be female. The Redstockings intended to put into action what they had shouted at the legislative committee, "Let's hear it from the real experts"—women. Irene Peslikis, a Redstocking member and chair of the speakout, commented at the beginning of the event, "all women are the experts . . . [so] we would really like to hear what women in the audience have to say."[33] Susan, who spoke in front of the legislative committee, echoed this goal in her testimony at the speakout: "No legislature would recognize my right to speak as an expert because it happens right inside of my body where that child grows. It happens in my body later on that I don't want that child and that I have to go through a period of time in which I have no function in society."[34]

Redstockings wanted both the small-group consciousness-raising sessions and the speakout to encourage women to collectively define their personal experiences as political issues. Through this process they believed women would directly address their oppression as active participants in the radical feminist movement, thus liberating themselves from the repressive effects of patriarchy. Ros Baxandall delineated some of the parallels between the speakout and the consciousness-raising method developed by Redstockings in her recollection of the March 1969 event:

After being ousted from City Hall [during the disruption of the legislative hearings], we rented Washington Square Methodist Church (whose ministers had been doing illegal abortion referral for years), sent out a press release, and held the first abortion speakout. We stood up before an overflowing crowd and remembered the details of our illegal abortions and made what had been private and personal, political and public. Keeping sexual secrets imprisons and isolates women. Sharing confidences empowers. We talked about abortion as a lived experience. Some told horror stories of back alley, sleazy procedures, others of wanting a child, but not being able to afford one mentally or economically.[35]

Susan Brownmiller also drew parallels between the speakout and consciousness raising: "For three hours, in the borrowed sanctuary of Rev. Finley Schaef's Washington Square Methodist Church, the group of women 'testified' from their own experience with unwanted pregnancy and illegal abortion." She continued:

> The "testifying" method was an outgrowth of the confessional style of the weekly meetings of the women's liberation groups, leaderless introspective sessions of free-form discussion where each woman is encouraged to "speak from your own experience, sister." The panelists had prepared no speeches. They set up an unobtrusive tape recorder, kept the lights comfortably dim to encourage conversation, and protected their anonymity by using first names only. The result, which could have been exhibitionistic or melodramatic, was neither—it was an honest rap. And it worked.[36]

Not only would women be collectively empowered through the process of testifying publicly as to their experiences with pregnancy and abortion at the speakout, but also the group could generate valuable feminist political theory on the topic of women's liberation. The speakout allowed a large group of women, many of whom may have been new to women's liberation, to participate in the process of formulating feminist political theory and analysis. They brought their own experiences to bear on the production of political ideology, which gave them a great sense of attachment to that ideology.

In defending the consciousness-raising format of the speakout against accusations that it encouraged complaints about personal problems, Peslikis announced that these so-called personal topics revealed relationships of power among men and women:

> A common accusation against women is that the things they say are too subjective, too personal. Actually men just call women's problems personal because women have not been considered part of the larger society. Really these are political problems—matters of power. We're not here to tell our troubles as such but to discuss our experiences in the light of the political problems confronting women.[37]

Peslikis felt it necessary to deflect the accusation that women's problems were not really politics. Both men in the New Left and the general public commonly accused feminists of making a political issue out of personal topics that ought to take a back seat to more urgent problems such as the Vietnam War or the race riots in Detroit, Los Angeles, and Newark. Peslikis and others countered such arguments by demanding recognition of the structures of political power and ideology that had effectively marginalized "half the population." Thus, the speakout functioned as an organizing tool, a media event publicizing the necessity of legal and affordable abortion in New York, and a process to help a group of women empower themselves politically.

At the speakout, a panel of a dozen women testified in front of the press and about three hundred observers. According to those who attended, the audience listened with rapt attention as one woman after another told her harrowing story about unwanted pregnancy or abortion. The panelists claimed their expertise on the topic of abortion because of these personal experiences. Many women in the audience had also had unwanted pregnancies and expressed loud support for the speakers as they heard stories that echoed their own. They clapped and laughed knowingly at the jokes the speakers made to illustrate what they saw as the insanity of allowing men, many of whom were beyond reproductive age, to decide the fate of a woman's pregnancy. The atmosphere in the room was one of camaraderie and shared experience. Many of the women also expressed wonder that there were so many others who had lived through similar traumas during an unexpected and unwanted pregnancy.[38]

Both Willis and Peslikis noted that several other women had wanted to speak but decided against it. Willis wrote in her journal documenting her introduction to feminism: "As a follow up to the abortion demonstration, we will hold our own hearings, at which women will testify about their abortions. About a dozen women agree to speak. Many others refuse because they are afraid of static from employers or families." Peslikis came to the same conclusion when she told the audience at the speakout that a lot of women who wanted to testify couldn't because they were afraid they would lose their jobs. She mourned, "there are reprisals for having an abortion . . . you don't really have any freedom to speakout on the issue." Fear of prosecution for illegal abortion, or apprehension about betraying an illegal abortionist who aided women desperate for assistance, were powerful deterrents for some women who otherwise might have wanted to testify. Brownmiller chose not to speak about her abortion because, at the time, she thought public testimony seemed too "confessional." After attending the speakout, she changed her mind, finding the testimony to be "incredibly powerful." Later in the year she and Barbara Susan both had a second chance to publicly reveal their abortion experiences in the *Abramowicz v. Lefkowitz* challenge to the New York State abortion law.[39]

The speakout gave women an opportunity to challenge prohibitions against speaking publicly about sexuality. In the tradition of consciousness raising, Willis and other Redstockings members believed that women needed to air their sexual and reproductive experiences in order to liberate themselves. Helen Kritzler, another Redstocking who helped disrupt the legislative hearings, testified about her experience with an unwanted pregnancy in college: "I know it is very hard for me to talk about abortion because I never really spoke about it before. I didn't really want to discuss it or talk about it. In fact, I have very rarely talked about it [because I was] afraid of disapproving looks. Most women don't talk about it or even think about it until it happens." Willis commented on some of the social prohibitions against public discussion of abortion and sexuality that kept women's experiences closeted. She wrote:

> If a woman speaks frankly about her sexual/reproductive life—which is as central to her oppression as the poor man's economic life—the standard response is pornographic enjoyment of what are considered highly intimate revelations. As a result we are inhibited about discussing sex with each other, let alone in public.[40]

As part of a feminist-sexual revolution, legal abortion would cease being an experience women felt ashamed of discussing outside of circles of trusted friends or family. The Redstockings abhorred the idea that a woman should ever be stigmatized for having an abortion and talking about it. Baxandall recalled that she worried about speaking publicly about an abortion she had had before she married; people might see her as a "cheap girl."[41] The shame associated with abortion had been part of the sexual double standard that the Redstockings rejected as oppressive for women. They believed that as sexual and reproductive individuals, women should be able to go public with their abortions in order to change the unacceptable abortion laws.

In looking back on the event, Brownmiller noted that "the political message of the emotion-charged evening was that *women* were the only true experts on unwanted pregnancy and abortion, and that every woman has an inalienable right to decide whether or not she wishes to bear a child." Furthermore, Brownmiller emphasized that women, not men, needed to have exclusive control over their female reproductive bodies. A man in the audience queried, "You keep talking about a woman's right to have a legal abortion. . . . What about a man's rights, in or out of wedlock? You didn't make yourselves pregnant." To which a member of Redstockings responded, "Women have the ultimate control over their own bodies." Brownmiller added, "Neither he nor any other male in the hall felt like challenging that simple yet not so obvious statement."[42] Willis also recounted her impression of the success of the speakout and the strength of the emphasis on personal experience made political and collective: "It works. In fact it's more effective than we had hoped. The testimony is honest and powerful and evokes strong reactions from the audience—empathy, anger and pain. Women stand up to give their own testimony."[43]

Personal Politics Goes to Court: Abramowicz v. Lefkowitz

Feminists organized in the Women's Health Collective (WHC) were inspired by the Redstockings speakout to expand upon a successful litigation drive that had begun in Washington, D.C. and California, in *United States v. Vuitch* and *People v. Belous*, which struck down those state abortion laws for vagueness.[44] They organized a class-action suit, *Abramowicz v. Lefkowitz*, to challenge the New York State abortion law. Three feminist lawyers and 350 female plaintiffs of childbearing age joined the Women's Health Collective suit.[45] Most of the plaintiffs were "young, white, [and] college-educated." Members of the WHC had been looking for a way to defeat the New York State abortion law and approached the feminist lawyer Nancy Stearns for advice. She invited two other female lawyers to begin a litigation drive to change the law. The suit came to be known as the women's case because of its all-female list of plaintiffs. The litigators for the women's case—Stearns, Diane Schulder, and Florynce Kennedy—were all associated with the Center for Constitutional Rights, which had provided litigation support for anti-segregationists during the civil rights movement. They considered themselves feminists although only Schulder had been involved with NYRW. Stearns had garnered her radical political background with SNCC from 1963 to

1964 in Mississippi. After litigating *Abramowicz*, she went on to help with the Connecticut class-action suit—*Abele v. Markle*—that successfully defeated the abortion law in that state.[46] Kennedy, a black civil rights lawyer, had been active in the civil rights movement, NY-NOW, and the Feminists, which split from NY-NOW under the leadership of Ti-Grace Atkinson.[47] The three litigators hoped their suit would eventually wind up in the Supreme Court and radically restructure women's reproductive choices by making abortion legal in all 50 states. Unexpectedly, however, by early 1970, the New York State legislature made abortion legal during the first 24 weeks of gestation with Cook's bill, invalidating the *Abramowicz* suit.

Before the legislature acted, the women's case was joined by three other suits filed at the same time: *Hall v. Lefkowitz*, a doctor's case litigated by Roy Lucas with support from the American Civil Liberties Union, *Lyons v. Lefkowitz*, a counselor's case involving clergy from CCS litigated by Cyril Means, and *John and Mary Doe v. Lefkowitz*, a poor person's suit litigated by Marsha Lowry. According to Stearns, the litigators believed that each of these cases represented a particular group of individuals whose constitutional rights had been violated by the New York State abortion law: women who claimed the right to control their reproductive lives using abortion; doctors who claimed the right to practice medicine; clergy counselors who claimed the right to recommend abortion; and poor people who suffered the deadly effects of illegal abortion more than any other group.[48]

The litigators for the women's case decided to help the WHC organize a class-action suit because they believed that the abortion law needed to be challenged on the basis of a woman's right to control her reproduction, rather than a doctor's right to practice medicine under the state laws that allowed abortion to preserve life or health. The latter defense had been used on behalf of physicians arrested for performing abortions in both the *Vuitch* and *Belous* cases and would be employed again in the doctor's companion case in *Abramowicz*. The women's case, however, marked the first time that a class-action suit pressing for a woman's reproductive freedom was organized by women themselves.[49]

Abramowicz was used as a model for additional class-action suits filed in the early 1970s, including the Georgia case, *Doe v. Bolton*, which, with *Roe v. Wade*, reached the Supreme Court and established a woman's constitutional right to abortion. Feminists organized class action suits in Connecticut, Florida, Massachusetts, New Jersey, and Rhode Island. In all these cases, women's lived experience was used as evidence to establish a woman's right to abortion. In *Abele v. Markle*, this strategy worked remarkably well: the Connecticut Court incorporated women's abortion and pregnancy experiences into their decision establishing legal abortion. Even more significant, Stearns asserted, the testimony from women utilized as evidence in *Abele* had direct bearing on the Supreme Court's abortion decision in *Roe v. Wade* in 1973. She wrote that Justice Blackmun's "description of the physical and emotional harm to women of an unwanted pregnancy, the stigma of an out-of-wedlock child bears a striking resemblance to the language used by the Connecticut court."[50] Stearns argued that "this strategy [originally used in *Abramowicz v. Lefkowitz*] became a crucial part of the groundswell of challenges to restrictive abortion statutes throughout the country between 1969 and 1973, when the Supreme Court issued its ruling in *Roe v. Wade*."[51]

The plaintiffs for *Abramowicz* were organized by the WHC. In order to gather plaintiffs to challenge the law, they held meetings around the city at which women told their stories about abortion, unwanted pregnancy, or the fear of unwanted pregnancy. Those who attended the meetings were asked to join the suit. Stearns decided to include women who had never been pregnant to demonstrate that "you never knew when you would get pregnant so you should not have to be pregnant to have standing" in the case. The WHC meetings were used to heighten consciousness about the problem of unwanted pregnancy, to give women the opportunity to share their experiences with each other and feel less isolated, and as an organizing tool for the class-action suit. Many of the plaintiffs involved in *Abramowicz* had participated in radical feminist politics elsewhere in New York City, primarily by attending consciousness-raising meetings and demonstrations. Some, like Susan Brownmiller and Barbara Susan, were involved with Redstockings.[52]

After gathering plaintiffs, Stearns, Schulder, and Kennedy sought an injunction preventing state authorities (Leon Lefkowitz was the state attorney general) from enforcing the New York State law and a declaratory judgment that would make the law unconstitutional. If successful, their strategy would have rendered abortion, like any other medical procedure, free of regulation by the state. On October 28, 1969, Stearns argued the plaintiffs' case in front of Judge Edward Weinfeld. In her argument she made reference to *Griswold v. Connecticut*, the 1965 Supreme Court case that first established a constitutional right to privacy for married couples who chose to use birth control. She also asserted that unwanted pregnancy obstructed a woman's constitutional right to liberty, due process, free speech, and equal protection under the law. The female plaintiffs' experiences with unwanted pregnancy were presented as evidence to establish these arguments.[53]

On November 5, 1969, Judge Weinfeld decided to convene a three-judge statutory court, including himself, Judge Harold Tyler, and Judge Henry Friendly. This act indicated there was a legitimate question as to the constitutionality of the state statute under review. Appeals from such a court go directly to the Supreme Court. Kennedy requested that three women judges be appointed to hear the arguments, but Judge Weinfeld reminded Kennedy, "You should know perfectly well there is only one woman judge in this district." To which Kennedy retorted, "That is, indeed, shocking."[54]

After Judge Weinfeld had convened a statutory court, a group of anti-abortion doctors, officially named the intervenors, entered the case. This group of white, male, and primarily Catholic physicians called themselves "the friends of the fetus."[55] Their justifications for refusing to perform abortions under any circumstances helped build the states' case against legal abortion.[56] In a departure from the usual anti-abortion rhetoric, they argued on behalf of the individual rights of the unborn. The "friends of the fetus" believed that when a pregnant woman came to them for treatment, they had an equal obligation to *two* patients. In 1969, very few people had made this claim. Most anti-abortion proponents had been Catholics, who believed that any form of birth control constituted a sin, but they rarely emphasized the fetus as a human life or abortion as murder.

The intervenors represented what was then a new anti-abortion position and one that was destined to gain in strength very quickly as abortion became legal and more widely available in New York and other states. In response to the intervenors' defense, Kennedy asserted that the plaintiffs might also make a case on behalf of the unborn, arguing that they "might not want to be brought into the world 'unless they could be born to rich parents' and thus enjoy all the benefits of life." This idea never became a substantial part of the pro-legal abortion argument in *Abramowicz*. Schulder, Kennedy, and Stearns believed strongly that the female plaintiffs in the case should publicly testify as to the barbarity of the New York State law. They wanted to build from the momentum of the Redstockings' speakout in order to bring women's experiences with unwanted pregnancy and abortion into the debate over abortion law. They believed that the law infringed upon women's constitutional rights, and women's personal experiences would prove this point. As in the Redstockings' disruption of the legislative hearings and the speakout, the litigators created a forum for women's voices and experiences where before there had been none. Also, like the Redstockings, the litigators believed that women's ability to become pregnant gave them priority in deciding matters that affected their bodies. They wanted women's personal experiences with abortion and pregnancy to form the concrete material for their legal challenge. Schulder and Kennedy attested that "it was [the speakout] that triggered the idea in our minds to have women testify, women as experts, in the Federal case to attack the constitutionality of the abortion law."[57]

On January 14, 1970, the litigators began taking deposition testimony from 14 plaintiff witnesses—including Barbara Susan and Susan Brownmiller—as to their experiences with unwanted pregnancy and/or abortion. These stories were used to demonstrate that the New York State abortion statute violated women's fundamental constitutional rights. All the witnesses were women, except for one rabbi who had written a book on birth control and abortion in Jewish law, which gave him status as an expert witness. The litigators chose their witnesses "on the basis of having each witness' situation illuminate a distinct kind of situation."[58]

By using female witnesses who had experienced illegal abortion or unwanted pregnancy, the plaintiffs' lawyers implicitly critiqued an entrenched legal tradition, wherein social science expertise had been used as legal evidence. Most often male professional experts had contributed to court cases.[59] The most frequently cited example of this evidentiary strategy was the 1908 Supreme Court case, *Muller v. Oregon*, where Louis Brandeis argued in support of an Oregon statute limiting the number of hours women could work in laundries. In a unique move, Brandeis constructed his brief from the "expert" evidence of "government labor statistics, reports from factory inspectors, testimony from psychological, economic, and medical treatises."[60] Brandeis was the first to utilize social scientific evidence to this great an extent in a legal brief. Thus, his brief marked a change in the sort of material introduced as evidence in support of a legal argument.

Drawing on Brandeis's legacy, the National Association for the Advancement of Colored People (NAACP) campaigned to desegregate southern public schools in the 1930s and 1940s, offering sociological evidence to prove their argument for integration. Primarily, they used Gunnar Myrdal's 1944 *An American Dilemma* to demonstrate that black children's educational experiences in segregated public schools compared unequally to those of white children.[61] Also, the NAACP encouraged those who had experienced civil rights abuses to testify in public in order to give evidence challenging the constitutionality of Jim Crow laws.[62]

By elevating women's personal experiences to the status of concrete material for a legal challenge to the anti-abortion laws, feminists looked to these legal precedents in pursuing their own civil rights agenda.[63] Kennedy, Schulder, and Stearns all referred to their recollection of the public civil rights movement testimonials when they explained their decision to take public depositions. They also explained that they wanted women to be the "experts" based on the fact of their sex. Like the Redstockings in their disruption and speakout, the litigators transformed the meaning of the term "experts" to make a new point about laws that affected women's bodies.

As in the Redstockings speakout, the attorneys would have preferred to interview the women at Washington Square Methodist Church. By holding the interviews in a public space, women would again have the opportunity to publicly address the problem of illegal abortion and reconstruct the popular discourse about reproductive choice. Also, the church would "accommodate over 300 plaintiffs and others interested in the case," including the press. Unfortunately for the plaintiffs, however, the attorneys for the state arrived and objected to the public proceedings as both "a circus" and "ridiculous."[64] The state objected to the public testimony on two levels: they rejected the women's experiences as irrelevant to the abortion law, and they protested that the deposition testimony should be taken in private. (Depositions are usually taken privately by the defense in order to gather information about the case.) According to Schulder and Kennedy, "the representatives from District Attorney Hogan's office delivered an immortal statement for the record, declaring that women were 'irrelevant' on the subject of abortion."[65] The strong reaction by the state against the public testimony suggested the threat they thought it posed to their argument. Sympathetic publicity for the witnesses' stories could aid the abortion rights movement in its growing popularity.

The interviews were subsequently moved to the Foley Square courthouse at the request of the state. The judge permitted the press to attend but prohibited cameras. Approximately 70 people, including plaintiffs, friends, and family members, packed into the small room to listen to the witnesses' testimonials.[66] According to Stearns, the women who crowded the courtroom carried coat hangers with them to dramatize the dangers of anti-abortion laws. Schulder and Kennedy recalled that at the close of the hearings they left the "coat hangers strewn about the room as a symbol of the instruments of illegal abortion and their brutal impact on women's lives." Stearns believed that the move to Foley Square actually aided their case. She said that they never would have been able to continue filling the Washington Square location, but the courthouse remained packed every day of the depositional hearings.[67]

Each woman deposed for *Abramowicz v. Lefkowitz* told a unique story that detailed problems created by the restrictive New York abortion law. Barbara Susan's testimony was chosen as an example of a woman who failed to get an abortion, despite great effort on her part to obtain one. Susan, a Redstocking and contributor to the Weather Underground Newsletter RAT, became pregnant during her first sexual encounter at seventeen.[68] She hoped that the man involved would help her to find an abortionist, but he decided he wanted Susan to carry the pregnancy to term. He was convinced that a child would cause them to mature faster. Despite her boyfriend's sentiments, Susan made several appointments with abortionists who claimed to be doctors, but none of them showed up at the appointed location or time. She testified that "the first thing that happened was I tried to find an abortionist, but since, in New York State, abortion is illegal and I wasn't a criminal and I didn't know any criminals, I had a hard time finding one."[69] About four months into the pregnancy Susan began to panic. When she could not find an abortionist in New York City she decided to fly to Puerto Rico, a popular spot for American middle-class women to obtain a reasonably safe illegal abortion. She confessed the pregnancy to her mother with the intention of borrowing money to leave the country. Her mother responded by becoming frantic. Susan testified that "[w]hen I realized that the one person I thought I could depend on couldn't help me, I just sort of completely broke down. The next thing I knew was that twenty-four hours later I was married to this guy who I didn't want to marry."[70] After her wedding, she took a full-time job at Columbia University but was soon fired because of her pregnancy. She was also forced to take a leave of absence from Queens College and thus forfeited her Regents' scholarship. This forced hiatus made it very difficult for her to finish her education when she decided to return to school after the pregnancy.

Susan emphasized her feelings of powerlessness in the face of her unwanted pregnancy. "We [Susan and her husband] stayed together for about a month and I really felt like I was imposed upon by the state, in that I didn't want this ordeal to happen to me." Furthermore, "the state was on the side of the people who were supporting my getting married and not on the side of my deciding what to do with my life." Susan gave the child up for adoption but she still had to pay for the doctor's and lawyer's fees. (The adoptive parents paid for her hospital stay.)[71]

Testimonials like Susan's illustrated the utter powerlessness a woman felt before abortion was made legal. The lawyers for the plaintiffs, like the Redstockings, decided to give prominence to this point by bringing women's abortion stories into the limelight. By confessing their powerlessness, women would gain power over their lives. They also revealed their own experiences to ensure that no other women would go through the horrors of unwanted pregnancy, illegal and unsafe abortion, or an unwanted marriage and a child. From now on, they declared in *Abramowicz*, as in the disruption and in the speakout, abortion needed to be a choice made by women and controlled by women. No doctor, judge, or husband had the authority to remove this right from a woman. Women would act as experts on matters affecting their own bodies.

Although the New York State legislature's unexpected legalization of abortion—up to 24 weeks—crushed the litigators' hopes that *Abramowicz v. Lefkowitz* would reach the Supreme Court, it paved the way for other challenges to state abortion laws. Most notably, a group of feminists at the University of Texas in Austin approached a young female lawyer, Sarah Weddington, about helping them to start an abortion referral service. They wanted to help women find doctors in the area willing to perform illegal abortions. This project led Weddington to try to use the courts to challenge the restrictive Texas law. Because the state legislature showed no signs of repealing the law, a court challenge seemed a solid alternative. The Texas case, *Roe v. Wade*, with the Georgia class-action suit, *Doe v. Bolton*, culminated in the legalization of abortion in all 50 states. In both these cases, a pregnant woman was at the center of the argument for changing the abortion laws.[72] Thus, the Redstockings strategy of bringing women's experiences with abortion and unwanted pregnancy to the center of the discussion about new abortion laws—rather than the "expertise" of doctors who had broken the laws—succeeded in laying the groundwork that would eventually become a part of the Supreme Court's decision on abortion.

A False Victory?
Radical Feminist Abortion Rights Ideology after Legalization

Although feminists disagreed among themselves as to the goals of the abortion rights movement, most radical feminists called for the total repeal of all abortion laws. They believed there should be no restrictions on a woman's ability to attain an abortion. Radical feminists, who adhered to this position, including those in Redstockings, were unhappy with the 1970 New York State abortion law and the restrictions on abortion provision that quickly followed. In the months after the legalization of abortion in New York, Lucinda Cisler, of New York Radical Women, NYC-NOW, and founder of New Yorkers for Abortion Law Repeal (NYALR), carefully elaborated the radical feminist abortion rights position in her widely read 1970 article, "Abortion Law Repeal (sort of): A Warning to Women." Cisler had been instrumental in promoting the repeal position and organizing the movement for the eradication of the outdated New York State abortion statute. Repealers like Cisler, and the activists in Redstockings and *Abramowicz*, wanted the old abortion law removed from the books entirely. They asserted that reproductive decisions belonged in the hands of pregnant women, not with the state or with physicians. To make this point, a group of radical feminists handed out flyers at an abortion rally with the picture of the ideal abortion law—a blank page.[73]

Cisler responded to the New York State legislature's passage of the new abortion law, scheduled to take effect in July of 1970, with grave misgivings about how beneficial it would be for women who needed an abortion. Other abortion rights activists disagreed with Cisler and viewed the New York State statute as remarkably liberal. After all, they argued, in most states abortion was still illegal.[74] But Cisler believed that her doubts were confirmed when, at the behest of anti-abortion Catholics and physicians interested in maintaining control over abortion services, both the New York State and the New York City health commissioners proposed a series of guidelines restricting abortion provision. The guidelines maintained that only doctors could perform abortions, that abortions would be restricted to hospitals, and would be limited to the first or second trimesters.[75]

Radical feminists feared that nonfeminist abortion rights reformers would accept the health commissioners' regulation of the New York State abortion law. They emphasized that only a feminist fight for abortion law repeal would ensure the availability of abortion for all women regardless of income. And only feminists understood that these demands rested on the struggle for women's equality. For Cisler and the Redstockings, abortion rights had to be addressed in the context of a feminist movement. The two were intimately intertwined because the one could not be achieved without the other.[76]

In order to bolster this position publicly, Cisler wrote her article on abortion law—published by Redstockings in 1970—that immediately gained recognition among radical feminists. In this article she attempted to steer the abortion rights movement onto the path of abortion law repeal by countering, in turn, each of the restrictions proposed by the health commissioners. The first restriction (and the one most likely to remain in force) made it illegal for anyone other than a physician to perform an abortion. Radical feminists opposed this restriction because they believed that female paramedical technicians in clinics could perform affordable abortions. They noted that since the nineteenth century doctors had fought to maintain their monopoly over abortion because it generated a lucrative income. According to Cisler and other feminists involved with abortion rights and women's health, the simplicity of the abortion procedure meant that women who were not physicians could easily master it. Radical feminists associated with the Chicago Women's Liberation Union (CWLU) in the Jane collective, as well as the Society for Humane Abortion in California, proved this point when they began to provide safe illegal abortions to women at a low cost. At first the Jane collective employed a man they thought was a doctor to perform the abortions. When they found that he was not a doctor, the Jane collective began to train themselves to perform abortions. They functioned for four years (1969–1973) without medical complications, performing hundreds of illegal, inexpensive, and medically safe abortions. For very poor women, Jane provided free abortions, believing that no woman should be prevented from terminating a pregnancy for financial reasons.[77]

Radical feminists also believed that doctors should give up their monopoly on abortion because so many still felt it was a stigma to be labeled an abortionist. Abortion, in the late 1960s and early 1970s, remained associated with illicit sexuality and crime, despite the pressure to make it legal. Redstockings confronted these negative stereotypes in their speakout and in their writings. They felt strongly that neither women who had abortions nor abortion providers should be stigmatized as criminals or sexual perverts. If women performed abortions, radical feminists reasoned, they would not be intimidated by these negative attitudes because they would be providing a service that they all needed.[78]

Cisler and other radical feminists argued that by restricting abortion to hospitals, the New York health commissioners discriminated against poor women. Clinics could provide safe abortions at much lower costs. Also, hospitals were not outfitted to provide for the large numbers of women who wanted a legal abortion. Eventually, profit and a limited concern for the health of poor women, who would be forced to continue to seek out cheap underground abortions, encouraged the establishment of low-cost abortion clinics. Manhattan Borough President Percy Sutton and NARAL fought for the legalization of freestanding clinics, which began to provide large numbers of safe, legal abortions at reasonable prices.[79]

Cisler rejected two more restrictions proposed by the New York City and New York State health commissioners: "abortions may not be performed beyond a certain time in pregnancy, unless the woman's life is at stake," and "abortions may only be performed when the married woman's husband or the young single woman's parents give their consent." Cisler contended that both restrictions compromised the feminist ideal that a woman needed to decide what to do with her body under any and all circumstances. She added that opposition to these restrictions required little explanation, however. As with the other restrictions she discussed, none but the pregnant woman—not husbands, parents, physicians, clergy, or the state—should ever decide whether to continue a woman's pregnancy.

Cisler worried that some abortion rights activists would accept the restrictions proposed by the health commissioners. Their blindness to the problems that restrictions could create for the least privileged women might produce class divisions within the movement, weakening it in the long run. Cisler explained this threat and her belief that radical feminists needed to take the lead within the abortion rights movement to ensure abortion rights for all women:

> All women are oppressed by the present abortion laws, by old style "reforms," and by seductive new fake-repeal bills and court decisions. But the possibility of fake repeal—if it becomes reality—is most dangerous: it will divide women from each other. It can buy off most middle-class women and make them believe things have really changed, while it

leaves poor women to suffer and keeps us all saddled with abortion laws for many more years to come. There are many nice people who would like to see abortion made more or less legal, but their reasons are fuzzy and their tactics acquiescent. Because no one else except the women's movement is going to cry out against these restrictions, it is up to feminists to make the strongest and most precise demands upon the lawmakers—who ostensibly exist to serve us. We will not accept insults and call them "steps in the right direction."[80]

This passage cuts to the core of the radical feminist position in the abortion rights movement and delineates some of the fault lines within that same movement. Cisler argued that restrictions placed on abortion access had an oppressive effect on all women, but they hurt poor women more severely than middle-class women. Some mainstream feminist abortion rights activists (including National NOW), however, adopted moderate abortion law reform, because they hoped to achieve easier access to abortion for themselves and other women in their immediate milieu. As a result, they ignored the needs of poor women. Radical feminists, who saw themselves as the most revolutionary and genuine part of the feminist movement, underlined the importance of including all women in their demands for gender equality.

Along the same lines, Kathie Sarachild of Redstockings argued that all women, but particularly poor women, needed to have access to abortion. She noted that even after the New York State legislature made abortion available for women who could pay, poor women continued to turn to illegal providers to obtain cheap abortions.

> The women who are not stopped from having an abortion by the accusations of murder . . . are stopped by the remaining legal prohibitions, the terrible financial requirements and the dangers of the "criminal" alternative. . . . Many in the great liberal state of New York still resort to the cheaper, illegal practitioners, not to mention coat-hangers and other dangerous gambles. City hospitals are still treating the victims of botched-up, back room jobs, although the number of these "incomplete" abortions, as the medical profession calls them, has fallen since the new law went through. According to New York City Health Service figures, they have only fallen by 50%. . . . Again this is further evidence that the new law discriminates against the less well to do.[81]

Radical feminist groups other than Redstockings also argued that re-strictions on abortion could endanger the lives of poor women. In an ar-ticle published by a D.C. women's liberation newsletter, a NARAL lawyer argued that restrictions on the new New York State abortion provision would "once again prove the inhuman nature of the health care system in America" by encouraging "the development of commercial abortion es-tablishments charging outrageous prices," which would "drive the poor back into the hands of the butchers who are maiming and killing them now."[82] Immediately before the new law took effect in New York, au-thors of an article published by the New York City radical feminist jour-nal *RAT* (affiliated with the Weather Underground) asserted that "abor-tion is a matter of economics. . . . The rich get rich and poor have chil-dren or mangled abortions or . . . die. Black and brown sisters, sisters without money, sisters without the right connections are the ones who most heavily bear the brunt of abortion laws."[83]

In all these articles, radical feminists concerned themselves with the "most oppressed" women. In her influential work on radical feminism during this period, Alice Echols argues that radical feminists sought to erase differences among women by championing the needs of those they saw as the most oppressed.[84] While it may be true that this strategy erased differences by including all women under the banner of feminism and ar-guing that all women's lives would be improved by a feminist revolution, it also recognized the important economic and social stratifications that divided women. Not all women had the same political priorities, radical feminists argued, because of socioeconomic divisions. To build an inclu-sive movement, radical feminists believed they had to find a way to pro-vide for a wide variety of social and political demands, particularly rec-ognizing the demands of the women who had been neglected by more mainstream feminist groups such as NOW.

The Sexual Revolution?—"Ok to fuck until it shows"

In addition to their claim that legal abortion needed to be available to all women regardless of economics, Redstockings used the abortion rights movement to explode myths about the sexual revolution. They rejected the idea that a sexual revolution could have arrived before women had gained control over their reproduction, despite claims to the contrary by the media and New Left men. Under the category "Punishment of women for sexual activity" in her notes for the Redstockings speakout on abortion rights, Irene Peslikis wrote: "What sexual revolution? Ok to fuck until it shows."[85] Redstockings radical feminists believed that a sexual revolution could not occur if women risked pregnancy, criminal activity, and death every time they had sex. For Redstockings, legal abortion affirmed female sexual pleasure by freeing women from the psychological and physical dangers that accompanied pregnancy as long as abortion remained illegal.

The Redstockings explained that a sexual revolution without a female liberation that included reproductive control left women open to sexual exploitation. In her journal, Ellen Willis admitted that after her mid-1960s divorce, she feared exploitation at the hands of men:

> There can be no sexual revolution in a vacuum. Our sexual status, like our economic and political status, has improved somewhat since the Victorian era, but the rhetoric of emancipation has far outstripped the social reality. The "liberated woman," like the "free world," is a fiction that obscures real power relations and defuses revolution. How can women, subordinate in every other sphere, be free and equal in bed? Men want us to be a *little* free—it's more exciting that way. But women who really take them at their word put them uptight and they show it— by their jokes, their gossip, their obvious or subtle putdowns of women who seem too aggressive or too "easy."

According to Willis, the myth of sexual liberation perpetuated the false idea that the sexually promiscuous woman was liberated. By telling women they could exercise their "freedom" by being sexual, men obscured the real inequalities challenged by feminists. Also, while the "sexual revolution" gave men easier access to sex with "liberated" women, it undermined women's traditional defenses against male exploitation—commitment and marriage. Willis lamented that even in the late 1960s, many women had no choice but to use romantic commitment and marriage as their only protection against social and financial vulnerability. She explained: "By denying that these attitudes still predominate, the s.r. [sexual revolution] propaganda has undermined our main defense against them, which was to insist, as a prerequisite to sex, that men love us or accept responsibility for us. . . . Not that there's anything wrong with casual pleasure. It must be nice to be able to be casual. But we've never had that option."[86] For Willis, abortion rights were most centrally about sexual liberation. She argued that the lack of access to birth control and abortion reinforced restrictive social prohibitions against women engaging in sex without being married.[87]

Shulamith Firestone agreed with Willis that the sexual revolution put women at a disadvantage in heterosexual relationships. In her chapter on love in *The Dialectic of Sex*, she wrote:

> But the rhetoric of the sexual revolution, if it brought no improvements for women, proved to have great value for men. By convincing women that the usual female games and demands were despicable, unfair, prudish, old-fashioned, puritanical, and self-destructive, a new reservoir of available females was created to expand the tight supply of sexual goods, disarming women of even the little protection they had so painfully acquired.[88]

Like Willis, Firestone underscored the perpetuation of a new double standard that prevented women from demanding the traditional protections of marriage and commitment in a sexual relationship. Suddenly, women had to compete to offer themselves as sexual commodities without receiving anything in return—even their pleasure was circumscribed by fear and insecurity. Many women complained that they could not enjoy sex because they worried constantly about pregnancy and what they would do if they needed an abortion. In order to address this imbalance, women needed to be able to control their reproduction. The Redstockings confronted the double standard and promoted the notion that women had as much right to enjoy sex as men without worrying about an unplanned and unwanted pregnancy.

Conclusion

Although they never achieved their goal of abortion law repeal—the blank page abortion law—the radical feminists in Redstockings succeeded in influencing popular opinion about abortion. Most clearly articulated in the abortion speakout, in *Abramowicz*, and in subsequent court cases challenging the antiquated anti-abortion laws, women who publicly exposed their experiences with abortion and the constant fear of unwanted pregnancy began to establish the idea that a forced pregnancy inhibited a woman's constitutional rights. Never again would abortion be thought of as merely the province of medical doctors, counselors, or psychiatrists, bent on granting a termination to certain deserving (usually middle-class and white) women. Nor would it be a decision made by husbands or boyfriends. Women would no longer need to prove their incompetence or insanity in order to gain some semblance of control over their reproductive systems.[89]

The right to choose an abortion changed the world for many women. Suddenly, they were able to pursue sexual pleasure without fear of being forced into an undesirable marriage or bearing an unwanted child. The young women who made up Redstockings and other radical feminist groups found themselves pursuing careers, sexual lives, and relationships not fully possible until reproductive control became a fact. On the other hand, other women's lives were less profoundly affected by the legalization of abortion. Poor women and women of color found themselves with problems that abortion could not solve. These women were unable to have children because of poverty, sterilization abuse, or even coerced abortion. For them, abortion was never a priority in the same way.

In the years immediately following the legalization of abortion in New York State, white feminists would be criticized by both black and Puerto Rican men and women who believed that abortion rights and population control often meant the same thing—the genocide of people of color. Black and Puerto Rican activists critiqued white feminists for failing to include a campaign against sterilization abuse in the abortion rights movement. However, members of Redstockings recalled addressing issues of race and discussing the particular problems of reproductive control facing African-American women, Latinas, and poor women.[90] They recognized that low-income women, black, and Puerto Rican women had a different perspective on reproduction and reproductive control. These issues did not come to the fore of the feminist campaign because legal abortion remained overwhelmingly the primary problem confronting young and middle-class women in the late 1960s. The movement against sterilization abuse and for a broad agenda of reproductive rights that focused on the needs of poor women would burst onto the political scene in the early part of the 1970s, as abortion became more available, and as black feminist and Black Power critiques of population control became more strident.[91]

2

"An act of valor for a woman need not take place inside of her"
Black Women, Feminism, and Reproductive Rights

Some Black Nationalists charge that the white power structure not only favors abortion law repeal, but is actually pushing it as a means of eliminating the black population, as well as all poor people. Of all the lies and moralism men have used to obligate women to bear more of their children, this one takes the cake. Not content with identifying a woman's freedom to terminate pregnancy with murder, as President Nixon does, these black reactionaries hold the accusation of genocide over every black woman who wants an abortion and over feminists of every race who fight for this right. A black woman who has an abortion is not merely committing murder, they charge. She is participating in the murder of her whole people.   —Kathie Sarachild of Redstockings

Black women are often afraid to permit any kind of necessary surgery because they know from bitter experience that they are more likely than not to come out of the hospital without their insides.   —Frances Beal of the Student Non-Violent
Coordinating Committee

Part of this struggle to control our own bodies is the fight against forced sterilization and population-control schemes. . . . [W]e will also fight the racist laws which have been proposed in some states, which stipulate that welfare mothers must be sterilized after they have had a certain number of children.
—Third World Women's Workshop

> Reproductive freedom means the freedom to have as well as not to have children. Policies that restrict women's right to have and raise children—through forced sterilization or the denial of adequate welfare benefits—are directly related to policies that compel women to have children, on the view that this is their primary human function.   —The Committee for Abortion Rights and Against Sterilization Abuse (CARASA)

Black men active in the Black Power movement of the late 1960s and early 1970s made strong and sometimes inflammatory statements about the use of contraception and abortion by black women. An initial investigation of the discourse surrounding black women's attempts to control their reproductive bodies suggests that black men dominated the emerging dialogue and made it a subset of the Black Nationalist impulse. Even white feminists, such as Kathie Sarachild of the radical feminist organization Redstockings, recognized that the pronatalist rhetoric of Black Nationalists was at the forefront of public conversation about black women and fertility control. In all this discussion of black women's fertility, black women's voices on how best to control their own reproduction often got lost.[1] Black women seldom receive proper credit for the work they have done on reproductive rights. Nor have white feminists often acknowledged the extent to which black women shaped the feminist reproductive rights movement.[2] What black women were saying about their reproductive bodies helps us to understand their views of reproductive control. In listening to black women, one discovers that they offered a more complicated view of reproductive control than did either Black Nationalists or white women's liberationists.

Politically active black women of the early 1970s carved out a reproductive rights discourse that involved relative autonomy over reproductive decisions not only in relation to black men but in relation to white feminists and white society as well. They rejected the Black Nationalist argument that the birth of children to black women reinforced black masculinity. They also disagreed with the claim that the use of birth control and abortion by black women spelled genocide for the race.[3] Moreover, they criticized abortion rights feminists for their narrow focus on legal abortion, insisting that feminists needed to bring reproductive abuses experienced by women of color—such as involuntary sterilization—to the forefront of their political agenda. Black women—some of whom identified themselves with the women's liberation movement—argued further that white feminists needed to forge an inclusive reproductive rights agenda that synthesized anti-poverty politics, welfare rights, and access to reproductive and basic health care if they wanted to include women of color in their movement. They proclaimed that improved access to total health care, a living wage, adequate housing, and subsidized child-care all needed to be present before a woman could know she had total control over her fertility. Although history has not acknowledged it, black women met with remarkable success in their effort to make their voices heard about their right to control over their reproductive bodies. By the end of the decade, mainstream feminists and other population planning organizations had adopted the reproductive rights discourse articulated by black women in a new movement for reproductive freedom.[4]

"The revolution needs numbers": Black Feminism and the Critique of the Theory of Genocide

Black women's position on reproductive control and their stance toward women's liberation emerged from contentious debates around gender roles in the black family that took place in black communities in the 1960s and early 1970s. Specifically, black women resisted stereotypes that characterized them as emasculating matriarchs—the role of the Sapphire—and criticized black men for asserting a form of machismo that insisted black women limit themselves to reproducing children for the revolution. Black women explicitly rejected these stereotyped gender roles when they criticized black militant and nationalist positions on birth control and abortion. For example, a black female hospital worker interviewed for an article on black women's attitudes toward birth control in *Ebony* explained that "the black man's opposition [to birth control] has a lot to do with his virility hang-up. They like to brag about the number of kids they've fathered. They think it's the ultimate proof of their manhood."[5]

Black women helped forge a new black feminism critical of certain aspects of Black Nationalist masculinity, yet still supportive of the united movement to end racial prejudice. In particular, black women were critical of the idea that they should stay in their place behind their men; they insisted that they had more to contribute to a social and political revolution than their fertility. They also criticized the image of the black man as the sole economic provider for the family. Black women had always struggled for the economic and emotional survival of their families and communities, they asserted.

The reproductive rights views of black women belong in the context of the hostility of Black Nationalist men, even to minimal forms of birth control. Black Nationalist men argued that African Americans needed to build an army of blacks to fight the white establishment. Whether this army picked up guns, marched to the voting booth, or built black institutions to serve black neighborhoods, numbers were high on the agenda. The more black people, the argument went, the more likely blacks could throw off the yoke of racism. The role of black women in this scenario was simple: Black Nationalist men wanted black women to produce and raise the (male) warriors for the revolution.

Assertions of black masculinity and aggression distinguished the Black Power/Nationalist movement of the second half of the 1960s from the older nonviolent civil rights movement.[6] To illustrate the radical transformation of the movement at this juncture, black militants used comparisons between the relative passivity of Martin Luther King and the confrontational character of the young Malcolm X or Stokely Carmichael. Rumbles of discontent with traditional nonviolent and integrationist strategies could be heard as early as the 1964 Freedom Summer, during which white college students traveled to Mississippi to help the black-led but interracial Student Non-Violent Coordinating Committee (SNCC) register rural blacks to vote. That summer some black organizers protested that white students tried to appropriate leadership positions in the organization. Also, black organizers objected that the rural blacks who lived in Mississippi and faced racist violence every day were neglected by the press as a result of the arrival of white students from the North. After the 1964 Mississippi Freedom Summer, some members of SNCC chose to expel whites from the organization. The younger members of the civil rights movement, represented by SNCC, decided that the goals of political integration as well as nonviolence were bankrupt. (The humiliation of the Mississippi Freedom Democratic Party at the 1964 Democratic Convention hammered home the futility of political integration for SNCC.) SNCC members decided to build black-controlled institutions, such as the Lowndes County Freedom Organization in Lowndes County, Mississippi. The Lowndes County group chose the image of a black panther to represent them in the election, and they chose to take up weapons in self-defense.[7]

The Black Panther Party for Self Defense, founded in 1966 in Oakland, California, acknowledged the influence of SNCC and the Lowndes County Freedom Organization on the Black Power movement by appropriating the symbol of the black panther for their new organization. The Black Panther Party epitomized the new masculinity of Black Power and Black Nationalism. Particularly in the early years of the organization, the Panthers made masculinity a symbol central to their political activities. One of the most public displays of masculine aggression occurred in 1967, when the Panthers mounted the California Supreme Court House stairs in Sacramento dressed in black leather jackets and berets and openly carried rifles and ammunition. Their display of firearms gave the Panthers new support among black Bay Area students and prompted the Black Nationalist poet LeRoi Jones (later called Amiri Baraka) to announce, "You better get yourself a gun if you want to survive the white man's wrath. . . . White policemen aren't here to protect you, they're here to kill you." Suddenly, the fight against racism required public displays of weapons, shooting melees with police, and competition within the ranks of the Black Panther Party to prove masculine prowess.[8]

Given their great contribution to civil rights organizing in the South—as members of SNCC black women headed up voter registration drives and suffered beatings from white racists equal to those meted out to black men—black women felt frustrated by the turn toward Black Power that often came at the expense of women's autonomy and voice in the movement. Black women had proved their dedication to a united effort to end Jim Crow segregation and disenfranchisement only to be rewarded with a newly constrained role.[9]

Out of these conflicts sprang the assertion that black feminism would be beneficial for both black women and the black movement against racism as a whole. Examples of black women's writings from the early 1970s exemplify some of the first attempts to mold the rhetoric of women's liberation to meet the needs of black women. The first black women's liberationists were critical of Black Power men for failing to recognize that sexism often perpetuated inequalities among men and women that paralleled the racism experienced by blacks. Reproductive control also topped the list of topics that black women believed they needed to grapple with in order to liberate themselves from both sexism and racist oppression. Black women's liberationists made strong statements in favor of the use of birth control and abortion. They insisted that contrary to assertions made by Black Nationalists, black women wanted to control their fertility. This stance did not necessarily lead to an easy alliance among black and white feminists.

Kay Lindsey, a black feminist writer, echoed other black women's criticism of the Black Power movement for marginalizing black women. She wrote:

> I'm not one of those who believes
> That an act of valor, for a woman
>   Need take place inside her.
>
> My womb is packed in mothballs
> And I hear that winter will be mild.
>
> Anyway I gave birth twice
> And my body deserves a medal for that
>   But I never got one.
>
> Mainly because they thought
> I was just answering the call of nature.
>
> But now that the revolution needs numbers
>   Motherhood got a new position
>   Five steps behind manhood.
>
> And I thought sittin' in the back of the bus
>   Went out with Martin Luther King.[10]

Lindsey underscored her critique by questioning black men about their failure to appreciate black women's past childbearing efforts. She noted that as long as reproduction was considered "natural" and immaterial to the struggle for radical social change, women would not be appreciated for the work (both emotional and physical) they put into childbearing and childrearing. Their reproduction only gained value as the civil rights struggle became increasingly gendered—as black virility began to symbolize black masculine power, and black women's reproduction and mothering of children began to be seen as women's primary revolutionary role. Black women activists have argued that as the movement shifted from civil rights to Black Power, women's political participation in the movement decreased. Lindsey's image of the revival of Jim Crow segregation captured the irony of a Black Power movement that claimed as its goal the end of racist oppression, yet limited black women's status within that movement.[11]

Although black women expressed outrage at the sexism of black men, Lindsey, and other black women, believed they needed to critique the Black Power movement as participants in it, in order to make it more effective. They believed that the sexism of the Black Power movement actually weakened it. Black women could not contribute fully to the struggle against white supremacy as long as black men insisted that black women's primary revolutionary role was the reproduction and care of black children. They hoped that by criticizing the sexism of the Black Power movement, black women would be able to contribute more fully to the realization of their own vision of a nonracist and nonsexist society.

In a widely circulated 1968 address to black men called "Statement on Birth Control," the Black Women's Liberation Group of Mount Vernon, New York asserted their right to fertility control, despite Black Nationalist rejections of contraception. The Mount Vernon group had roots going back to 1960, when they formed as a network of women concerned with expanding black women's access to birth control. They were composed primarily of working-class women and women on welfare. They placed a strong emphasis on black women's role as mothers, which included the traditional mothering role of caring for children, as well as fighting to pave the way for a better future for their community. They demanded welfare rights and access to decent housing and education. They defined these demands as issues fundamental to women's liberation. Like other black women who had been active in the civil rights movement, those who organized with the Black Women's Liberation Group argued that black women needed to be leaders within the black movement for an end to racial oppression. And black women needed to define the issues of concern to them and their children.[12]

In their "Statement on Birth Control," the Black Women's Liberation Group expressed a great deal of resentment toward black men for their alleged abandonment of black families. The authors of this "letter," which included "two welfare recipients, two housewives, a domestic, a grandmother, a psychotherapist, and others who read, agreed, but did not help to compose," argued that black men who had abandoned their families made it necessary for black women to control their fertility. They declared that "if we take the Pills or practice birth control in other ways, it's because of poor black men." The Mount Vernon authors added that "black women have always been told by black men that we were black, ugly, evil bitches and whores—in other words we were the real niggers in this society—oppressed by whites, male and female, and the black man, too." The Mount Vernon group argued that if black men could not demonstrate that they would stand with black women, black women would take matters into their own hands by limiting their fertility out of necessity. They wrote, "So when Whitey put out the Pill, and poor black sisters spread the word, we saw how simple it was not to be a fool for men any more (politically we would say men could no longer exploit us sexually or for money and leave the babies with us to bring up)." To the Mount Vernon group, it was hypocritical for Black Nationalist men to urge women to have babies and then walk away when the time came to support them. The Mount Vernon group thus used a racial stereotype about black men—that they walked out on black women and children in large numbers—to strengthen their pro–birth control argument. This sort of rhetorical stance likely fueled the strained relations between black activist men and women in the early 1970s.[13]

Frances Beal, an organizer for SNCC's Black Women's Liberation Committee (BWLC) and a black feminist, also denounced the sexism of Black Nationalist men and argued that black women required voluntary fertility control. In 1968, Beal helped found the BWLC in order to address the triple oppressions—race, sex, and class—experienced by black women. BWLC members reported that Black Nationalist gender politics represented a marked and disturbing increase in sexism in the civil rights movement. To prove their assertion, BWLC members pointed out that Black Nationalist men accepted damaging myths about black women, particularly the myth of a black matriarchy put forth by Daniel Patrick Moynihan in 1965. Beal argued that black women could not give up power in order to empower their black brothers. Rather, they needed to be full participants in the black struggle to end racist oppression. To achieve this goal, black women needed to empower themselves by addressing both racism and sexism.[14]

In 1970, the BWLC became the Third World Women's Alliance (TWWA) in order to expand their politics to encompass all Third World women. TWWA further developed the political analysis laid out by BWLC. They asserted that women of color were equally oppressed by sexism, racism, and capitalist exploitation as workers.[15] In their journal, *Triple Jeopardy*, published from 1971 through 1975, TWWA devoted numerous articles to women's health care, with particular attention to reproductive abuses experienced by Third World women. For example, in 1975, *Triple Jeopardy* editors included two articles on sterilization abuse: one that addressed the abuse of Puerto Rican women and the second about Native American women forcibly sterilized in federal government hospitals. In both cases, the authors argued that manipulating the reproduction of poor Third World women bolstered U.S. colonialist efforts.[16]

Like members of TWWA, Cellestine Ware, author of *Woman Power*, argued that despite their vehement criticism of Black Nationalist men, black women still needed to make the fight against racist oppression central to their feminist agendas. She argued that this meant that black women had to pursue a drastically different political agenda from white women. Black women, she wrote, "are too occupied struggling for essentials: shelter, food and clothing to organize themselves around the issue of women's rights." Thus, black women saw the necessity of creating political liaisons with black men "in the struggle for racial equality." Feminist demands seemed individualistic and trivial when compared to the fight against racism. Ware concluded that "feminist goals, like abortion on demand and easily obtainable birth control, are viewed with paranoid suspicion by some black militants at a time when they are literally fighting for their lives and looking everywhere to increase their numbers." In other words, many black women politicos shied away from the white feminist movement because they feared splitting a united front against racism and they had a stronger commitment to ending race oppression. They often preferred to address sexism among black liberationists without the intervention of whites.[17]

In her 1970 article, "The Black Movement and Women's Liberation," Linda La Rue, a graduate student in political science at Purdue University, concurred with the notion that black women should put their energy into criticizing black male sexism within the civil rights movement and should refrain from joining the white women's liberation movement. She believed that white and black women's experiences and political interests were too far apart to unite in any common struggle against sexism. On the subject of abortion rights, La Rue noted that black and white women both wanted to limit their fertility but for very different reasons. She wrote that white feminists "assert that all women have the right to decide if and when they want children and thus fail to catch the flavor of the actual circumstances. Actual circumstances boil down to middle-class women deciding when it is convenient to have children, while poor women decide the prudence of bringing into a world of already scarce resources another mouth to feed." Black women were concerned about ending poverty so they could raise their children in a healthy environment. Having the means to prevent conception or terminate a pregnancy was not enough by itself.[18]

Thus, support for a broad reproductive rights agenda underlay the development of a black feminism that stood somewhat apart from most white women's conceptions of feminism and the abortion rights movement. Within this context, the black writer Toni Bambara composed one of the most well-known articles in support of birth control for black women. In this piece she maintained that black women needed to take on revolutionary roles within the Black Power movement that paralleled those filled by black men. She wrote, "Seems to me the Brother does us all a great disservice by telling [the black woman] to fight the man with her womb. Better to fight with the gun and the mind."[19]

While the reproduction of revolutionaries had to be accomplished, Bambara expressed skepticism that a woman could best contribute to the Black Power movement by having babies indiscriminately. She explained why she thought black women could empower themselves by using birth control:

> It is a noble thing, the rearing of warriors for the revolution. I can find no fault with the idea. I do, however, find fault with the notion that dumping the pill is the way to do it. You don't prepare yourself for the raising of super-people by making yourself vulnerable—chance fertilization, chance support, chance tomorrow—nor by being celibate until you stumble across the right stock to breed with. You prepare yourself by being healthy and confident, by having options that give you confidence, by getting yourself together, by being together enough to attract a together cat whose notions of fatherhood rise above the Disney caliber of man-in-the-world-and-woman-in-the-home, by being committed to the new consciousness, by being intellectually and spiritually and financially self-sufficient to do the thing right. You prepare yourself by being in control of yourself. The pill gives the woman, as well as the man, some control. Simple as that.[20]

Bambara believed that black women should refuse to perpetuate the stereotype of docile woman behind her revolutionary man. But this refusal did not mean a rejection of the revolutionary struggle. Rather, black women wanted to play many parts in the transformation of a racist society into an egalitarian one. One way to begin making changes was to demand access to fertility control. Bambara asserted, "It is a sinister thing for the state to tell anyone not to have a child." Instead,

> Time, money, energy could be invested in taking care of her health so that the champion she plans to raise isn't faced from the jump with the possibility of brain damage because of her poor nutrition; could be invested in a safe home, so the baby isn't hazarded by lead poison in the falling plaster and by rats; in the acquiring of skills and knowledge and a groovy sense of the self so the child isn't menaced by stupidity and other child-abuse practices so common among people grown ugly and dangerous from being nobody for so long.[21]

For Bambara and other black women demanding access to fertility control measures in the early 1970s, birth control and abortion could not satisfy their requirements alone.

Involuntary Fertility Control: The Problem of Sterilization Abuse

Black women required birth control and abortion for themselves, but they also warned that sterilization abuse posed a particular threat to women of African descent.[22] The Third World Women's Workshop—constituted at a 1971 national abortion conference held by the National Abortion Coalition of Michigan—crafted a vituperative critique of sterilization and population-control abuses declaring, "Part of this struggle to control our own bodies is the fight against forced sterilization and population-control schemes." They continued their statement, emphasizing the necessity of combining a pro–legal abortion politic with one that opposed sterilization abuse: "The campaign to get rid of the abortion laws is one of the best ways to fight forced sterilization because the lack of legal abortion has been used for years to force women to undergo sterilization." Some women of color and poor women had experienced sterilization after a physician had agreed to perform an illegal abortion; others were pressured into sterilization after receiving a legal hospital abortion. If this woman could not care for a child, a doctor might reason, she had no right to her fertility.[23]

As we have seen, in 1973, one case brought mainstream attention to the problem of forced sterilization. Twelve-year-old Minnie Lee Relf was sterilized in a federally funded (Health, Education, and Welfare [HEW]) health clinic—the Montgomery Family Planning Clinic—in Montgomery, Alabama. A state eugenics statute authorized the procedure for the "mentally incompetent" without requiring the girl's or her family's consent. Caseworkers had diagnosed Minnie Lee as mentally retarded, although the basis for this diagnosis was spurious. Before her sterilization, Minnie Lee had been provided with Depo-Provera shots to prevent conception. Clinic staff presumed that the girl could not make responsible decisions about her sexuality and reproductive capacities, so they prescribed this controversial drug to control her reproduction. They argued that Depo-Provera proved advantageous in cases of mental incompetence because patients had no active role in its administration. When the clinic where she had received the Depo-Provera shots discontinued that treatment (because Depo-Provera caused cancer in lab rats), it was recommended that Minnie Lee be sterilized. Despite the suspicions of welfare caseworkers, there was no evidence that Minnie Lee Relf was sexually active at the time of the Depo-Provera provision or the sterilization.[24]

Minnie Lee's mother believed that she had authorized the continued administration of Depo-Provera, not her daughter's sterilization, by signing a consent form with her "X." (As a woman who had spent most of her life sharecropping in Alabama, Mrs. Relf had never learned how to read or write.) To prove that Minnie Lee did not understand the consequences of her operation, one of the lawyers in the class-action suit filed against HEW on her behalf (*Relf v. Weinberger*), asked her if she planned to have children. She replied, yes, she planned to have a little girl.[25]

In response to Minnie Lee Relf's sterilization, the National Welfare Rights Organization (NWRO) filed a suit against HEW for violating regulations created by the Nixon administration that prohibited the sterilization of minors using federal funds. The Montgomery Southern Poverty Law Center joined the NWRO suit with attorney Joseph Levin as the chief litigator. After the Relf scandal became a sensation in the mainstream press, Senator Edward Kennedy of the Health Subcommittee also pressed for a hearing on the forced sterilization of minors and the failure of HEW to comply with the existing sterilization regulations.[26]

Members of NWRO accused HEW of using federal funds "to pay for the involuntary sterilizations of juveniles and those alleged to be incompetent." They claimed that the sterilization regulations failed to protect public assistance recipients from threats that they would lose their welfare funds if they declined a sterilization procedure. NWRO also asserted that poor and black women should control their own fertility. This included providing them with the means to bear as many children as they wanted. In order to secure this demand, poor and black women required resources, including a living wage.[27]

At the end of March 1974, Judge Gerhard Arnold Gesell of the U.S. District Court for the District of Columbia—who also decided the landmark 1969 case that made abortion legal in Washington, D.C.—handed down his decision in *NWRO v. Weinberger*. He ruled that HEW must cease funding sterilizations for minors and the mentally incompetent. He also ordered HEW to redraft its regulations for sterilizations performed on welfare patients. In April, HEW issued a set of "interim regulations" that prohibited federally funded sterilization of any incompetent persons without their "uncoerced" consent. These guidelines stayed in effect until 1978 when, after a long battle, feminist reproductive rights activists against sterilization abuse strengthened them further.[28]

Statistical evidence indicated that black women had reason to worry about sterilization abuse. In 1970, black women were sterilized at over twice the rate of white women, 9 per 1,000 for black women as compared to 4.1 per 1,000 for white women. Like Minnie Lee Relf, many of these women were low-income and relied on federally subsidized clinics or Medicaid funds for their health care. Their dependence on the federal government for reproductive health care made them vulnerable to the workings of a system that often neglected the needs of low-income women. It also made them vulnerable to the prejudices and biases of state providers, who sometimes subscribed to the notion that black and poor women had no right to make choices about their personal fertility.[29] A 1972 study by the Center for Disease Control of the Department of Health, Education and Welfare in Alabama found that women of Latin American descent, black women, and public assistance recipients were sterilized in higher numbers than white women and women who had never received welfare benefits. Another 1973 survey reported that 43 percent of women sterilized in federally financed family planning programs were black.[30] Data gathered in 1975–1976 indicated that poor women and women with education limited to high school or below experienced high rates of sterilization. Women receiving Medicaid payments, in particular, were sterilized at a rate two to four times greater than nonrecipients.[31] These statistics suggest that some doctors pushed sterilization on women they deemed unworthy of the right to reproduce.[32] Even when doctors did not force poor and nonwhite women to accept sterilization as a method of contraception, social and cultural factors—such as poverty, limited access to health care, lack of education, or inability to speak English—often influenced their decision to "choose" sterilization over other methods of birth control.[33]

Black civil rights activists throughout the 1960s documented sterilization abuse among black women, particularly poor and unmarried black women. In 1964, the Student Non-Violent Coordinating Committee (SNCC) issued a pamphlet called "Genocide in Mississippi" that contained critical information about a punitive sterilization bill in Mississippi, making it a felony to give birth to a second or subsequent illegitimate child. Anyone convicted under this statute would have had the option of becoming sterilized instead of serving prison time. The Mississippi state legislature had been trying to pass a punitive sterilization law since 1958, arguing that sterilization would help prevent illegitimacy. A successful campaign against this bill waged by SNCC and members of the mainstream media, including *Newsweek*, forced the state senate to drop the sterilization provision of the bill.[34]

Fannie Lou Hamer—the civil rights activist who served as a delegate for the Mississippi Freedom Democratic Party (MFDP) at the 1964 Democratic Convention in Atlantic City—testified about her own forced sterilization. She wanted to publicize the reality of compulsory sterilization in the South. Her sterilization took place when she had to be hospitalized for the removal of a uterine tumor. Through the hospital grapevine, Hamer heard that her uterus had been excised (hysterectomy) during the operation. No doctor had informed her about the nature of her surgery or acquired her consent for the procedure. In a speech before the Women's International League for Peace and Freedom, Hamer reported that 60 percent of black women who passed through Sunflower City Hospital in her hometown in Mississippi were sterilized, many of them without their knowledge. In her speech before an audience of white women, Hamer connected female sterilization abuse with other civil rights abuses. Just as the right to vote was necessary to achieve social equality, the right to reproduce needed equal affirmation. Hysterectomy had become so common in Mississippi that it had gained the nickname "Mississippi appendectomy" by physicians practicing in the region.[35]

During the 1960s and 1970s, to reduce the numbers of illegitimate and poor children, punitive sterilization laws were proposed in California, Connecticut, Delaware, Georgia, Illinois, Iowa, Louisiana, Maryland,

Mississippi, Ohio, South Carolina, Tennessee, and Virginia. For example, in 1971, Lucius N. Porth, a Republican legislator in South Carolina, submitted a proposal for a bill that would force a woman on welfare with more than two children to give up her entitlement or submit to sterilization. The legislators who proposed these measures believed that women receiving AFDC (Aid to Families with Dependent Children) and Medicaid benefits drained public coffers by breeding irresponsibly. They intoned that the poor women for whom these laws had been designed could only understand punitive and dehumanizing measures such as forced sterilization. Because black women made up a relatively high percentage of poor people who received AFDC or Medicaid benefits, these proposals would affect them disproportionately. Legislators with a population control agenda suggested that poor and black women lacked the capacity to make their own reproductive decisions—to choose to bear a child or to control their fertility using birth control. Gene Damschroder, state representative of Ohio, betrayed this sentiment when he described a proposed bill forcing women on welfare with more than two children to undergo sterilization. He told reporters, "If a man decides to live like an animal he should be treated like an animal."[36]

Black women's organized opposition to legislation that proposed withholding welfare benefits from women with illegitimate children proved fundamental to the development of a feminist reproductive rights movement sensitive to the demands of low-income women. Black women shifted the dominant feminist discourse on reproductive control away from a singular focus on legal abortion and access to contraception to a more inclusive discourse that emphasized the right to bear children regardless of economic class or race. For example, from 1968 to the early 1970s, poor black women organized in the NWRO fought for the right to welfare entitlements for poor women with children, particularly a living wage paid directly to recipients. They identified poverty, sexism, and racism as barriers preventing black women from having as many children as they wanted. NWRO activists countered the prevailing notion of who constituted the "deserving poor" and who required regulation to prevent a drain on society. They argued that women on welfare with small children deserved state support to care for their families, no matter how small or large. In addition to state support, they demanded jobs that paid enough to survive comfortably, as well as state-supported child-care services. They also demanded access to safe and effective birth control and legal abortion. Regardless of her economic status, NWRO members believed that every woman had an inalienable right to bear children or limit her childbearing if she chose to do so.[37]

NWRO linked the right to welfare entitlements with the right to voluntary fertility control in their political literature and campaigns. In a 1968 article published in *NOW! The National Welfare Leaders Newsletter* (the newsletter of the NWRO), Doris Bland linked sterilization abuse to demands for state subsidized child-care. Bland believed that federally funded daycare was a necessary accompaniment to a poor black woman's right to her fertility. Black women needed the means to bear children and care for them even if they were poor. Johnny Tillmon, executive director of NWRO in 1972 and once a long-term AFDC recipient, told a reporter that a social worker had tried to convince her to take birth control pills. She replied that poor women never have children to get extra benefits.[38] In 1971, the NWRO successfully organized opposition to a Tennessee bill that would "force women with one or more 'illegitimate' children to submit to sterilization or lose all welfare benefits." In 1973, NWRO brought the suit on behalf of Minnie Lee Relf against HEW demanding stringent regulation of all federally funded sterilizations.[39]

Although NWRO supported voluntary sterilization, they expressed the importance that federal regulations be strengthened to protect poor women and women of color from involuntary sterilization. Ann Carson of the Research Department of NWRO explained, "NWRO is for voluntary sterilization. However, in light of recent developments we feel federal regulations on sterilization are necessary. . . . Unfortunately such regulations may make it difficult for those seeking voluntary sterilizations, but we feel the most important thing is that individuals rights are guarded and there is no possibility for coercion." Another welfare rights organization based in Jackson, Mississippi, the Rural Coalition of Mississippi, also reviewed the federal regulations after the Relf sterilization came to light. Members of the Mississippi group argued that they had studied the HEW guidelines on sterilization and expressed alarm at its vagueness. They explained their opposition to the guidelines, "Recent experiences and practices indicate that sterilization is being used for economic purposes, to reduce the welfare roll."[40]

Minnie Lee Relf's was the most well-known involuntary sterilization of the 1970s, but other women of color also came forward to claim that they had been coerced into giving up their ability to bear children. Newspaper reports indicated that at least 80 minors were sterilized by government funds in a 15-month period between 1972 and 1973.[41] In 1971, the University of Southern California, Los Angeles Medical Center allegedly sterilized 10 Chicanas under suspicious circumstances. The 10 women testified in a class-action suit (*Dolores Madrigal et al. v. E.J. Quilligan*, director of obstetrics at USC-L.A. county et al.) against the medical center and anonymous doctors who performed the sterilizations. All the female plaintiffs in the case held that they had been forced to sign consent forms authorizing the procedure during labor and while under anesthesia. Clearly, they argued, at this moment they lacked the ability to make an informed and thoughtful decision about their desire for future children. Furthermore, doctors presented consent forms written in English, even though all the women spoke Spanish as their first and primary language. The sterilized women insisted that consent under these conditions did not constitute a voluntary decision for the medical procedure. Unfortunately, the sterilized women lost their suit. The judge argued that there had been a miscommunication but the doctors could not be held responsible for it.[42]

Despite the ruling in favor of Director of Obstetrics Quilligan and the Los Angeles Medical Center, *Madrigal*, like Relf, made it impossible to ignore that women of color had been sterilized coercively. Claudia Dreifus, a white feminist writer and reporter, and Dr. Bernard Rosenfeld, coauthor of a study on forced sterilization published in 1973, decided to further investigate the problem of sterilization abuse at Los Angeles County Hospital. They suspected that there were an inordinately high number of sterilizations among women of color at that institution. In his previous study, Rosenfeld found that physicians and interns sterilized women against their wishes in order to practice their surgical skills or because they believed these women had too many children. His study also revealed that many physicians failed to inform their patients of the permanence of sterilization surgery. One physician interviewed by Dreifus and Rosenfeld betrayed the patronizing and hostile attitude doctors took toward low-income minority patients. He stated that

> most of our patient population was black, inner city. . . . We had a lot of young girls come in . . . thirteen and sixteen and they'd have two or three children. In those cases, we'd ask 'em, often when they were in labor, if they wanted tubal ligations. There were so many young girls and most of them had a real low mentality. We'd tell them about birth control and they wouldn't take it. It would get some of the residents really mad.[43]

In the same year that the Relf case exploded onto the pages of American newspapers, Nial Ruth Cox, a black woman, came forward to say that she had been sterilized coercively at age 18, eight years earlier, when pregnant with her only child. Her mother had been told that Cox's surgery was not permanent—it would wear off. According to Cox, clinic workers had explained to her that she risked losing the welfare benefits that supported her, her mother, and her 10 siblings if she rejected the sterilization procedure. In order to protect this essential income, she went ahead and authorized the sterilization for herself. The physician who performed the surgery declared her "mentally deficient" in order to make use of a North Carolina eugenic statute that allowed sterilization surgery without a hearing or psychological examination in cases of permanent mental incompetence. (Federal family planning clinic officials used a very similar law to sterilize Minnie Lee Relf). The Eugenics Board of North Carolina routinely authorized sterilization procedures for mental incompetence.[44] Architects of the North Carolina statute, and those similar to it in other states, believed that mental deficiency could be transmitted to the next generation.[45] Cox confided to an interviewer that her sterilization made her "feel like half a woman." With this statement, she expressed a sentiment shared by many women who found themselves sterilized involuntarily. She continued, "No man wants half a woman. A man is going to look for someone who can give him a child. I don't even look anymore." Cox had not known that her sterilization had rendered her infertile until the fall of 1970. When she discovered her infertility, her fiancé broke their engagement. The American Civil Liberties Union (ACLU) used Cox's case to challenge the North Carolina statute. They argued that Cox was sterilized because she was black, poor, a member of a family that received welfare benefits, and a minor.[46]

A similar North Carolina case involved a 14-year-old black girl, Elaine Riddick Trent, who was sterilized after she gave birth to a son. At the time of her sterilization, Trent and her family received welfare assistance. Neither Trent nor her husband learned of her sterilization until 1973, after she had tried to get pregnant for a year. According to ACLU reports, the Eugenics Board of North Carolina approved 1,620 sterilizations between 1960 and 1968. The vast majority of these sterilizations—1,023—were performed on black women and nearly 56 percent on those under 20 years of age.[47]

Also in 1973, reports circulated that, in the previous year, an Aiken, South Carolina physician, Dr. Clovis Pierce, had accepted federal money to sterilize 18 Medicaid patients in his clinic. He told the women that he would deliver their third pregnancy only if they submitted to sterilization afterward. As the only doctor in the region to accept Medicaid as payment for a delivery (he had earned over $60,000 in Medicaid payments in one 18-month period), the women he served had little choice but to patronize Dr. Pierce. Sixteen of the 18 women sterilized by Pierce were black and 10 were under 25 years old. One 20-year-old black mother of three children, Marietta Williams, feared that she would never marry again after her sterilization. "Who would want me, knowing I cannot have children?" she despaired. Carol Brown, a 30-year-old white woman and mother of four children, refused sterilization by Pierce. She reported Pierce to the South Carolina social services after he insisted that her obstetrical care depended upon her sterilization.[48]

Brown and another woman sterilized by Pierce brought a suit against him, but Pierce succeeded in defending himself against all allegations of coercion. He justified his actions with a letter written in 1973 to Dr. Archie Ellis, commissioner of the South Carolina Department of Social Services: "I feel that a patient who has already demonstrated that two or more fatherless children have been brought into this world and that the same practice will be continued in the future deserves the benefit of sterilization." The Social Services department forbade Pierce from delivering Medicaid patients, unless he ended his sterilization requirement. But the South Carolina State branch of the American Medical Association (AMA) unanimously supported Pierce's actions against the women.[49]

Drawing on their experiences of reproductive abuses, black women criticized white second wave feminists for failing to make forced or coerced population control in the United States a central issue alongside their campaigns for legal birth control and abortion. Angela Davis illustrated what she believed was missing from the birth control movements of the twentieth century:

Birth control—individual choice, safe contraceptive methods, as well as abortions when necessary—is a fundamental prerequisite for the emancipation of women. Since the right of birth control is obviously advantageous to women of all classes and races, it would appear that even vastly dissimilar women's groups would have attempted to unite around this issue. In reality, however, the birth control movement has seldom succeeded in uniting women of different social backgrounds, and rarely have the movement's leaders popularized the genuine concerns of work-ing-class women. Moreover, arguments advanced by birth control advo-cates have sometimes been based on blatantly racist premises. The pro-gressive potential of birth control remains indisputable. But in actuality, the historical record of this movement leaves much to be desired in the realm of challenges to racism and class exploitation.[50]

Although Davis did not acknowledge the progressive claims to birth con-trol made on behalf of working-class women by early twentieth-century birth control leaders such as Emma Goldman and the young Margaret Sanger, Davis's criticisms reflected many black women's perception of the racist and class-biased nature of the birth control and pro-abortion move-ments. Davis maintained that feminists in the abortion rights movement needed to distance themselves from eugenics and population control rhetoric before black women would feel comfortable with the struggle for reproductive control.[51]

White and black women had very different experiences with fertility control that determined at which point they entered the political dis-course on fertility control and reproductive rights that took shape during the early and mid-1970s. Unlike women of color, white women often viewed sterilization as one more option for voluntary fertility regulation. Even poor white women who struggled to raise children without daycare or health care did not experience reproductive abuses at the same rate as did women of color in the 1960s and early 1970s. By the early 1970s, vol-untary sterilization, among both white men and women, had become the most popular method of birth control. (Black men were the least likely to choose permanent sterilization.) Despite the increases in requests for ster-ilization among middle-class white women, however, physicians balked at performing the surgery on those who had a long period of fertility still ahead of them. These women experienced the pronatalist side of a race-sex bias that promoted the birth of children to white middle-class women, in an era when women increasingly chose to defer childbearing in favor of educational and career pursuits. Miriam Stone wrote about the diffi-culties that she had finding a doctor to sterilize her: "I went to my gyne-cologist to make arrangements, only to get my first big surprise. While he found me physically capable of having the operation, he refused to per-form it, and, in one of those fatherly I-know-what's-best-for-my-little-girl speeches, assured me I would be sorry when it was too late."[52]

For some women who were finished with their childbearing, or for those who had never wanted to bear children in the first place, sterilization presented an excellent alternative to the dilemma of unwanted fertility. In a letter appearing in the *Boston Female Liberation Newsletter*, a woman discussed her campaign to make sterilization available on demand. She declared that, as with abortion, "Sterilization is a right that must not be denied to anyone desiring it, whether that person has ten children or none at all."[53] While her assertion made sense to women who wanted to end their capacity to reproduce, the letter-writer did not acknowledge the complexities of such a demand in a context in which some women were sterilized without their consent.

Many physicians would not sterilize a white woman until the number of children she had given birth to multiplied by her age added up to 120. For women who wanted to become sterilized, this random formula suggested that physicians did not trust them to make their own reproductive decisions. In 1971, to address this bias, the ACLU brought a suit against Peekskill (New York) Community Hospital to press doctors to voluntarily sterilize a young white woman, Mrs. Cafarelli, who already had three children. ACLU lawyers reasoned that if women had the right to control their reproduction using abortion and birth control (abortion became legal in New York in 1970), they should "also be guaranteed the right to prevent pregnancies permanently." Ira Glasser, executive director of the ACLU, argued that voluntary sterilization represented "a major women's rights issue." He added that doctors either "permit sterilization only when pregnancy will endanger the mother's life or health, or they apply special formulas to determine eligibility."

Those in favor of easier access to voluntary sterilization invoked both the right to privacy and the problem of class discrimination in arguments that built on abortion and contraceptive rights litigation such as *Griswold v. Connecticut*, *Abromowicz v. Lefkowitz*, and *Abele v. Markle*. Jeremiah S. Gutman, one of Cafarelli's lawyers, stated that, as in *Griswold*—the 1965 Supreme Court decision recognizing the right of married couples to use contraception—"voluntary sterilization . . . falls under the constitutional protection of a 'right of marital privacy.'"[54] Cafarelli's lawyers explained further that prohibitions against voluntary methods of contraception, such as sterilization, violated the constitutional right to equal protection of the law because "wealthy women can easily go to a different hospital while poorer women can leave the Peekskill area for medical care only at an economic sacrifice." If one viewed prohibition against sterilization as parallel to illegal abortion, this position made sense. Poor women needed greater access to affordable fertility control. Unfortunately, poor women of color too often received permanent sterilization in lieu of nonpermanent forms of birth control or abortion.[55]

Black Feminism and Reproductive Rights

Politically active black women believed that they needed to combine their opposition to sterilization abuse with solid support for safe, legal abortion and birth control. Holding this belief meant walking a line between white feminists who put most of their political energy behind the fight for legal abortion and birth control and Black Nationalist men who declared all contraception, including abortion, to be genocidal. The Third World Women's Workshop of the 1971 national abortion conference in Michigan released one of the first public pro–fertility control statements of the decade made by black women. In this statement, the Workshop rejected the Black Nationalist contention that black women did not want access to abortion. They argued:

> There is a myth that Third World women do not want to control our bodies, that we do not want the right to contraception and abortion. But we know that Third World women have suffered the most because of this denial of our rights and will continue to suffer as long as the anti-abortion laws remain on the books. We know that more Third World women die every year from illegal back-street abortions than the rest of the female population.[56]

The Third World Women's Workshop concluded that black women needed to stake out an autonomous reproductive rights discourse that demanded safe, legal abortion in order to protect black women's lives.

Before 1973, many black women entered the debate over fertility control silently, yet forcefully, by having abortions or using birth control. In the years before legalization, black women died having inexpensive illegal abortions in far higher numbers than white women because they had very limited access to private physicians or hospital committees granting therapeutic abortions. Historian Leslie Reagan found that women of color died during abortion procedures at four times the rate of white women before the procedure was legalized. By 1971, after several states had legalized abortion, including New York, California, Hawaii, and Washington, black women began to have legal abortions at twice the rate of white women.[57]

The numbers of black women having abortions continued to increase after the Supreme Court found abortion to be a constitutionally protected right in 1973.[58] Soon after the Supreme Court ruling, black female political activists leapt to defend their right to abortion as it came under attack by the religious right. One statement, signed by six prominent black women leaders—June Christmas, M.D., Commissioner of Mental Health and Retardation, City of New York; Dorothy I. Height, President of the National Council of Negro Women; Aileen C. Hernandez, Task Force on Minority Women and Women's Rights of the National Organization for Women; Eleanor Holmes Norton, Commissioner of Human Rights, City of New York; Inez Smith Reid, Black Women's Community Development Corporation; and Margaret Sloan, Chairwoman of the National Black Feminist Organization—demanded that Congress reject an anti-abortion bill that would prohibit Medicaid coverage for abortion. Because black women were disproportionately among the poor, they argued, a bill that prevented federal funding for abortion would result in the deaths of women of color. To prove that an anti-abortion bill put women of color at risk, they asserted further that "the vast majority" of women "who died at the hands of incompetent practitioners in the days before abortion was legal were Black and Brown."[59]

Other prominent black women also voiced their opposition to Black Nationalist characterizations of abortion as genocide. Representative Shirley Chisolm, from the Bedford-Stuyvesant neighborhood in Brooklyn, New York, emphasized the importance of black women's support of legal abortion and safe and affordable birth control in her 1970 autobiography *Unbought and Unbossed*. At first, Chisolm explained, she refused to endorse Representative Albert Blumenthal's 1969 pro–legal abortion bill despite requests for support from the National Association for the Repeal of Abortion Laws (NARAL). She changed her mind, however, when several women she knew experienced illegal abortions that rendered them sterile or left them with chronic complications. She wrote that "it had begun to seem to me that the question was not whether the law should allow abortions. Experience shows that pregnant women who feel they have compelling reasons for not having a baby, or another baby, will break the law and, even worse, risk injury and death if they must to get one." Since abortions had not disappeared by making them illegal, Chisolm argued that "the question becomes simply that of what kind of abortions society wants women to have—clean, competent ones performed by licensed physicians or septic, dangerous ones done by incompetent practitioners."[60] Chisolm felt that as "a black woman legislator, far from avoiding the abortion question, [she] was compelled to face it and deal with it."[61]

Soon thereafter, Chisolm decided that she had a moral and political responsibility to protect the health of black women by ensuring the legalization of abortion in New York. Yet, she knew that as a black representative she took an unusual political risk by supporting a pro-abortion bill. She recalled that "for me to take the lead in abortion repeal would be an even more serious step than for a white politician to do so, because there is a deep and angry suspicion among many blacks that even birth control clinics are a plot by the white power structure to keep down the numbers of blacks, and this opinion is even more strongly held by some in regard to legalizing abortions."[62] Although she struggled with her fear of alienating black men, Chisolm regarded the decision to have an abortion as a woman's prerogative and chose to respond to the desperate needs of the black women in her district. Without legal abortion some of the women she represented might die attempting to terminate a pregnancy.

Thus, Chisolm characterized black genocide declarations as "male rhetoric, for male ears." She explained:

> It falls flat to female listeners, and to thoughtful male ones. Women know, and so do many men, that two or three children who are wanted, prepared for, reared amid love and stability, and educated to the limit of their ability will mean more for the future of the black and brown races from which they come than any number of neglected, hungry, ill-housed and ill-clothed youngsters. Pride in one's race, as well as simply humanity, supports this view. Poor women of every race feel as I do, I believe.[63]

By pointing out that fewer children would garner greater care from their parents, Chisolm provided a reasoned argument defending fertility control against criticisms of black genocide. Her comments echoed those made by other fertility control advocates. Voluntary motherhood advocates of the late nineteenth century made similar cases for controlling their fertility. They argued that fewer children would be better loved and healthier.[64]

Chisolm recognized, however, that black women often felt uncomfortable joining the movement for abortion rights, even if their lives were at stake. For this reason, she participated in the campaign as their representative, aiming her criticism at Black Nationalist men opposed to birth control and abortion. She questioned any political ideology that would sacrifice the lives of black women in the name of racial power:

> Which is more like genocide, I have asked some of my black brothers— this, the way things are, or the conditions I am fighting for in which the full range of family planning services is freely available to women of all classes and colors, starting with effective contraception and extending to safe legal termination of undesired pregnancies, at a price they can afford.

Chisolm asked why the deaths of black women from illegal abortion would be any less genocidal for blacks than the abortion of a black fetus.[65]

Frances Beal noted the paradox of the Black Nationalist opposition to legal abortion. She pointed out that it was black women who died from illegal abortions. She declared, "The rigid laws concerning abortions in this country are another vicious means . . . of outright murder. Rich white women somehow manage to obtain these operations with little or no difficulty. It is the poor Black and Puerto Rican women who are at the mercy of the local butcher."[66]

Mary Treadwell, a black activist in Washington, D.C. and former spouse of civil rights activist and D.C. Mayor Marion Barry, elaborated on the pro–birth control and abortion sentiment put forth by Beal, Chisolm, and other black women in the public arena, when she asserted that a black woman needed the means to conceive a child as well as prevent conception. She said, "Every woman should have the right to control her body and its usage, as she so chooses. Every woman should have the right to conceive, when she so chooses." Treadwell explained her reasons for supporting fertility control and rejecting the Black Nationalist notion that large numbers of black babies would solve black peoples' problems: "There is no magic in a home where someone has reproduced five or more black babies and cannot manage economically, educationally, spiritually nor socially to see that these five black babies become five highly trained black minds." Furthermore, black women needed the "freedom to be able to fulfill themselves sexually without fear of conception."[67]

Frances Beal wrote a 1970 essay that laid the groundwork for a black women's reproductive rights discourse that departed from both Black Nationalist and mainstream feminist reproductive politics up to that point. Beal concurred with black female activists such as Treadwell when she insisted that black women needed access to contraception and legal abortion as well as protection from reproductive abuses. And she passionately rejected the Black Nationalist notion that black women should have babies for the sake of racial progress. This article paved the way for a new discourse on reproductive rights that made the demands for legal abortion, contraception, and an end to sterilization abuse central to the feminist campaign for reproductive rights. Beal wrote:

> We are not saying that Black women should not practice birth control. Black women have the right and the responsibility to determine when it is [in] the interest of the struggle to have children or not to have them, and this right must not be relinquished to anyone. It is also her right and responsibility to determine when it is in her own best interests to have children, how many she will have and how far apart. The lack of the availability of safe birth control methods, the forced sterilization practices, and the inability to obtain legal abortions are all symptoms of a decadent society that jeopardizes the health of Black women (and thereby the entire Black race) in its attempts to control the very life processes of human beings. This is a symptom of a society that believes it has the right to bring political factors into the privacy of the bedchamber. The elimination of these horrendous conditions will free Black women for full participation in the revolution, and thereafter, in the building of the new society.[68]

Unlike most women's liberationists, few black women could support abortion and birth control without acknowledging the dangers of sterilization abuse. Beal held that just the threat of sterilization abuse adversely affected black women's health. First, because they feared forced sterilization, "Black women are often afraid to permit any kind of necessary surgery because they know from bitter experience that they are more likely than not to come out of the hospital without their insides. (Both salpingectomies and hysterectomies are performed.)"[69] In a perverse reversal of the role black women were forced to play during antebellum slavery—that of breeders valued primarily for their ability to produce slave children—black women's health and well-being once again became linked to their reproductive functioning, or, in this case, the lack of it.[70]

Throughout the first half of the 1970s, black women organized to address their unique reproductive rights demands. In so doing, they contributed to the creation of a new inclusive movement for reproductive freedom. In 1973, Margaret Sloan and Florynce Kennedy, a prominent civil rights lawyer, black feminist, and abortion rights activist, organized the National Black Feminist Organization (NBFO), in which they addressed black women's need for access to safe legal abortion and an end to sterilization abuse. Kennedy and Sloan gained support from Doris Wright, a black feminist writer, Shirley Chisholm, Alice Walker, and Eleanor Holmes Norton. The NBFO supported Dr. Kenneth Edelin, a black physician who was arrested in 1975 for performing an illegal abortion. In 1975, Barbara Smith and other black feminist activists in Boston formed the Combahee River Collective. Members of Combahee also combined activism for abortion rights and against sterilization abuse.[71]

Black feminists argued that black women not only needed access to safe and legal abortion, but they also required a number of other demands before they could claim true reproductive freedom. For example, the health problems that caused black people to die, on average, years before affluent whites, which also inflated maternal death rates and infant mortality rates, needed to be addressed before many blacks would accept family planning as other than genocidal. For this reason, black women and men demanded that the federal government improve general health care and living conditions in poverty neighborhoods before contributing to family planning programs. Ideally, the state would contribute to both. Naomi Gray, a black family-planning consultant and former vice president of Planned Parenthood World Population, explained this perspective: "The challenge is to illustrate everyday that rats, roaches, and hunger pangs are viewed by all society as more of a menace than an accidental pregnancy." She continued, lending her support to family planning within the context of improved health conditions for the poor: "If we are to do that [improve general health care], we can enlist more and more of the black, brown, and the poor who can then . . . preach with a clear conscience about the problems and dangers of cluttering up this weary planet with too many people." According to Gray, blacks were receptive to personal fertility control. She emphasized, however, that for black women and men, federally subsidized birth control seemed superfluous, at best, when basic health needs had not been met in poor communities.[72]

Given the lack of health care for low-income and poor blacks, Gray, even more than Chisolm, sympathized with black militant suspicions of genocide and population control. After leaving her position at Planned Parenthood, she spoke on "Population Control—a Form of Black Genocide" at various forums around the country. In her talk, Gray characterized population control in the United States as "legislation for sterilization of welfare mothers made by Southern states," "coercive sterilization induced on black mothers during delivery time in Southern hospitals," and "attempts made by the Federal government to limit the number of children for which support could be received." Rather than limiting the size of black families, Gray argued, these measures discouraged any use of contraception whatsoever because black people had become fearful that the government meant to eradicate African Americans as a group. She added that blacks wanted to limit their families, "but without white coercion."[73]

Gray concluded her discussion with a simple list of requirements that needed to be met before black people—particularly low-income blacks and black militants—would accept family planning in their neighborhoods:

> It is important that the negative approach of population control, high cost of welfare, etc., be de-emphasized and the positive emphasis of the reduction of high incidence of maternal and infant mortality and morbidity among the nonwhite population be stressed. . . . Concern must also be stressed for other, more urgent needs and priorities such as better housing, nutrition, educational and employment opportunities, economic and community development, etc. These are the "bread and butter" issues confronting blacks and other minorities with regard to their own survival.[74]

For Gray and other black women who advocated a broad perspective on health care provision, one that included family planning but was not limited to it, this list of priorities appeared straightforward.

Mary Treadwell echoed Gray's notion of reproductive freedom when she insisted that feminists needed to take into account the economic needs of poor women of color when they spoke of abortion rights. She noted that the U.S. federal government forbade abortion but failed to provide support for the children born to poor women. In 1972, Treadwell argued that white male legislators "reject[ed] legalized abortion" and, at the same time, refused

> to provide an adequate guaranteed annual income for these children born to women without financial and social access to safe abortion. . . . [They] refuse to fund quality, inexpensive prenatal and postnatal care to women without access to abortion . . . refuse to fund quality education and training for the children of the women without access to abortion.[75]

Poor women—who were disproportionately black and Hispanic—were caught between a pronatalist and moralistic ethic that restricted legal birth control options for women and an anti-welfare drive that rejected claims made by women for public support for their children. Treadwell and other black women believed that women of color could not achieve reproductive control without both access to abortion and economic security for themselves and their families.

The Transformation of the Feminist Abortion Rights Movement

In the early part of the 1970s, the feminist abortion rights movement had not incorporated the demands made by Gray, Treadwell, and other black women. Their emphasis remained on a woman's right to terminate or prevent a pregnancy. The most ubiquitous radical feminist pro–legal abortion slogan was "Free Abortion on Demand." Most white feminists believed it was essential to place the bulk of their political energies behind the movement for legal abortion. Certainly, this position was understandable in an era when an estimated one million illegal abortions were performed every year on American women. Before 1973, most women who contemplated the termination of an unwanted pregnancy also contemplated risking their lives to end that pregnancy. For mainstream feminists in the early part of the 1970s, challenging the arcane laws that prohibited abortion was a priority. Eventually, however, feminist abortion rights activists became more receptive to criticisms by black women and men, and reproductive politics began to shift its focus.[76]

3

"An instrument of genocide"
The Black Nationalist Campaign against Birth Control

These [sterilization] clinics claim to be "aiding the indigent," (the poor and black) but the obvious aim is surgical genocide, as effective in a long term sense as Nazi Germany's gas chambers and with the same objective.   —*Muhammad Speaks*

Birth control is nothing more than part and parcel of the anti-human practices of the fascist racist and U.S. government and their genocidal war effort.   —*The Black Panther*

There is growing evidence that there is an organized plot on the part of the Montgomery Community Action Committee (MCAC) and the Montgomery Family Planning Center (MFPC) to employ mass sterilizations of Black people in Alabama. The Planning Center has arranged sterilization for 11 persons during the past year.
                                                       —*The Black Panther*

As we have seen, in the late 1960s and early 1970s, the Nation of Islam and the Black Panther Party claimed that any contraceptive use among blacks would inevitably lead to the genocide of the population. This was the anti–fertility control rhetoric criticized by black and white feminists in the previous chapters. The Nation of Islam, founded in the early 1930s in Detroit and united under Elijah Muhammad in Chicago, and the Black Panther Party, a Black Power group organized in Oakland in 1966, both protested against what they saw as the pernicious aims of government funded family planners and those who supported them, including white feminist abortion rights activists. For the most part, Black Nationalist men were opposed to any promotion of personal fertility control until black feminists pressured them into changing their position. At the same time, the Black Muslims and the Black Panthers contributed to the development of a new public discourse on *involuntary* reproductive control that foregrounded problems of sterilization abuse and population control among people of color.

Background

Black Nationalist and Black Power opposition to fertility control came to prominent public attention after the sterilization of Minne Lee Relf in 1973. But the Panthers and the Black Muslims had already vocalized opposition to federally funded birth control in poor black neighborhoods for over half a decade. The Black Panther Party for Self-Defense responded to Relf's sterilization with the scathing accusation that "the actions of the Montgomery Family Planning Clinic are genocidal."[1] According to the Black Panthers the Montgomery Family Planning Clinic had contributed to the genocide of the black race by sterilizing a total of 11 women who received federal health subsidies in 1973. The Nation of Islam similarly alleged, "This is but one known case of sterilization: many Blacks are aware of the genocidal program of the federal government against Blacks. This case here in Montgomery which has gained publicity is simply one 'manifestation.'"[2]

The responses to the Relf sterilization by the Black Panthers and the Nation of Islam represented some of the most negative and severe black attitudes toward family planning in the United States. Research done in the 1970s suggested that the majority of blacks supported government involvement in fertility control, although in lower numbers than white respondents. Young black men had the least positive response to fertility control and were the most likely to link fertility control with black genocide.[3]

The Black Panthers and the Black Muslims saw Minnie Lee Relf's plight as one instance of a national, and possibly international, conspiracy by whites to eradicate people of color. All federally supported fertility control programs in poor communities came under fire as methods meant to gradually destroy black populations. As one writer for the Black Panther paper wrote, "no pill, loop, or treatment short of mass sterilization will restrict our growth . . . each child born will be one more revolutionary that the power structure will have to try to deal with."[4]

Black Panthers and members of the Nation of Islam placed sterilization abuse and other birth control methods, viewed as coerced population
control, within a larger context of concern about the overall welfare of
blacks. A broad view of their concern for black racial survival allows for
a better understanding of some of their vehement rejection of birth control and abortion. Black feminist and pro–fertility control advocate,
Frances Ruffin, expressed her understanding of the black militant's legitimate paranoia about genocide:

> In a country which has a history of being a hostile environment for
> Black people, militants felt that it was necessary to reject this society's
> attempt to use birth control as the answer in dealing with the outstand-
> ing problems of poverty, unemployment, unequal education, and inade-
> quate housing conditions. . . . [O]n the minds of many, was the realiza-
> tion that the thrust of governmental funds to public and private birth
> control programs followed on the heels of urban upheavals of the mid
> 60's—such programs were previously out of reach for many Black
> women.[5]

Ruffin emphasized that blacks only gained access to birth control and
abortion after the political and social rebellions of the civil rights movement, Black Power, and riots in Detroit, Newark, and Watts. She suggested that that sort of "benevolence" on the part of a white government
reticent about granting blacks any kind of real political or economic
power spawned theories of genocidal intentions among blacks. For Ruffin, blacks reasonably suspected that white paranoia about black political organizing and violence motivated federal government sponsorship of
fertility control programs.

According to former Black Panther Kathleen Cleaver, fears about a
dangerously shrinking black population had been expressed throughout
the 1960s, particularly as the civil rights movement shifted to Black
Power and became more violent.[6] When the Black Panthers found themselves the target of the FBI's counterintelligence (COINTELPRO) efforts,
their suspicions of a genocidal plot grew. Revelations in 1972 about the
U.S. Public Health Service's research experiments on syphilitic black men
in Tuskegee, Alabama whose condition was left untreated further fed suspicions that the U.S. government intended to destroy the black population.[7] The Panthers also published articles in *The Black Panther* accusing
the federal government of spreading heroin in poor black neighborhoods

and imprisoning black men in order to wipe out the black population. Likewise, the Nation of Islam believed that whites had tried to eradicate blacks by keeping them poor, by supplying drugs to black neighborhoods, by jailing black men, and by promoting the use of fertility control.

Like black feminists, both the Panthers and the Muslims also argued that white population controllers threatened the survival of people of color by offering them birth control without other health care measures, such as public clinics specializing in preventive medicine and hospitals providing pre- and postnatal care, nutrition advice, and dentistry. According to Black Nationalists, African Americans needed other resources too, such as decent housing, opportunities for work and education, and day care, all aimed at the wellness of the entire population. They believed that a total health care program that took into account the extensive needs of poor blacks was central to the promotion of stable and thriving black communities. Without an end to the health care problems linked to poverty, Nationalists argued, birth control services remained harmful.

Too often Black Nationalists are represented as a uniform group without contradictory or conflicting beliefs about the best way to fight racist oppression. Yet, a more precise representation of Nationalist beliefs recognizes that they articulated varied opinions as to the best strategy for ending racist oppression. This is particularly true when looking at Black Nationalist positions concerning health care and fertility control. Compared with the Black Panthers, the Black Muslims articulated a relatively weak plan for total health care. Their warnings of a genocidal conspiracy, published in their paper *Muhammad Speaks*, often sounded more like science fiction than rational political editorializing. Still, concrete evidence of sterilization abuse in black communities in America convinced many non-Muslim blacks that the Black Muslims were not entirely wrong when they cried "genocide." Even the National Medical Association, a society of black physicians, voiced their suspicions that federally funded family planning programs were not in the black community's best interest, particularly when blacks lacked basic health care facilities.[8]

By contrast, the Black Panthers offered advice for total health care in their publications and set up their own community-controlled clinics to stem the tide of ill health in poor African-American neighborhoods. The Panther warnings of genocide accompanied a political agenda that advocated black community-controlled health care. Ideally, this program would include prenatal care, preventive health care such as vaccinations against childhood diseases and screenings for sickle cell anemia, community-based child-care, and prekindergarten education for children. The Panthers believed that blacks could best provide medical services in their own communities. These programs helped maintain a popular following for the Black Panthers, particularly among black women.

The Black Panther emphasis on total health care led them to reverse their anti–birth control and abortion position without disrupting their most popular programs set up to strengthen black communities. In the early years of the debate, the Black Panthers argued that all fertility control—sterilization, abortion and contraception—equaled genocide for people of color. As the feminist message of a woman's fundamental right to abortion became more widespread, and as black women began to forge a feminism of their own, the Panthers refined their criticism to accept birth control and abortion when voluntarily chosen. This gradual transformation came at the behest of black women, both in the Party and outside of it, who rejected the total condemnation of reproductive control for people of color as genocidal. By the mid-1970s, black criticism of population control focused almost exclusively on the federally supported sterilization of black, Latina, and Native American women. Most of the conspiratorial rhetoric about black genocide had disappeared from Black Panther literature.

Other factors also contributed to the shift in the Black Panther's attitudes toward birth control and abortion. By the mid-1970s, the federal government had reduced funding for fertility control. Public support for family planning was less acceptable after *Roe v. Wade*, due to a concerted campaign on the part of the Catholic Church and other New Right anti-abortion organizations. Also, the Health, Education and Welfare (HEW) department adopted a set of guidelines regulating sterilization in federally funded clinics. Finally, accusations of genocide by Black Nationalists (both in the U.S. and internationally) convinced the population establishment to refashion their rhetoric. They began to promote the idea that every individual should exercise full control over his or her fertility; this included the right to bear children as well as the right to prevent or terminate pregnancy. All these forces combined, contributed to a context in which the Black Panthers felt free to promote abortion and birth control as beneficial to the black community, a reversal of their earlier position.[9]

In the 1960s and early 1970s, however, other prominent blacks joined the Nation of Islam and the Black Panthers in their criticism of black birth control programs. Black scholars, in particular, argued that "family planning" institutions failed to ameliorate the causes of hunger, poverty, and ill health in black communities. Ronald Walters, chairman of the department of political science at Howard University, became one of the most outspoken critics of population control aimed at African Americans. Walters decided to explain his position when he rejected a request to become a member of the Advisory Board of the World Population Society. In his essay, originally appearing in the *Black Scholar*, he detailed some of the reasons blacks felt that birth control programs were not in their interests. First, Walters asserted that population control rhetoric emanated from "the richest nation in the world, a nation which might be able to feed its population and wipe out its poverty except for the fact that this would require basic changes in its system of the distribution of resources." Furthermore, the richest nation in the world aimed their population control rhetoric at poor nations and poor residents of the United States, all of whom consumed fewer resources than well-to-do Americans. Walters offered an alternative strategy for improving the lives of the poor. He advised, "It should be clear that the need is not for population limiting programs but for the expansion of political and economic opportunity" in the Third World and among low-income Americans. By refusing to exercise this option, Walters believed the U.S. government "admits its inability or its unwillingness to accomplish the humane task."[10] Finally, Walters argued that, "since black and Third World communities appear to be the target communities for family planning, and it is their survival which is at stake . . . such programs should be determined by them and their peoples and no one else." Walters asserted that communities of color and poor people should take responsibility for defining their own fertility programs to fit their needs as they perceived them. This notion of community control was a key element in Black Power discussions of fertility control without coercion.[11]

Other prominent black leaders, including members of the Urban League, officials of the NAACP, members of the Southern Christian Leadership Conference (SCLC) led by Martin Luther King, and the Student Non-Violent Coordinating Committee (SNCC), criticized birth control programs in the 1960s. In particular, Whitney Young, head of the Urban League in 1962, worried that Planned Parenthood consciously obscured their population control aims with rhetoric about aiding the black community. He believed that an absence of minority representation in Planned Parenthood's local programs betrayed their hostile attitude toward the black population. Roy Innis, National Director of the Congress of Racial Equality (CORE), criticized both domestic and international population control programs and, like Walters, noted the high density of populations in European countries in comparison to the rest of the world. Based on this evidence, he questioned the motivations of population control programs aimed at African and other Third World countries inhabited by people of color. Furthermore, Innis argued, the percentage of blacks in America had dropped since the eighteenth and nineteenth centuries—from 20 percent of the population to 10 percent. He maintained that "this catastrophe . . . was caused, in part, by the genocidal action of Europe and her offspring in America against 'Africans at home and abroad.'" Innis concluded, "Overpopulation is a white man's problem. In his limited space, he squanders an extremely disproportionate share of the world's resources."[12]

Evidence that others in the black community were suspicious of family planning programs came in 1966 when SCLC held a workshop on family planning in South Carolina. Participants voiced their negative attitudes about federal birth control programs in black neighborhoods. Comments ranged from the belief that God intended women to bear children to fears that the state conspired to keep black people powerless by controlling their numbers. For example, one woman testified, "I am a mother of 12—8 living and I don't believe in birth control because if God meant me to have 12 children I should and God will provide." Another argued that "birth control is a plot just as segregation was a plot to keep the Negro down." A third activist at the workshop concurred that "it [birth control] is a plot rather than a solution. Instead of working for us and giving us our rights—reduce us in numbers and not have to give us anything." At the same time, other civil rights activists in SCLC stated that blacks wanted to control their fertility, but distrusted agencies such as Planned Parenthood that presumably promoted fertility control without taking into consideration the wide range of more pressing needs in poor black communities.[13]

There were also strident black voices affirming the importance of birth control to the black community in the 1960s and early 1970s. Julius Lester of SNCC believed that forced childbearing was akin to slavery. He wrote, "Those black militants who stand up and tell women, 'Produce black babies!' are telling black women to be slaves." Stressing the positive benefits of birth control for blacks, Lester continued, "If blacks within the movement are seriously concerned about revolution, then they should be urging women to postpone having children, because women need to be free for the fullest participation in the struggle."[14] In concert with Lester, Dr. Martin Luther King denounced anti–birth control rhetoric as similar to the forced breeding of slave women by antebellum slaveholders.[15]

When the Black Panthers and members of the Nation of Islam raised the specter of genocide, they responded to what they viewed as a long history of state and corporate-sponsored eugenic population control in the United States.[16] Granted, from the 1930s onward, even the most avid advocates of eugenic population control avoided any rhetoric that might associate them with Nazi eugenic policies.[17] Some population control advocates believed, however, that contraceptives, often including sterilization, could help eradicate the poverty found in black and Latino communities.[18] Furthermore, some population controllers championed birth control as a palliative against rebellions and riots among urban blacks as the civil rights movement shifted toward Black Power in the mid-1960s. As society appeared to be crumbling around them, and people of color threatened to overturn racial hierarchies by bringing armed-revolution to the streets, some white Americans climbed onto the population control bandwagon, supporting greater government funding for birth control in communities of color.[19]

Contemporary forms of population policy date to the end of World War II and to the formation of John D. Rockefeller III's influential Population Council in 1952, although the U.S. federal government did not back population programs financially until the 1960s because of opposition from the Roman Catholic Church. In the 1960s, the United States reversed their family planning policy as concerns about ecology, a "population bomb," and political upheaval grew both abroad and at home. In 1963, Secretary of State Dean Rusk gave authorization to the Agency for International Development (AID) for the creation of family planning programs. Also in 1963, Senator Ernest Gruening of Alaska introduced legislation that would amend the foreign aid bill, allowing AID to research the problem of population increase. By 1964, Planned Parenthood affiliates had acquired Organization for Economic Opportunity (OEO) funding from President Johnson for welfare programs. In 1965, the Johnson administration provided OEO with additional funds for family planning—excluding abortion—and maternal health programs. In the same year, Senator Gruening convened hearings on S. 1676, which addressed expenditures to deal with the "population explosion" both abroad and in the United States. Witnesses who testified at the hearings connected what they believed was a dire problem with overpopulation in poor and black neighborhoods to the riot in the Watts neighborhood of Los Angeles. Finally, the year 1967 included congressional passage of the Child Health Act, which mandated that at least 6 percent of maternal-child health grants to public health agencies be reserved for family planning. Through initiatives such as these, birth control became state policy. Birth controllers justified the provision of contraceptives to the poor with the logic that not only the rich should be able to regulate their fertility.[20]

The Nixon administration expanded state involvement in population politics even further. With Daniel Patrick Moynihan as his social policy director, President Nixon established a five-year goal to provide contraception to all people unable to afford it. He proposed increased spending on family planning from $48 million to $150 million over the course of those five years. In 1970, responding to the administration's policy on family planning, Congress passed the Family Planning Services and Population Research Act that would help achieve Nixon's goal of providing contraceptive services to every poor woman on a voluntary basis.

Federal population policy went through another sea change, however, just as achievement of the goal of providing contraception to a broad representation of the American poor was in sight. The introduction of abortion into the population control equation was central to this transformation. When the Commission on Population Growth and the American Future, established by Congress in 1970, endorsed the use of legal abortion to control population, Nixon distanced himself from the birth control issue in response to criticism from the Catholic Church. Although abortion was legal in New York State, Washington State, and Hawaii, it was still too controversial to be introduced as federal policy.[21] It was also during the Nixon administration that a federal clinic had involuntarily sterilized Minnie Lee Relf. As the press popularized this case and others similar to it, the Nixon administration received a barrage of criticism for its failure to regulate the OEO-HEW federal sterilization programs. As a result of these two public controversies over federal contraceptive programs, the Nixon administration back-pedaled on its earlier commitment to provide contraceptives to poor women.[22]

In and of itself, there would appear to be no complaint against an administration that made it a goal to provide birth control equally to rich and poor. Both black and white and rich and poor women had need for voluntary fertility control measures. For many Black Nationalists, however, the idea that the federal government would use birth control to prevent social unrest further fed theories about genocide. Suspicions among black leaders of racial prejudice and demographic manipulation were spawned when government funds for fertility control increased in 1965, the same year that saw the Voting Rights Act passed.[23] Both the Black Panthers and Black Muslims believed that attempts to quell urban riots or to end poverty through family planning were palliatives used by the federal government to avoid more sincere efforts to change the circumstances that caused poverty in communities of color. They argued, rather than curb the poor black population through fertility services, government planners should end poverty by helping strengthen the economy in neighborhoods of color and incorporating blacks and Hispanics into the national political process. After these goals had been achieved, people of color would consider limiting their fertility for their own reasons. Neither the Black Muslims nor the Black Panthers trusted a white government to help them meet these ends, however; both agreed that if blacks wanted more power, they would have to take it for themselves.[24]

A "Sin" against Allah: The Nation of Islam and Genocide Rhetoric

The Nation of Islam espoused a conservative theology that at its foundation opposed any form of population limitation within the black community. The Black Muslims inherited their animosity for any form of fertility control from an earlier twentieth century Black Nationalist movement founded by Marcus Garvey and his Universal Negro Improvement Association. In 1934, the Garveyites passed a resolution condemning all use of birth control. Likewise, in 1976, Elijah Muhammad, the foremost "Prophet" and spiritual leader of the Nation of Islam wrote of birth control: "Using the birth control scheme against the production of human beings is a sin that Allah (God) is against and for which he will punish the guilty on the Day of Judgment. Both the Bible and Holy Qur-an's teachings are against birth control."[25]

Elijah Muhammad traced the "sin" of birth control to the creation of the white race. He used this mythology to illustrate his opposition to fertility control among blacks: "The white race is a race that was produced by using the birth control law, says God to me. Do not accept this death plan of the devils to destroy and keep from being a people."[26] The Black Muslims believed that Yakub, a black scientist who tampered with biological reproduction by taking grafts from black people to create a new race, created whites. According to the myth, blacks consisted of two parts, one brown and one black. "The brown germ can be grafted into its last stage, and the last stage is white." Elijah Muhammad preached that God gave the white race six thousand years to rule over blacks as punishment for Yakub's manipulation of God's creation. That rule ended in 1914. From that year on, it fell to black people to overthrow whites and take their divine place as leaders.[27]

Despite their extreme racial views, and a marginal place in American politics, the Black Muslims articulated an argument about black genocide that drew upon fears already present in American black communities. The Black Muslims incorporated these fears into their brand of racial politics and religious doctrine. In a study published in the *American Journal of Public Health* in 1973, Castellano Turner and William Darity found that young black men with less than average educations most often believed that family planning was a form of black genocide. Expressing sympathy for this sentiment, they wrote, "The young, lower status, northern black male (the most expressive of genocide fears) has every reason to wonder why white America is pushing family planning in the black community at the same time that it fails to push for equity in education and in occupational opportunity." Additionally, Turner and Darity found that most blacks supported family planning when under their personal control, and black women expressed desire for birth control more often than black men. Turner and Darity theorized that because fears of genocide created ambivalence about family planning, it had an overall negative effect on the use of birth control among blacks.[28]

Black Muslims also created an elaborate history that narrated white attempts to exterminate blacks, which resonated for many people of color who did not join the Nation of Islam. They traced the genocidal plot against black people to the international slave trade of the seventeenth and eighteenth centuries. In a condemnation of the historical colonial exploitation of Africa, one Nation of Islam reporter for *Muhammad Speaks* proposed that if it had not been "for the incredibly ruthless and genocidal slave trade which raped and wrecked Africa for centuries—Africa today would be the world's most populous continent and perhaps the most prosperous and thriving."[29] As this passage suggested, the Nation of Islam twinned black population growth with economic growth. They believed that because they were greater in numbers, people of color united could overwhelm whites of European descent, appropriating both economic and political power. Greater numbers would also confirm the prophecy that blacks and other nonwhites were destined to rule over whites. "The slavemasters envy their once-slaves' future and want to destroy it," Elijah Muhammad preached. Black Muslims conjectured that if white people had no reason to fear blacks and other people of color, they would leave them to prosper. The Black Muslims believed that whites knew that when the tables would be turned, people of color would rise up against them, so they fashioned methods to keep blacks and other people of color weak.[30]

Anti-birth control rhetoric figured centrally in Muhammad's political diatribe against the white man. In one 1967 address to his followers, he gave evidence that he believed proved that whites used birth control to reduce the number of Third World people. He wrote, "Birth control has become a major phase of America's foreign 'aid' program—in some cases, the 'hook' on which all other aid to underdeveloped countries hangs."[31] He used India as an example: "The cynically overt way in which famine-plagued India was forced to accept birth control, in the form of devices and sterilization, shocked civilized people everywhere, even among some white nations."[32] In fact, after droughts and an economic crisis in 1966, the Indian government transformed what had been a voluntary program for population reduction into one that operated on the basis of incentives to both individuals and communities to reduce their fertility. Compulsory sterilization was part of the state population control package, particularly in the 1970s. Muhammad argued, however, that India was "forced" to accept these measures. While the whole story of Indian state-sponsored birth control is much more complex, it is true that after 1966 USAID and the World Bank pressured India to step up their population reduction efforts.[33]

Muhammad gave special warning about the dangers of birth control to the women in the Nation of Islam. Because Black Muslims believed that women held the ultimate responsibility for bearing and rearing a strong and large black population, they needed to be extra vigilant when it came to temptations to use birth control. Perhaps Muhammad also understood that black women had relatively positive notions about birth control and would want to limit their reproduction if given the opportunity. He wrote, "To the Lost-Found members of the tribe of Shabazz (the so-called Negroes), I warn you my people—and especially the women. Be aware of the tricks the devils are using to instill the idea of a false birth control in their clinics and hospitals." Muhammad avowed that women lost their value if they could not reproduce. He asked, "Who wants a sterile woman? . . . No man wants a non-productive woman. Though he may not want children for a time, he does want a woman who can produce a child if he changes his mind. Using birth control for promiscuous behavior is a sin." Muhammad described most black women as incapable of making their own personal decisions about fertility control. He stated that they were "ignorant of the real motive behind the so-called birth control schemes proposed and demanded by white officials." According to Muhammad, Black Muslim women should count themselves lucky to receive his warnings about fertility control; with this knowledge they could fulfill their god-given childbearing role (at the behest of their husbands) and contribute to the fight against black genocide.[34]

According to Black Muslims, whites used sterilization as their primary weapon in the genocidal war against Third World peoples in America and internationally. In 1967, Lonnie 2X, writing for *Muhammad Speaks*, reported that "Black leaders across the country have pointed to this state's [Virginia] sterilization clinics as proof that there is a deliberate effort to destroy the Negro population of America by surgically stripping young black women of their ability to bear children." He believed that the "United States has sponsored sterilization clinics and other 'birth control' programs in nonwhite countries throughout the world. Already some three million young men and boys in and around New Delhi, India, have been sterilized" by the United States Peace Corps.[35] Although the author overestimated the number of sterilizations at this point in Indian population control history and I have found no evidence that the United States Peace Corps carried out sterilizations, the significance of his statement lay in the author's attempt to connect the oppression experienced by African Americans—experiences of reproductive abuses that included coerced sterilization—within the borders of the United States to that of Third World peoples subjected to what the Nation of Islam viewed as neocolonialism.[36]

The Nation of Islam made explicit the parallels between what they saw as genocidal population control in the United States and in developing nations. According to Black Muslims, John D. Rockefeller III sponsored this program with the aid of his Population Council. Black Muslims believed that because Rockefeller was "[a]ware that the skyrocketing growth of political knowledge among the world's poor is directly threatening his profits," he plotted to institute a worldwide program of population control.[37] An uncredited article in *Muhammad Speaks* declared, "the most hated and bitterly opposed scheme the U.S. Government has plotted since the enslavement of Africans and the near-extinction of North and South American Indians and Eskimos is the world wide birth control program." The article continued, "This 'contribution' according to a study financed by the Ford Foundation, involves wiping out 2 billion potential liberation army soldiers in the systematically de-developed nations of Asia, Africa, Central and South America." President Nixon, too, the article intoned, had jumped on the population control bandwagon despite his public opposition to abortion by "cutting aid to living poor people" and maintaining "LBJ's level of birth control budgeting" siphoned into the OEO/HEW clinics.[38]

Although the Nation of Islam produced some of the most heated critiques of state population planning in the United States and in the Third World, other people of color and feminists agreed with the essence of the Black Muslim protest against population control efforts. The reproductive rights critique of population control put forth by feminists and other people of color that would gain influence in the mid-1970s was partially articulated by members of the Nation of Islam in the late 1960s. The general argument was that population policy-makers within the United States government believed that world population growth needed to be limited in order to stem the tide of poverty and violence among people of color both in U.S. borders and in developing countries. The United States, and developing nations influenced by the United States, sponsored population planning that focused on limiting fertility by any means, sometimes coercively through incentives and sometimes by force. They argued further that health care measures that could have been influential in reducing infant and maternal mortality rates among the poor, both domestically and internationally, were bypassed in favor of fertility limitation.

Despite their critique of Third World population control programs, the Black Muslims' primary concern remained with low-income black Americans. Lonnie 2X reported that "now so-called 'Maternity Clinics'—specifically outfitted to purge women or men of their reproductive possibilities—are cropping up in hospitals across this state (Virginia)." According to Lonnie 2X, a Virginia clinic sterilized one woman whose husband had recently died. He described her experience of being pressured into the procedure:

> First they go easy . . . by explaining the surgery and trying to persuade
> you that it's all very harmless. If you don't go for this, they say your re-

lief checks might be cut off. Soon the attitude of the doctors and welfare people changes. Where they asked you to be sterilized at first, they start telling you to be sterilized later.

The sterilized woman told Lonnie 2X that she immediately regretted her "choice." She expressed the fear that no man would want to marry her now that she had lost her ability to reproduce. When she returned to the clinic that had sterilized her to ask if her reproductive organs could be restored, "'[t]hey actually laughed at me,' she went on, tears swelling in her eyes. 'To make a long story short,' she continued, 'there is no way to restore my womanhood. The operation was the greatest mistake of my life.'"[39]

Black Muslim rhetoric about genocide and coercive population control measures failed to balance the dangers of reproductive abuses with the benefits of individual control over reproduction. Their opposition to any form of reproductive control had a conspiratorial tone that tended to alienate those who did not ascribe to the general teachings of Elijah Muhammad—specifically white women's liberationists—who were otherwise sympathetic to a critique of domestic and international population policy. For example, writing for *Muhammad Speaks*, Dr. Charles Greenlee, proclaimed that the "genocide tool that the white man is counting on most heavily now is a procedure he labels, 'Population Control.'" He argued, "Population Control is broken down into two categories." One that attempted to control nonwhite people by limiting their numbers, and a second, which attempted to control "the kind of people who populate this earth." Greenlee described "Quality Population Control" as "the ultimate weapon of Black genocide . . . it is a few years off and for that reason, the U.S. along with other white governments is pushing Numerical Control to the nonwhite races." Greenlee continued, weaving a conspiracy he believed whites and "Uncle Tom" blacks waged against nonwhites:

Today, the liberal, money oriented whites, backstopped by the black "butler" group ("anything you say white folks"—Blacks), have seized upon the noble sounding cause of the individual right of every mother to have her family with whatever spacing she desires, and have converted this noble cause to an instrument of Black genocide in the same manner that the church converted the brotherhood of men and the fatherhood of God into an instrument of mass murder during the crusades.[40]

By couching anti–population control rhetoric in such conspiratorial and generalized terms, Black Muslims discouraged multiracial protests against the forced sterilization of women of color. Rather than jump to defend black women against forced sterilization, many white women's liberation activists understandably opposed genocide arguments that equated all reproductive control with population control. The vehemence of the Black Muslim genocide argument may have delayed feminist participation in the anti-sterilization abuse campaign by forcing them to defend all fertility control programs regardless of their sympathy for women of color and the problem of sterilization abuse.

Despite their sometimes-fantastic warnings against genocide, however, the Nation of Islam contributed an important perspective to discussions of reproductive health care. Like the Black Panthers and black feminists, they believed that blacks had the right to have as many children as they wanted, they needed to have comprehensive health care, and there needed to be an end to poverty and its effects in black communities before many African Americans could look on reproductive control positively.

Contributors to *Muhammad Speaks* were some of the first to outline the dual demands for an end to reproductive abuses and improvement of total health care in poor communities—and to push it as an alternative to federally sponsored birth control clinics. For example, writers for *Muhammad Speaks* reported on the inordinately high rate of infant deaths among blacks. One author maintained that "despite the fact that the death of babies in the United States has reached 'an all-time low for the nation,' black infants continue to die at an alarmingly faster rate than white babies."[41] Another article provided statistics on high infant mortality rates, linking them to poverty in black neighborhoods. This author connected birth control and poverty and argued that both contributed to the genocide of blacks: "the 'pill' is but a latter-day adjunct to a long-time weapon of genocide against Black people in the ghettos—poverty and all its ramifications."[42] A similar article entitled "Nutrition Expert Surveys Pre-Natal U.S.A.: Pigs Get Better Care Than Pregnant Women" summed up the problems faced by poor women offered birth control over prenatal care: inadequate nutrition, low birth weight babies, and a high infant mortality rate.[43] A final article discussed the effects of poverty that had become an intrinsic part of life for many black urban dwellers. The author quoted the director of the Health Services of the National Urban League to assert that "'there is sufficient evidence . . . that ill health and poverty reinforce each other.'" The doctor continued, "'The poor, particularly the Negro poor . . . live in conditions which assault both physical and mental health in terms of malnutrition, crowded and unclean housing, substandard heating and sanitary facilities as well as poor personal hygiene and family disorganization.'"[44] Rosalind Petchesky, feminist activist and historian of the reproductive rights movement, reported that in 1979 black American rates of infant mortality still stood at nearly twice the rate of the white majority. For Black Muslims, who felt that black people were already struggling for survival in a country that valued African Americans for little more than their cheap labor, federally funded family planning services seemed to only exacerbate their already dire health problems.[45]

Ogun Kokanfo, writing for *Muhammad Speaks* in 1969, tempered the hostility often directed at birth control programs in this publication but still drew a connection between the lack of government efforts to combat poverty and black suspicions of genocide. Kokanfo discussed "the fact that while welfare for the living is held in suspension, the money spent on birth control had already been increased and is slated to be increased even further." Kokanfo maintained that HEW officials justified funding family planning by claiming to provide for those who needed birth control but did not have the resources to pay for it. Their motives, however, might not be all that benevolent, he argued: "They say that they simply want 'poor families to have the same choice that families in middle- or upper-income levels have: to plan the size and spacing of their families.'" Agreeing with this goal, Kokanfo expressed a position reiterated by Black Nationalists and black and white feminists in the 1970s:

> Certainly poor families should have this right. But shouldn't they also have the same right not to be poor: Shouldn't they have a right to the same education, the same adequate diet, the same medical treatment and the same sanitary and roomy housing conditions as middle- and upper-income levels have: to plan the size and spacing of their families.[46]

Although Kokanfo still invoked a language of genocide—the article is entitled "Why Blacks Must Resist Govt.'s Genocidal Birth Control Programs"—he opened the door to an acceptance of fertility control in conjunction with an end to poverty among blacks. This perspective, that a program for total health care must accompany personal reproductive control, would become popular with both black and white feminists in the 1970s.

The Black Panther Party and Fertility Control— The *"weapon of the pigs"* or a Woman's Right?

In the first few years of the organization's existence, the Black Panthers rejected all forms of reproductive control as genocidal for blacks. Thomas "Blood" McCreary, a member of the New York City Black Panther Party from its inception in 1968 and the Black Liberation Army, the military wing of the party, recalled, "abortion was considered genocidal." He said that the Panthers worried about population controllers imposing birth control and abortion on black women. He added that he now thinks "women should be able to have children if they want them. People don't have babies to get more welfare money and laws that restrict the number of children a woman can have when on welfare are" more likely to be "genocidal than legal abortion or contraception used voluntarily." He continued, "We wanted numbers for political power although we now realize that numbers don't make all the difference. I believe women should have the choice, but should never be coerced into abortion or sterilization."[47]

Like the Black Muslims, some Black Panthers believed that an armed revolution by blacks against the white power structure was possible, if not inevitable. Large numbers of soldiers would be required to win the struggle. The Panthers also agreed with the Black Muslims that the U.S. government plotted to reduce the number of nonwhites in America in order to prevent an armed revolt. McCreary and others also believed that, if blacks were to exercise their civil rights, they would require large numbers of political participants to have any positive effect.[48]

This attitude was to change for several reasons. First, in 1971, the party began to reconsider their anti–birth control position as women in the party articulated some of the barriers to large families. For example, they noted that large families were costly in terms of both time and money. If both men and women were going to be involved in the movement, they argued, less energy could be devoted to raising large families. Second, in 1974, Elaine Brown took over the leadership of the party after Huey Newton went into exile. With Brown in a leadership position, women gained more influence in the organization. Women also became more important as men in the party were killed or serving long-term prison sentences, as a result of the FBI's crackdown on the Black Power movement.[49] Additionally, feminism began to have a more positive impact on Black Panther politics, as black women articulated their own black feminist agenda and expressed their demand for voluntary methods of contraception.[50] At this stage, the Panthers continued to report and condemn reproductive abuses, involving forced sterilization or incompetent abortions performed on black, Latina, and Native American women; at the same time, however, they supported the voluntary practice of fertility control by women of color. In the late 1970s, they took a firm stand against congressional measures making it more difficult for poor women to obtain legal abortions, particularly the Hyde Amendment, first passed in 1976 as a rider to an HEW appropriations bill that banned federal Medicaid support for abortion.

Huey Newton and Bobby Seales had founded the Black Panther Party in 1966 in Oakland, California, as northern urban blacks became the focus for Black Power organizing in the late 1960s. At this point, and for the first year, the party was entirely male. Newton argued that he wanted to organize the "brothers off the block." They drafted a 10-point party platform that articulated their political ideology. The last point of the platform called for economic security for blacks and a nationalist program that united blacks around the world as colonized subjects. They also called for black exemption from military service, an end to police brutality, freedom for black men held in jail, and juries of black peers for black people brought to court.[51]

Newton had a charismatic style that captured wide media attention and the fascination of a trendy Hollywood coterie of film and other entertainment personalities able to give the Black Panthers substantial financial backing. White (male and female) new leftists were also drawn to the urban Black Power movement's display of weapons and revolutionary rhetoric, as the anti-war movement became more militant, violent, and many argue, masculine. Black Panthers and new leftists often worked together to oppose the Vietnam War, exchanging political ideas in the process of building an anti-war coalition. These alliances allowed Newton to establish a diverse following that popularized the Panthers in both black and white grassroots political circles (including radical feminist ones).[52]

When Huey Newton left the country for exile in Cuba in 1973 (he had been accused of murder), making Elaine Brown the head of the party, the Panthers began to develop in a less violent direction, focusing on community-controlled institutions to build local black political power. Brown expanded upon Newton's "Survival Programs," which included a free health clinic, responsible for testing hundreds of blacks for sickle-cell anemia, a free ambulance service, a free shoe program, prisoner support facilities, free breakfast programs for children, and a Black Panther elementary school. The party also developed programs for senior citizens (SAFE—Seniors Against a Fearful Environment), programs for teens (GED classes and peer counseling), and early childhood education (a day-care center and a child development center). Newton believed that black-run social services could be used to build a revolutionary following by educating the community. Blacks would begin to wonder "why the party can do so much with so little, and the capitalists so little with so much. That'll motivate them to start making some demands—not begging—for more concessions . . . the programs are another tactic for revolution."[53]

When Elaine Brown took over the party, she placed women in key positions in the organization and expanded Newton's Survival Programs. She found new methods for raising funds, particularly for the elementary school, which became the Panthers' showcase program. At this point in the development of the party, Brown also decided the Panthers needed to become more involved in electoral politics; Bobby Seale had already run for mayor and Brown for city council. After a second bid for a city council seat in 1974, Brown served as a delegate for Jerry Brown in the 1976 presidential election.[54]

By changing the direction of party organizing and placing women in powerful positions, Brown risked the enmity of some Black Panther men who believed women should support their men, not lead them. Brown noted that "a woman in the Black Power movement was considered at best, irrelevant. A woman asserting herself was a pariah. A woman attempting the role of leadership was, to my proud black Brothers, making an alliance with the 'counter-revolutionary, man-hating, lesbian, feminist white bitches.'"[55] Despite open hostility, Brown persisted in making Beth Meador, a law student, her campaign manager; Phyllis Jackson, a coordinator of Panther campaign workers; Ericka Huggins, administrator of the school; Joan Kelley, administrator of the nonmilitary apparatus, in particular, the Survival Programs; and Norma Armour, the minister of finance for the party.[56]

Newton's return to the United States in 1976 quashed female leadership in the party. Elaine Brown explains in her memoir that she fled the Bay Area in fear of reprisal for transforming the party into an organization focused on gradual social change rather than armed revolution. According to Brown, Newton felt pressure from the "brothers" in the organization to reassert masculine leadership by physically "disciplining" women who ran the social programs. This ugly display of masculine aggression drove important female members of the party to cut all ties with the Panthers.[57]

Despite the reassertion of masculine dominance in the party in the late 1970s, black women had helped to transform Black Power attitudes toward birth control and abortion. Elaine Brown's tenure as head of the Black Panther Party from 1974 to 1976 accompanied a new attitude toward reproductive control for black women that included both anti–sterilization abuse and pro–birth control and abortion positions.

In the early 1970s, articles appeared in the Black Panther Party paper condemning all forms of birth control for blacks. A 1970 article entitled "Birth Control" discussed the need for economic changes that addressed poverty before blacks concerned themselves with fertility limitation. This article echoed those published by the Black Muslims in *Muhammad Speaks*, in that the Black Panthers questioned "family planning" policy that recommended ending poverty through fertility control. The author wrote, "The relevant question is not, 'If you have all those babies, how will you care for them?' But 'Why can't we all get enough to care for our children?'" The author described the pill as "the weapon of the pigs" because it stifled the growth of the black community and added that government rhetoric about the "'population explosion' is only another attempt at deceiving the masses." He asserted that it was wrong to prevent births because it "dealt with overpopulation rather than capitalism and imperialism. Capitalism is the problem, not too many people." He continued, challenging any attempt to reduce the black population: "no pill, loop, or treatment short of mass sterilization will restrict our growth . . . each child born will be one more revolutionary that the power structure will have to try to deal with."[58]

Other articles published in the early 1970s Black Panther Party paper speculated as to the genocidal intentions of white medical practitioners in publicly funded hospitals. One article described a pregnant black woman's experience at San Francisco General Hospital. After finding out about her pregnancy, she wrote, "The doctor thinks you wouldn't possibly want another kid for the state to support so he tells you how to go about getting a therapeutic abortion. You explode and tell him a few things about genocide." The author criticized a physician who tacitly assumed that low-income black women with children should be granted abortions, whereas a white woman might have difficulty obtaining one.[59]

At this point in their history, the Black Panthers opposed any relaxation of the anti-abortion laws as genocidal. The Panthers ran an article on the 1970 New York State abortion reform law that described the theoretical dangers that legal abortion posed for black women. The New York law allowed a woman to terminate her pregnancy up to 24 weeks gestation as long as a doctor performed the procedure. The Black Panthers considered the new abortion law the most recent chapter in a genocidal history of European domination over people of color:

> A victory for the oppressive ruling class who will use this law to kill off Black and other oppressed people before they are born. To the black woman, the Welfare mothers, it is an announcement of death before birth. Black women love children, and in order to see to it that they do not starve, that they do not have to be ashamed of having to wear improper clothing, they will kill them before they are born.

At the same time, the Black Panthers argued for increased entitlements for the poor, explaining that black poverty stemmed from a racist and capitalist system that exploited poor blacks as laborers. If black people were going hungry, it had little to do with overpopulation. Instead, according to the Black Panthers' Marxist analysis of capitalism and poverty, fewer laborers were needed in an economy that had shifted to service from production. The Panthers believed that the government used legal abortion to reduce the worker population, resulting in genocide for blacks.

Like the Nation of Islam, the Panthers suggested that abortion should be illegal because black women could not be trusted to make their own reproductive decisions. The Panthers maintained that some black women might be fooled into believing the feminist "dogma" that legal abortion could save them from illegal and unsafe abortions. They amended the argument that black women suffered most often at the hands of dangerous illegal abortionists with evidence that black women did not receive quality health care in hospitals either. With abortion legal, the Panthers predicted, black women might be subject to abuses by medical doctors. One Panther wrote that the "abortion law hides behind the guise of helping women when in reality it will attempt to destroy our people. How long do you think it will take for voluntary abortion to turn involuntary."[60]

The Black Panthers also educated their readers about the dangers of forced sterilization among indigent women of color as incidents of abuse became public. In a 1971 article, the Black Panther Party reported on a punitive sterilization bill proposed in the state of Tennessee. As we already saw, bills of this sort were proposed in many states nationwide during the 1960s and early 1970s. The Panthers noted that the Tennessee bill would address "'the problem' of families with 'dependent children' by reducing or eliminating the very possibility of children for black and poor people. The number of 'illegitimate' children would be controlled by involuntary sterilization of women." The Tennessee bill stipulated that all unmarried welfare mothers of two or more children be sterilized or forfeit their benefits and give up their children to the state. The writer for the Black Panther paper described the sterilization law as "the state's insurance against a large young generation of blacks and other poor people swelling the welfare rolls."[61] A coalition of organizations including black doctors, black legislators, and welfare rights groups successfully fought the Tennessee sterilization bill. Some of the most committed protesters against this bill were a group of about 200 mostly black welfare women associated with the local branch of the National Welfare Rights Organization. All of these activists held that the state had a responsibility to provide a living wage for the poor, not reduce their numbers.[62]

The Panthers addressed further the coerced sterilization of black women who received Medicaid benefits in their report on Dr. Pierce of Aiken, South Carolina, the doctor who had required that indigent women with two or more children be sterilized if they wanted to use his obstetrical services. The Panthers argued that "what continues to go on with state and local financing, as well as private, is clearly a racist, genocidal extermination directed at poor, Black girls and women. Every evidence of such a policy, in every corner of this country must be exposed, condemned and destroyed."[63]

The Black Panthers recognized that Puerto Rican, other Latina, and Native American women suffered from the highest rates of abuse. Like the Nation of Islam, the Black Panthers linked sterilization abuse in the United States among women of color with the violation of women's reproductive rights in parts of the Third World. For example, in an article supporting the Committee to End Sterilization Abuse (CESA), a New York City anti-sterilization abuse group that included black, Latina, and white activists, the Black Panthers asserted that over one-third of Puerto Rican women had been sterilized as well as 20 percent of black women in the United States. They compared these figures to the high numbers (40,000) of women sterilized in Colombia in the late 1960s with support of the Population Council. In another example, the Black Panther paper reported the story of a Puerto Rican woman who consulted her doctor about fibroid tumors. The doctor ordered sterilization even though this condition never required it. The Panthers also criticized international and domestic family planning programs, supported by the United States, that discouraged abortion and barrier methods of birth control in favor of sterilization and more permanent methods of contraception such as the IUD or the pill, both of which have contributed to dangerous side-effects in women.[64]

By 1974, after Newton's exodus and Brown's accession, the Black Panther Party had shifted their rhetoric away from the genocide argument to focus on the importance of health care and safe, legal abortion provision in the black community. In a radical reversal, the Panthers emphasized the complementary nature of health care and abortion, arguing that black women needed quality health care in addition to legal abortion. Elaine Brown described her advocacy of abortion rights in her autobiography, testifying that "I would support every assertion of human rights by women—from the right to abortion to the right of equality with men as laborers and leaders."[65] Both Brown and the Black Panthers owed their new support for birth control and abortion, in part, to black feminists like Toni Cade, Linda La Rue, Frances Beal, and the women organized in the Black Women's Liberation Group of Mount Vernon who began to speak out in favor of reproductive rights in the 1970s. Beginning with just a few voices in the early 1970s, black women were a fundamental part of the feminist movement that combined the fight for abortion rights with an anti-sterilization abuse movement. The Black Panther support of abortion rights coupled with demands for access to general health care reflected the persuasive powers of this group of black women.

In 1974, an article appeared in the Panther paper that explicitly reflected the new feminist influence on the party. The article instructed women on how to do their own breast exams so that they would have greater control over their personal health. The same information had been distributed by feminists both to facilitate early breast cancer detection and to illustrate that women need not depend on a male medical profession for all their health care. Both the Panthers and feminists involved in the women's health movement understood that knowledge about the body gave individuals and communities power.[66] Finally, the Panthers developed a program to bolster AFDC support by offering welfare recipients medical care, free food, nutrition information, and help in applying for Women, Infants, and Children (WIC) supplements.[67]

Two years after the Supreme Court found abortion to be a constitutional right, the Black Panthers placed themselves firmly in the feminist pro-abortion camp by protesting the persecution of a black abortion doctor accused by Right-to-Life activists of aborting a viable fetus. Dr. Kenneth Edelin, coordinator of Boston City Hospital's (BCH) ob/gyn department, was one of two doctors willing to perform legal abortions at this hospital. BCH physicians treated a largely poor and minority clientele unable to pay for abortions at private clinics. Edelin argued that low-income and black women died from illegal abortion in large numbers before 1973 and continued to have difficulty affording safe, legal abortion after *Roe*. The Black Panther paper quoted Edelin as saying, "'During illegal abortions, not only did the fetuses die, but many women died. . . . The problem is, the women who die are poor women, mainly Black women.'"[68]

As black feminists became increasingly outspoken in their support for abortion rights, the Black Panthers followed their lead. Like black feminists, the Panthers addressed the particular needs of poor and black women. For example, in 1977, after the Hyde Amendment cut federal Medicaid funding for abortion, the Black Panthers ran a series of articles on how these restrictions would damage black women. One author wrote, "Black and poor women on welfare will suffer the most from this ruling, as Medicaid funds that were previously used for abortions may be denied."[69] When President Carter stated that he opposed federal abortion funding, the Panthers publicly criticized his position.[70]

The Black Panther health care agenda diverged from the mainstream feminist one, however, in that the Panthers did not make abortion and birth control their first priority. By 1975, abortion was just one aspect of a total health care plan. Like black feminists, Panthers emphasized the need for jobs, comprehensive health care, child-care, housing, welfare entitlements, an end to imperialism, and prevention of police violence against blacks. Furthermore, the Panthers focused on the importance of maintaining welfare entitlements for poor women, a disproportionate number of whom were black.[71]

By 1975, the Black Panthers began promoting women's liberation as a racially inclusive movement with the potential to benefit both black and white women. Like their stance on abortion, the Panther attitude toward feminism transformed under the leadership of Elaine Brown and as black feminists gained influence and power in both mainstream and radical feminist organizations and began to form their own feminist groups, such as the National Black Women's Health Project, an umbrella organization of women's health groups, which grew out of the National Women's Health Network founded in 1975. To showcase their new feminist stance, one Panther author quoted Margaret Sloan, president of the National Black Feminist Organization, stating that "we Black feminists say very clearly that we are part of the women's liberation movement. Many of us feel very insulted that the women's lib movement is called White because we were there from the beginning."[72]

In the early part of 1977, the Panthers articulated a working-class feminist agenda by running an article protesting a Supreme Court ruling that allowed employers to refuse disability payments for pregnancy-related disorders or childbirth. Similar to their defense of Medicaid abortions for poor women, the Panthers supported pregnancy disability coverage because the issue addressed economic disparities among women. The 1976 case involved women workers at General Electric who argued that the "failure to include pregnancy in the company's disability coverage programs constituted discrimination on the basis of sex." General Electric countered that payment for childbirth and pregnancy complications added significantly to their health care costs. The Supreme Court, siding with GE, disagreed with Equal Employment Opportunity Commission (EEOC) findings that equated discrimination on the basis of pregnancy with sex discrimination. The Court called pregnancy a "unique" and "voluntary" status, making GE's refusal to cover medical costs legitimate. In opposition to this ruling, the Black Panther paper editorialized, "In the worst possible sense employers can now treat pregnant women as badly as they like—can fire them, refuse to hire them, or force long leaves of absence." By taking this position, the Panthers staked out a feminist reproductive politics that prioritized working-class women's economic access to reproductive control, including the right to bear children. Black women had pioneered this notion when they argued that women had a right to bear children regardless of economic status. Some white feminists would adopt this political stance as they attempted to build an inclusive reproductive rights movement.[73]

Despite their earlier anti–fertility control rhetoric, the Black Panthers aided in the transformation of an abortion rights campaign into one for reproductive rights. Due to the combined efforts of the Black Panthers, Black Muslims, and black feminists involved in the movement against population control abuses both in the United States and abroad, organizations concerned with population policy and abortion rights found it increasingly difficult to advocate fertility control for the indigent without including demands for improved health care and resources for the poor. American Black Nationalist links to Pan-Africanist and other nationalist movements in the developing world helped create an international coalition against reproductive coercion. The Panthers and Black Muslims were not the only American nationalist organizations to demand that fertility control accompany improved health care, however. In the late 1960s and early 1970s, the Young Lords, a Puerto Rican nationalist group, fought for an end to sterilization abuse among women of color, access to safe abortion for poor and minority women, community-controlled health care, and an end to machismo and equal treatment for women as we will see in the next chapter.

4

"Abortions under community control"

Feminism, Nationalism, and the Politics of Reproduction among New York City's Young Lords

Eighteen days after a new abortion law went into effect in New York State—on July 1, 1970—the heart of a 31-year-old Puerto Rican woman, Carmen Rodriguez, stopped during a saline-induced second-trimester abortion at Lincoln Hospital in the South Bronx. She was the first woman to die from a legal abortion after the reformed New York State abortion law—legalizing termination up to 24 weeks—became effective.[1] This tragic event immediately became a lightning rod for criticism of both national and local reproductive policies and the conditions of public hospitals serving the poor in New York City. It also helped to crystallize an original reproductive rights discourse combining both feminism and nationalism stridently put forth by women in the Young Lords Party (YLP), a New York City–based Puerto Rican nationalist organization.

The YLP, echoing similar claims made by Black Nationalists and Black Muslims, pointed to Rodriguez's death as evidence that Puerto Ricans and other people of color were targets for mass genocide through population control. For example, after Rodriguez's death, Gloria Cruz, health captain of the YLP, warned that the new state abortion law, in the context of the dangerous medical environment of New York City public hospitals, was an essential part of an attempt to reduce the population of low-income Puerto Ricans. Cruz announced: "A new plan for the limitation of our population was passed—the abortion law. Under this new method we are now supposed to be able to go to any of the city butcher shops (the municipal hospitals) and receive an abortion. These are the same hospitals that have been killing our people for years."[2]

As we have seen, the belief that people of color were being subjected to a genocidal plot was a popular political position in nationalist circles in the late 1960s and early 1970s. This view was extreme, and no evidence confirms that population control reduced the numbers of people of color in America. But the realities of inadequate health care at Lincoln and other public hospitals—long waits for emergency room care, exhausted and hurried interns as medical staff, the lack of provisions for drug treatment or pre- and postnatal care, run-down accommodations, and Carmen Rodriguez's death—provided a context for the dire warnings espoused by Cruz and other people of color.

At the same time, the YLP distinguished themselves from other nationalist organizations active during this period by demanding a broad reproductive rights agenda, which included the right to legal abortion. As we have seen, most nationalist organizations of the early 1970s, like the Black Panther Party or the Nation of Islam, were staunchly opposed to abortion or any other form of reproductive control, even if chosen voluntarily. They insisted that by increasing their numbers, people of color would gain political power. By contrast, the Young Lords' pro–fertility control position developed as a result of the actions of a few very outspoken and powerful women within the organization who were sympathetic to feminism. These women ensured that feminist demands for safe, legal contraception, abortion, and other reproductive rights were an integral part of the Young Lords' politics. Although, at first, women were not taken seriously by most of the male members, by 1970—the first anniversary of the group's existence—they had radically altered the political ideology of the group. For the first time, a nationalist organization composed of people of color made an explicitly feminist position central to their political ideology.

The reproductive rights agenda developed by the female Young Lords between 1969 and 1974 was inclusive: it encompassed access to voluntary birth control, safe and legal abortion, a quality public health care system, free day care, and an end to poverty among Puerto Ricans and other people of color. It also combined two distinct strands of political thought: the first was a nationalist politics—emphasizing the right of poor people of color to control over local institutions, an end to poverty among people of color, and an anti-genocide rhetoric—most stridently articulated by the Black Panther Party and the Nation of Islam in the late

1960s and early 1970s. The second was a feminist politics that demanded a woman's right to control her own reproduction, articulated by women's liberationists during the same period.[3] As female Young Lords pushed feminism to the center of the Young Lords' nationalist political ideology, reproductive rights demands gained increasing importance. After their first year, the YLP openly demanded that Puerto Rican women had a right to bear the number of children they wanted and the right to raise them in a prosperous environment.[4]

At least one group of Puerto Ricans thus developed a unique radical politics during the early 1970s that encompassed both feminism and nationalism. The coexistence of these two political positions within one organization may come as a surprise. There has been a presumption that nationalism and feminism cannot coexist, that a group's nationalism inevitably renders any feminist expression insincere. This perspective is not a product of careful historical examination, however. Not only did women in the YLP push the group to embrace both nationalism and feminism, but they also did so without contradiction, although not without conflict. They drew from both nationalist and feminist political ideologies to forge a libratory reproductive politics. Their standpoint as Puerto Rican feminists active in a nationalist organization that emphasized the needs of poor people of color allowed YLP women to develop this unique version of reproductive politics. In short, their particular position within the YLP fostered an original and inclusive reproductive politics.

The Young Lords Party: Background

Cha Cha Jimenez, a young Puerto Rican activist, and a group of Puerto Ricans allied in the Young Patriots Organization, a politicized street gang, founded the Young Lords Organization (YLO) in Chicago in 1968. The YLO drafted a 13-point platform at the founding that echoed the Black Panther Party's 10-point platform. The first point demanded Puerto Rican independence. Independence for the island was important to Young Lords (both Chicago and New York) politics for the entirety of their existence but became more so after the first three years. Early on, the group focused on improving and empowering poor Puerto Ricans in the barrios of Chicago and New York City. They encouraged individuals with diverse backgrounds to join the group, including people of European, Native-American, and African descent. They wanted their organization to reflect the variegated cultural and racial demography of Puerto Rico and the barrios without the prejudice or class inequity that plagued both the island and mainland United States.[5]

Meanwhile, in New York City, a group of young New Left and civil rights activists, including Denise Oliver, Robert Ortiz, and Mickey Melendez, joined an organization called the Real Great Society (RGS)—an anti-poverty program funded by Vista—that quickly became known as *the* Puerto Rican radical group in New York City.[6] In May 1969, Oliver, Ortiz, and Melendez, along with a group of students of color at the State University of New York, Old Westbury, heard about Jimenez's successes organizing Puerto Ricans into a nationalist party in Chicago and decided to establish a Young Lords Organization branch in New York City.

The New York YLO created a central committee of five individuals—all men—including Felipe Luciano, deputy chairman; Juan Gonzalez, deputy minister of education; Pablo "Yoruba" Guzman, deputy minister of information; David Perez, deputy minister of defense; and Juan "Fi" Ortiz, deputy minister of finance. With about 30 active members at the beginning, the New York group quickly superseded the Chicago YLO as the most prominent branch and began to call themselves the Young Lords Party. Their journal, *Palante*, enjoyed a wide readership among Puerto Ricans and other New Yorkers interested in radical and New Left politics.[7]

The New York Lords' first public political action, in July 1969, was a protest against the New York City Sanitation Department. According to the Lords, the New York City Sanitation Department neglected to provide service to poor black and Latino neighborhoods. To address this problem, they decided to begin a community sanitation project. YLP work groups piled the refuse in heaps in the streets, blocking traffic, to force the city to collect it.[8]

The next protest was a takeover of the 111th and Lexington Avenue Methodist Church on December 28, 1969. The New York Lords had formally requested the use of the church basement to provide free community services, such as a free breakfast program, health clinic, and day-care center, modeled on the Black Panther social programs.[9] When the church authorities refused the request, the New York Lords took over the church. For 11 days after the initial takeover, they used the church for clothing drives, breakfast programs, a liberation school, political education classes, a day care, free health care, and evening entertainment. Hundreds of people from the community joined the protest and became involved in the direct service programs.

Feminist Philosophy: "We want equality for women"

The women present in the YLP at its founding and in the first year were a powerful force in the group. They shaped the agenda to include both feminism and reproductive rights demands. The first women to become involved were Iris Morales, the education captain and now a documentary filmmaker, Denise Oliver, the minister of finance for the YLP, a Black Panther, and now a medical anthropologist, and Gloria Fontanez, a stalwart supporter of the Puerto Rican Nationalist Party, a member of the Health Revolutionary Unity Movement (HRUM)—an organization of health-care workers—and a field marshal for the YLP. Although women composed nearly half of the YLP from the beginning, these three women were particularly influential in forcing feminism to the center of YLP ideology.

At first, gender was not a matter of great importance for the YLP. Women joined the party for many of the same reasons that men did; they identified as Puerto Ricans and believed that poverty, racism, and disempowerment among Puerto Rican New Yorkers was unacceptable and had to be fought. Just as young black men and women across the country had been mobilized by the explosive cries for "Black Power!", Puerto Rican New Yorkers joined together to transform their status. Within months of their founding, however, gender became central to their politics as women decided they wanted a greater role in determining the direction of the movement. Women became discouraged with male displays of machismo and sexism and decided to force the issue within the political forum created by the Lords.[10]

Oliver recalls that a series of particularly heated clashes with YLP men helped mobilize women in the group to bring feminist demands to the group. Several months after the founding, a schism developed among the (male) leadership. Felipe Luciano expressed dissatisfaction with the Lord's ideological alliance to the Black Panther Party and their "national socialist politics," which was diametrically opposed to a cultural nationalism that celebrated "African" identity. He was particularly inspired by the poet Amiri Baraka who lived in Newark, New Jersey and advocated an Afrocentric politics. Luciano and several central committee members arranged a meeting with Baraka in Newark to explore the possibility of a stronger alliance with the Lords. Although she was not a central committee member yet, Luciano asked Oliver to join the meeting as one of the founding members of the YLP. She was the only female Lord to attend.

Oliver described her shock and outrage at the scene that unfolded when the Lords arrived at Baraka's headquarters: "Women crawled into the room on their hands and knees wearing elaborate headdresses decorated with fruit. They accompanied Baraka's coterie of male guards and supporters who wore dashikis and gave power handshakes to the male Lords." She immediately began to fire questions at Baraka about women's role in his organization, but he wouldn't answer her. Pablo Guzman, one of the Lords invited to attend the meeting, then asked the same questions of Baraka, but Oliver became so furious she marched out of the room without waiting for his answers.[11]

Oliver returned to New York City and immediately held a women's caucus meeting with other women in the Lords. She explained what had happened with Baraka. She recalls, "I told them [YLP women] that if we didn't do something we would end up on our hands and knees with fruit on our heads." The women's caucus decided that it was time to force men in the Lords to take feminism seriously. Shortly before the incident with Baraka, several female YLP members, including Oliver and Iris Morales, had become active in the women's liberation movement and participated in a feminist takeover of the left movement journal *Rat*. But the YLP women were unwilling to form their own feminist group apart from the YLP men. They decided, instead, to use a strategy that they hoped would convince the YLP men to yield to their demands. Influenced by Aristophenes' play, *Lysistrata*, they declared they would have no sexual relations with YLP men until the central committee met their demands, which included adding women to the central committee, elevating women to other positions of power, eradicating the call for revolutionary machismo from the platform, and integrating the defense committee by gender.[12]

Many of the YLP, including Oliver, joined the party as part of a couple. Others formed romantic and sexual partnerships within the group over time. For security reasons, the central committee not only encouraged these sexual liaisons among members, but they also forbade extra-group sexual relations. Violation of this rule constituted an offense worthy of disciplinary measures and possible expulsion from the organization. With rumors of FBI infiltration within radical groups running rampant, the Lords feared any intrusion by outsiders not committed to the ideals held by the group.

After the "no sex" strike had been in effect for several weeks, a few central committee members, including Luciano, disappeared. Oliver remembers worrying that the central committee members had been arrested when nobody heard from them for over 24 hours. When they finally turned up after several days, their security guards confessed that the central committee members had been meeting with women outside of the YLP. It turned out that all of the central committee members were privy to the offense, although not all of them had engaged in extraorganization sexual relations.[13]

As the highest-ranking noncentral committee member, it fell to Oliver to decide the central committee's punishment. She demoted the entire central committee to cadre status. Eventually, they could be reinstated, but not until they took time to think over their transgression. Oliver enjoyed full support from the female YLP and some support from the men who had adhered to the rules. With the central committee members humbled, the women's caucus took the opportunity to push their demands: Oliver and Gloria Fontanez joined the central committee and women in the Lords began holding evening seminars to teach men in the group how to treat women as equals.[14]

Most of the YLP women were sympathetic to the goals of second wave feminists, including demands for safe, legal abortion and contraception. A few had been involved in women's liberation organizations. Women in the Lords distinguished themselves from many second wave feminists, however, by stressing what they viewed as the absolute right of all women to have as many children as they wanted—to rid themselves of the poverty that could discourage childbearing and to end involuntary sterilization or any other form of coerced fertility control. While women's liberationists were declaring an absolute right to safe, legal, and free abortion, women in the YLP argued that Puerto Rican and black populations needed to have the freedom to grow and to thrive free from the poverty that affected a woman's choice to bear children or caused illness in children after they were born.[15]

After the demotion of the central committee members, the YLP revised the call for "revolutionary machismo" on the platform so that it disavowed both sexism and traditional machismo. It stated:

WE WANT EQUALITY FOR WOMEN, MACHISMO MUST BE REVOLU-
TIONARY . . . NOT OPPRESSIVE

Under capitalism, our people have been oppressed by both society and
our own men. The doctrine of machismo has been used by our men to
take out their frustrations against their wives, sisters, mothers, and children. Our men must support their women in their fight for economic
and social equality, and must recognize that our women are equals in
every way within the revolutionary ranks.

FORWARD, SISTERS, IN THE STRUGGLE![16]

Although "revolutionary machismo" seemed like a contradiction, YLP
men and women appropriated the traditional Latino concept of
machismo for the purposes of revolution. They literally stood the term on
its head so that machismo took on a connotation directly opposed to its
traditional usage. After feminism became part of the YLP ideology,
machismo for a YLP man now meant treating women as comrades and
equals.[17]

By 1971, the YLP explicitly and vocally supported the women's liberation movement. They stated: "We say right on to any women who are
revolutionaries. They're getting their shit together, they have to deal with
the white man, who is probably at the top of the heap in terms of being
a capitalist oppressor, and they've got a heavy battle—they've got to fight
their husbands and their fathers."[18] Angie Sanabria, who became a self-
described "foot soldier" for the YLP in 1972 after leaving high school,
agreed that the organization had a positive outlook on women's liberation. She recalled that members of the YLP had an "awareness that you
were a woman and wanted to be treated as an equal." And, they made a
"conscious effort to have women and children in the forefront. People
were not allowed to be chauvinistic. Women were not on the back
burner."[19]

Over time, the YLP recognized a political symbiosis between feminism and anti-racism: a sense that the two movements were necessarily
interconnected. The YLP 1970 Position Paper on Women stated that
"Third World women have an integral role to play in the liberation of
all oppressed people as well as in the struggle for liberation of women."
And, more plainly, "We [YLP women] support them, and they should
support us [YLP men] in our struggle."[20] The YLP believed that men and
women of color needed to unite to fight problems of poverty and racism.
Sexism, too, needed to be addressed within a framework that made anti-

racism, anti-poverty, and gender inequality equal priorities. The Lords added:

> The basic criticism we have of our sisters in Women's Liberation is that they shouldn't isolate themselves, because in isolating yourselves from your brothers, and in not educating your brothers, you're making the struggle separate—that's again another division, the same way that capitalism has divided Blacks from Puerto Ricans, and Puerto Ricans from whites, and Blacks from whites.[21]

From the Young Lords' perspective, white women had created a separatist feminism that excluded women and men of color because it made white middle-class women's progress the priority. Preferably, women would lead men to reject sexism, not by excluding them, but by teaching them about power imbalances that involved sexual difference. The Lords argued that the division of feminism from the anti-racism movement prevented the real revolution from taking place; if white women just garnered power for themselves, nothing would really change. They asserted that "racism has to be eliminated, and that whole division of male from female has to be eliminated, and the only way you can do that is through political education. I don't believe that a group of women should get together just to educate themselves, and then not go out and educate the brothers."[22]

Reproductive Rights: *"End all genocide. Abortions under community control!"*

The Young Lords' feminism was essential to their support of a broad reproductive rights agenda. Unlike other nationalist groups, the Lords linked an anti-sterilization position, which originated with their criticism of high sterilization rates in Puerto Rico, with a pro-abortion stance. Feminist Lords argued that Puerto Rican women on the island and in New York required access to safe and legal methods of fertility control, including safe abortion and a variety of birth control methods from which to choose. These methods needed to be distributed in publicly funded health facilities under community control. The Lords believed that if fertility control measures fell into the wrong hands, they could become dangerously coercive, even genocidal. Thus, they announced, all Puerto

Rican women needed to be able to choose freely how many children they wanted, whether this meant never bearing children or bearing 10.

Although most of the YLP were born on the mainland, Puerto Rican New Yorkers were still very much affected by their cultural and historical ties to the island. A massive out-migration of Puerto Ricans to the mainland United States—primarily to New York City—began during World War II, when factory laborers were needed for war production. With improved transportation and communications between the island and the mainland after the war, migration increased through the decade of the 1950s. Despite efforts to attract industry to Puerto Rico in "Operation Bootstrap," Puerto Ricans poured off the island because of high unemployment and greater economic opportunity in the States. By the 1960s, migration began to level off, and some Puerto Rican New Yorkers returned to the island. But the constant contact between the two locales ensured strong bonds between people living in Puerto Rico and in the United States.[23]

The YLP traced the history of sterilization abuse among Puerto Rican women in New York to what they viewed as a tradition of coerced and forced sterilization on the island.[24] The Puerto Rican legislature legalized sterilization as a method of birth control in 1937. Interest in birth control, however, as a measure to stem a growing poor population in Puerto Rico dated to the early 1920s. In 1922, Luis Munoz Marin, who eventually became the first elected governor of the island, began writing a series of articles supporting birth control in *La Democracia*, the newspaper of the Union Party. He argued that the birth control ideas promoted by Margaret Sanger would save the island from becoming overrun with too many mouths to feed, too many children to clothe, and too few resources.[25]

Faith in the potential of birth control to help control unemployment and poverty in Puerto Rico continued to grow throughout the decade of the 1920s, particularly among Puerto Rican physicians and other members of the professions. Dr. Jose Lanauze Rolon founded the Puerto Rican branch of Sanger's organization, the American Birth Control League (ABCL), in Ponce in 1925. The Puerto Rican ABCL faced fierce opposition, however, from the Catholic Church. As a result, the ABCL of Puerto Rico dissolved in 1928. Still, many local physicians continued to lobby the legislature for the legalization of birth control.[26]

Puerto Rican professional women—nurses and social workers—also became active in the movement for birth control on the island. In 1932,

Violet Callendar—who had trained as a nurse at Margaret Sanger's Birth Control Clinical Research Bureau in Harlem—opened a birth control clinic in San Juan. Unfortunately, Sanger never favored Callendar and refused to support her effort to distribute the diaphragm to Puerto Rican women. Callendar's clinic failed within a month. Rosa Gonzalez, a Puerto Rican feminist leader, opened another clinic in Lares, which also quickly closed. Without support from the mainland, feminist attempts to establish birth control clinics modeled on the Sanger clinics ended in failure.[27]

In 1937, birth controllers met with greater success through the efforts of members of the privately funded Maternal and Child Health Association, founded by the Procter and Gamble heir Dr. Clarence J. Gamble. The association opened with 3 private clinics and at its peak directed 12 birth control clinics on sugar plantations throughout the island. In addition to contraceptive distribution, the association successfully lobbied for pro-birth control legislation, including the repeal of article 268—Puerto Rico's version of the "Comstock" laws[28]—that legalized birth control. At the same time, the legislature passed Law 116, which created a eugenics board to evaluate legal sterilization cases.[29]

With the legalization of birth control, sterilization became increasingly popular among Puerto Rican women. For some women, the highly medicalized aspect of the sterilization procedure helped overcome the sense that birth control was immoral.[30] Many women also chose sterilization because they believed that other contraceptives were dangerous, dirty, only for use by prostitutes, or the cause of infidelity. Puerto Rican men, on the other hand, rarely consented to a vasectomy for fear it would hinder their potency. Puerto Rican women who chose sterilization had an average of 6 children and a mean age of 32. Most sterilizations occurred after labor; by 1949, 17.8 percent of all deliveries were followed by sterilization.[31]

Sterilization was by far the most heavily promoted method of contraception in Puerto Rico. Surgeons in hospitals around the island promoted sterilization surgery as the most effective method of contraception for women with several children. They argued that other methods required too much responsibility by the user and ultimately led to contraceptive failure. One study of 850 Puerto Rican unmarried women revealed that 22 percent knew about sterilization, or "la operacion," while only 1 percent knew about the diaphragm and 12 percent knew about the condom. At first, sterilization was most common among higher income women who could pay for the cost of surgery in a hospital facility. Eventually, however, sterilization became the chosen method of middle-income Puerto Rican women as the procedure became more available and less taboo. The most privileged and well-educated women chose temporary methods of birth control, while the majority of extremely poor women remained outside of the medical establishment altogether.[32]

The theory that Puerto Rican women lacked the ability to choose how they regulated their fertility was reinforced in the mid-1950s, when several American contraceptive researchers, including Dr. Gregory Pincus, Hale H. Cook, Dr. Clarence J. Gamble, and Adaline P. Satterthwaite, under the aegis of Margaret Sanger's Planned Parenthood Federation of America, tested the birth control pill in Puerto Rico. The researchers chose Puerto Rico as the locale for the pill tests for 3 reasons: first, they believed that overpopulation and poverty threatened public health on the island. Second, as a U.S. commonwealth they could more easily gain the support of the local government. And, third, poverty and a high population density provided ample justification among neo-Malthusian birth controllers for using the island as a laboratory for the pill. One pro–birth control commentator described the island as "crowded, impoverished and ripe for an intensive birth control program—a prototype underdeveloped country on America's own doorstep."[33] As of November 1958, 850 Puerto Rican women had participated in the birth control trials in San Juan, Humacao, Puerto Rico and also Port-au-Prince, Haiti.[34]

The YLP believed that the pill tests, in conjunction with high rates of sterilization, revealed the genocidal intentions of U.S. birth controllers.[35] While there is no evidence of an actual genocidal campaign against Puerto Ricans or people of color in general, for the YLP and other nationalist organizations, there was a perception that people of color did not have the option of choosing when or how to control their fertility.[36] Fertility rates were high among Puerto Rican women, but rather than encourage choice among a variety of nonpermanent forms of contraception, birth controllers, the Puerto Rican state, and the Catholic Church limited contraceptive choice. Also, birth controllers often offered contraception as a tool for ameliorating poverty. To people of color, reducing the numbers of poor people was not the same as ending poverty.

Anti-eugenics politics have a long tradition in Puerto Rico among Puerto Rican Nationalists. Decades before the pill tests, the Puerto Rican Nationalist Party feared that eugenicists intended to drastically reduce the Puerto Rican population. In 1932, Nationalist Party members learned that Dr. Cornelius Rhoads, who worked in the San Juan Presbyterian

Hospital under a Rockefeller Foundation grant, advocated the elimination of Puerto Ricans in a private letter. *El Mundo*, a leading daily newspaper on the island, published the letter after its discovery by one of Rhoads's lab assistants. There was no evidence that Rhoads succeeded in carrying out his genocidal mission. But the U.S.-appointed governor of the island, James R. Beverly, exacerbated the situation when he announced in his 1932 inaugural address that the population problem on the island would have to be addressed sooner or later. Nationalist Party members were particularly incensed when Beverly stated that the problem was not only the quantity but also the quality of the Puerto Rican population. Nationalists suspected that Rhoads's and Beverly's sentiments were not uncommon among influential Americans living and working on the island.[37]

Echoing Nationalist Party criticisms, the Lords spoke and wrote of what they called an international conspiracy of genocide waged by U.S. imperialists against all Third World peoples. The Lords drew parallels between reproductive abuses occurring in Puerto Rico, Africa, and elsewhere in the Third World. In 1971, Gloria Colon wrote that "the birth control pill was first used in Puerto Rico; the 'morning after' pill is being experimented on women in Africa. Poor Third World women are continuously being used as guinea pigs, not for our own good, but for the destruction of our people. The proper word for it is 'genocide' (mass murder)." In all of these nations, Colon postulated, the United States had a vested interest in limiting the population both to sustain the abundant natural resources that kept the American economy afloat and to reduce the possibility of organized rebellion in Third World nations.[38]

Writing in 1970, Iris Morales raised the specter of genocide when she discussed the history of high rates of sterilization among Puerto Rican women. She asserted that "genocide is being committed against the Puerto Rican Nation through the mass sterilization of Puerto Rican women! In no other nation has sterilization been so prevalent as a means of genocide against an oppressed people." According to Morales, Puerto Rico had become a "military stronghold" and base from which the United States could assert control over the rest of Latin America. She added: "One way to control a nation of vital importance is to limit its population size. The u.s.[*sic*] is doing exactly this through sterilization."[39]

The Young Lords' anti-genocide rhetoric stemmed from their criticism of international population control policy. They rejected neo-Malthusian theories espoused by birth controllers that Third World poverty could be eradicated through population limitation. The YLP and other nationalists argued that population controllers really wanted to reduce or eradicate groups of "undesirable" or "unfit" people rather than put an end to poverty.[40] The Lords also emphasized that Puerto Rican men and women lacked personal control over their reproduction. Social biases discouraged many women from choosing nonpermanent methods of fertility control, such as a diaphragm or condoms, the pill caused unpleasant side effects (including death), and female sterilization was more available than any of the nonpermanent methods. Under these circumstances, Puerto Rican women had no real choice about birth control.[41]

High rates of sterilization in New York City were also of great concern to the YLP, particularly in the first few years of the 1970s when they focused almost all of their political energies on organizing working-class and low-income Puerto Ricans living in the South Bronx, Harlem, and on the Lower East Side. The Lords argued that when poor Puerto Rican women appeared to choose sterilization they did so under very restrictive circumstances. In New York City, Puerto Rican women had seven times the sterilization rate of white women and twice the rate of black women. Many of these women had been sterilized in Puerto Rico; but a significant number were sterilized after arriving in New York City. In her 1970 article on sterilization abuse, Morales explained: "Genocide through sterilization is not only confined to the island of Puerto Rico. It is also carried out within the barrio; sterilization is still practiced as a form of contraception among women, especially young Sisters." Morales posited that one in four Puerto Rican women in New York City were sterilized, and many of these had the operation when still in their twenties. She added that "the system justifies the shit saying the Sisters go to Puerto Rico to get it done. Yet the evidence says that over half the Sisters get the operation done right here in New York City and are strongly encouraged by their doctors to do so." Morales concluded that many Puerto Rican women felt severe disappointment when they could not have all the children they wanted because they had been sterilized before making an informed decision to end their childbearing.[42]

Other evidence confirmed Morales's claims that poor Puerto Rican women in New York were sterilized in high numbers and at a young age. Puerto Rican women tended to have their children early, so they opted to restrict their childbearing while still in their twenties. Puerto Rican women "chose" sterilization when they wanted to restrict their childbearing because they often felt uncomfortable with, or did not know about, other methods such as the diaphragm—condoms were often rejected by male partners—and legal abortion was not an option in New York until 1970. The vast majority—80 percent—of Puerto Rican women sterilized in New York did so for socioeconomic reasons. If they had been given the economic means to have more children, many of them might have made that decision.[43]

Women in the YLP believed that sterilization had negative psychological effects and they worked to combat the stereotypes about femininity that fed this psychology. For example, many Puerto Rican women who opted for sterilization without fully realizing its permanence, or without total confidence in their decision, expressed the sense that they only counted for "half a woman" after the surgery. Writing in 1974, Lopez explained that "unfortunately, men also feel this way. They think that if a woman can't have children or menstruate monthly that she is not a complete woman." Female YLP members argued that these stereotypes constituted a myth about womanhood that required reevaluation. Lopez continued, "Due to his ignorance and 'machismo' a man may leave his wife after she has been sterilized. It is wrong for both men and women to believe that the sole purpose of a woman is to bring children into this world." Women in the Young Lords articulated a feminist rhetoric that deconstructed stereotypes about womanhood and reproduction traditionally popular among Puerto Ricans. They believed that women needed to be able to make autonomous reproductive choices, without coercion from either birth controllers or their male partners.[44]

The YLP reproductive rights position included demands for safe, legal abortion, although the right to legal abortion often seemed secondary to ending sterilization abuse and ensuring that poor Puerto Rican women received proper health care in public hospitals. Denise Oliver recalled that abortion was not central to the Young Lords' political program. She pointed out that "sterilization was the main thing because of the great number of women sterilized in Puerto Rico." Olgie Robles, who joined the YLP in 1969 after dropping out of high school at the age of 16, remembered being strongly pro–legal abortion at the time. She believed that poor women needed the means to limit their reproduction when they could not afford to raise another child. She added, however, that most women in the barrio would not have chosen abortion if they had had the resources to care for an additional child.[45]

After Carmen Rodriguez's death, the Lords feared that unsafe abortion in public hospitals might become the rule despite the new law legalizing abortion. The YLP alleged that doctors had carelessly given Rodriguez the wrong medication to control her asthma, which resulted in a heart attack. Supposedly, none of the staff noticed that she had a heart condition that could be aggravated by asthma medication. The Lords claimed that an inexperienced student intern without proper supervision had treated her. According to the Lords, the Rodriguez case proved that legal abortion was not the answer for poor and Third World women who did not have access to quality health care. The YLP did not trust the new abortion law to radically change these statistics. In 1971 they argued, "Abortions in hospitals that are butcher shops are little better than the illegal abortions our women used to get."[46]

In response to the Young Lords' allegations, the Lincoln Hospital administration denied responsibility for Rodriguez's death. They released an autopsy report disclosing that she died from a rare reaction to the saline solution that was injected into "[her] uterus to induce the abortion."[47] They admitted that she had a heart condition that was aggravated by the abortion. But the hospital administration insisted that the death was unavoidable because they had no previous knowledge of Rodriguez's vulnerable condition.[48]

The YLP and a coalition of other groups, including members of the Black Panther Party and hospital workers from the Health Revolutionary Union Movement (HRUM), called a community meeting to discuss their reaction to the Lincoln Hospital findings. At the meeting, Mike Smith, a Lincoln Hospital intern and member of the Medical Committee for Human Rights (MCHR)—a group of medical students allied in an informal national network to address health problems in low-income and underserved areas—presented a chart, or "clinical pathological conference" (cpc), that summarized Rodriguez's case history. Records of an autopsy appeared in the cpc, demonstrating that the patient died of medical neglect. The Lords called the meeting "the People's cpc" in order to claim the community's right to control medical decisions that affected them; they wanted to appropriate the hospital medical staff's exclusive access to and manipulation of medical information.[49]

As with other medical services, the YLP asserted that the community needed to control their own abortion provision to ensure safety for women of color. In their 1970 "Position Paper on Women," they insisted that women needed to have the option of controlling their fertility using abortion in healthy conditions. They stated: "We believe that abortions should be legal if they are community controlled, if they are safe, if our people are educated about the risks, and if doctors do not sterilize our sisters while performing abortions." In some circumstances, they argued, abortion was a necessity, particularly when poor women did not have adequate resources for more children: "We realize that under capitalism our sisters and brothers cannot support large families and the more children we have the harder it is to get support for them."[50]

Rather than oppose abortion, the YLP asserted that poor Puerto Rican and African-American women needed greater access to safe abortion and total health care or else they would end up in Rodriguez's predicament; she was so far along in the pregnancy she required a dangerous saline procedure, which turned out to be life-threatening in her condition. One writer for *Palante* described the difficulty of acquiring an abortion in a municipal hospital in the first months following legal abortion in New York City:

> Lincoln Hospital has an abortion waiting list of over 300, but provision has been made for only 3 abortions a day. This means that many of our sisters will be in advanced stages of pregnancy when the abortion is performed; this makes the abortion more dangerous. In addition, these operations are not even performed in a well-equipped, sterile operating room, but rather in a small room that had previously been used as a storeroom.[51]

Abortion provision quickly improved as freestanding clinics became the norm in the 1970s. After legal abortion became more available, low-income women experienced a tremendous improvement in survival rates for termination of pregnancy. One study from 1982 indicated that abortion fatality dropped by 73 percent in the decade following *Roe v. Wade*. But after Rodriguez's death in 1970, legal abortion appeared as if it would be as dangerous to minority women as illegal abortion had been for all women before *Roe*.[52]

According to the YLP, safe and accessible abortion needed to accompany a total health care program that allowed Third World women to have all the children they wanted: "We say, change the system so that women can be freely allowed to have as many children as they want without suffering any consequences."[53] This scenario constituted true reproductive freedom for the YLP. Colon illustrated this point in a discussion of the circumstances of another Puerto Rican woman who attempted to get an abortion for economic reasons but became frustrated in the end because of the poor abortion services in New York City clinics and hospitals. When the woman Colon described first went to a clinic, she discovered that her pregnancy had progressed too far for a first trimester abortion. A hospital would perform a late-term saline abortion but only after she had reached her fourth month. According to Colon, her situation worsened when she discovered that without money to pay for an abortion, she would have to go to a city hospital for the late procedure. (Clinics were not prepared to perform the more difficult second trimester surgical procedure.) At the city hospital a doctor told her that she had reached 6 1/2 months: too late to terminate her pregnancy at all. "The sister returned home to her other children and her unemployed husband to do more hustling to allow her future child to survive when she gives birth." According to Colon, the woman felt great relief when she was finally forced to forego the abortion. She explained that "being a Puerto Rican woman, she knew that for her entering an abortion clinic in a New York City hospital was either risking her life or the possibilities of ever being pregnant again. And she was scared!" Colon proposed that Puerto Rican women were not alone in risking their lives for abortion—other women of color confronted the same circumstances. She postulated that "the case of this sister is no different from that of other Third World (Puerto Rican, Black, Chicana, Asian, Native American) women who face the situation of choosing between the risk of an abortion from a racist hospital administration, or of inventing new ways of hustling to clothe, feed, and shelter an addition to her family." Pregnancy without adequate health care measures or economic security left a minority woman "holding on to her pregnant body, watching her already born children nibble on lead paint in place of food, watching the rats that gather to nibble on the toes of her children, worrying about having her insides ripped-up during an abortion."[54]

The only way to adequately provide health and fertility care for Puerto Ricans and other people of color, the YLP declared, was to gain control over the hospitals and other health care facilities in their neighborhoods. Colon detailed her understanding of this nationalist requirement:

Point Number 6 of the Young Lords Party 13-Point Platform and program states: "We want community control of our institutions and land." This means that we want institutions, like hospitals where sisters go to have abortions, to be under the control of our people to be sure that they really serve our needs. Until we struggle together to change our present situation, women will not be allowed to have the children they can support without suffering any consequences.[55]

The slogan "End all genocide. Abortions under community control" encapsulated the notion of truly voluntary fertility control for Puerto Rican nationalist activists in the YLP. Real fertility control could only be achieved when both of these demands were met: that is, when women of color and poor women could choose to limit their fertility when and how they wanted, could have as many children as they wanted, and had economic access to quality overall health care. The YLP believed that Puerto Rican women needed to wrest control of their bodies and reproductive capacities from institutions and individuals preventing them from making their own reproductive decisions. In this sense, the YLP embraced a feminist politics sympathetic to many of the demands made by radical feminists and women's liberationists active at the end of the 1960s and in the early 1970s. They argued that women needed to decide—without any outside pressure—what to do with their own bodies. At the same time, institutions that provided health care to Puerto Rican women needed to be collectively controlled by Puerto Rican communities to ensure that they were safe from medical abuses. For the YLP, reproductive and health care decisions were never strictly limited to the individual; they recognized that a woman's right to abortion needed to be guaranteed by a politicized community that could protect both individual rights and the interests of the larger group.[56]

Several factors allowed the Young Lords to adopt this quite remarkable position that distinguished them from other nationalist organizations such as the Black Panther Party. First, a few powerful female Lords—notably Denise Oliver and Iris Morales—led the way by forcefully arguing that true liberation of people of color needed to include an end to sexist oppression. These women became empowered to speak out against machismo by involving themselves in the women's liberation movement. The second factor is a matter of timing and political context: The first members of the Young Lords founded the organization in 1969, just as women's liberation emerged as a popular political discourse among those affiliated with the New Left. The parallel development of second wave feminism with the YLP's particular brand of nationalist politics allowed the Lords to become sympathetically acquainted with feminism while they forged their political ideology. By contrast, the Black Panther Party members founded their organization several years before women's liberation emerged. As a result, it took much longer for the Black Panthers to incorporate feminism into their political ideology.[57]

Finally, in 1970, Young Lords men were in a better position to lend a sympathetic ear to women's liberation than Black Panther men. Throughout the twentieth century, black men experienced a cultural emasculation—the Black Sambo stereotype—while black women were stereotyped as emasculating and unwomanly. The response among Black Panther men was to embrace a hypermasculinized identity.[58] Puerto Rican men did not carry the same stigma and Puerto Rican women were not burdened with having committed the crime of emasculation. As a result, the deconstruction of machismo within the YLP occurred much more swiftly than it did among the Black Panthers.[59]

Therefore, women in the Young Lords carved out a politics of multiple identity positions—as nationalists and as feminists of color.[60] This stance allowed them to develop their unique reproductive rights position, which embraced both a gender-based politics and a race- and class-based politics. While much of early 1970s New Left politics centered on a singular identification with racial oppression, gender oppression, or oppression by sexual identity, the YLP women were able to construct a politics that took into account race, class, and gender oppression. An inclusive reproductive rights agenda that addressed the needs of women of different identity positions was the result. By the middle of the 1970s, socialist feminists—most notably feminists organized into the Committee for Abortion Rights and Against Sterilization Abuse (CARASA)—adopted much of the YLP politics of reproductive freedom. But in the early part of the decade, the Lords were among the first to demand both an end to sterilization abuse and a right to abortion and contraception on demand within an organization whose politics grew from both nationalist and feminist roots.[61]

5

Race, Class, and Sexuality
Reproductive Rights and the
Campaign for an Inclusive Feminism

Reproductive freedom means the freedom to have as well as not to have children. Policies that restrict women's right to have and raise children—through forced sterilization or the denial of adequate welfare benefits—are directly related to policies that compel women to have children, on the view that this is their primary human function. Both kinds of policies constitute reproduction control by the state and affect the rights of all women insofar as women are the reproducers of children. But state-sponsored reproduction control also affects different groups of women differently. In a period of economic crisis, many white middle-class and working-class women are pressured to resume the "woman's role" of full-time motherhood and housework. At the same time, low-income women—particularly those on welfare and those who are black, Hispanic, and Native American—are targets of systematic, heavily funded programs of "population control" as well as programs that aim to remove their children from them and into "foster care" or state institutions.   —The Committee for Abortion Rights and
                    Against Sterilization Abuse (CARASA)

This statement—written in 1979 by the Committee for Abortion Rights and Against Sterilization Abuse (CARASA) and published in the pamphlet "Women Under Attack"—represented a political high point in nearly two decades of feminist struggle to establish reproductive rights for women. The movement began in the late 1960s with the pre-*Roe v. Wade* feminist campaign for legal abortion that emphasized a woman's sovereignty over her reproducing body. It culminated in the 1980s with the fight to stem the tide of conservative legislation and Supreme Court decisions, limiting hard-fought abortion and contraceptive rights.

CARASA entered this fight in the mid-1970s to oppose the Hyde amendment, which restricted federal funding for Medicaid abortions. For the most part, CARASA members defined themselves as socialist feminists. They focused on the economic bases of women's oppression. Unlike Marxists, however, they believed that it was not enough to address class without also focusing on patriarchy as a system of gender oppression that interacts with (but is semi-independent from) class and race oppressions. According to Barbara Smith of the Combahee River Collective and a reproductive rights organizer in Boston, in the mid-1970s, "socialist feminists were trying to address the issue of race and class." They also believed that "capitalism puts certain limits on how healthy anyone can be."[1]

Many CARASA members had earned their political experience with the civil rights and the anti–Vietnam War movements of the 1960s and early 1970s. These political origins made CARASA feminists aware of links between racial and class oppression in the United States and in the Third World. Furthermore, their anti-war and civil rights activism made them particularly sympathetic to the anti-imperialist ideologies put forth by Black and Latino Nationalist organizations like the Black Panther Party and the Young Lords. Finally, and most important, CARASA members' political orientation made them sensitive to the experiences and perspective of women of color, who insisted that without economic guarantees, reproductive freedom was nonexistent for anyone but the middle class.[2]

CARASA's most central campaigns demonstrated that socialist feminists successfully made demands for economic access to personal fertility control an ideological priority for the reproductive rights movement. They fought for federally funded abortion (primarily in the form of opposition to the Hyde and the Human Life amendments), an end to sterilization abuse, and for occupational health and safety and state-subsidized high quality child-care. Their broad focus was a substantial shift from pre-*Roe v. Wade* feminist abortion rights organizing, in that they identified a nexus of political demands centering on economics that had to be secured before reproductive freedom could become a reality.

At the same time, the anti-abortion movement, first organized by the Catholic Church, but quickly joined by conservative fundamentalist Protestants, identified economic access to abortion as a strategic place to begin chipping away at abortion rights. Specifically, anti-abortion activists began to challenge federal Medicaid provisions for abortion. These efforts culminated in the Hyde Amendment (proposed by Representative Henry Hyde, R-IL) and the 1980 Supreme Court decision—*Harris v. McRae*—that upheld Hyde. Passed by Congress in 1976 as a rider to the HEW appropriations bill, the Hyde Amendment cut off federal funds for Medicaid abortion with exceptions only "where 'the mother's' life is endangered; where she would suffer 'severe and long-lasting health damage' if she gave birth, as determined by two physicians; or where pregnancy is due to rape or incest, and the incident has been reported to a law enforcement agency or public health service." In cases of rape or incest, a woman could receive a Medicaid abortion if she reported the attack within 60 days of the crime.[3]

Reproductive rights feminists, like those organized in CARASA, identified these fundamentalist attacks on women's economic access to abortion as further evidence that a woman's income and economic assets determined her ability to control her reproduction in a capitalist society. They argued that denying a person reproductive control based on her class position was an egregious form of discrimination that needed to be addressed to create a more just society. They also pointed out that many abortion rights feminists had neglected to put economics at the center of their politics of "choice," which left poor women vulnerable to conservative attacks on reproductive freedom.

Background

On June 28, 1977, seven days after the Supreme Court upheld the Hyde Amendment, more than one hundred socialist feminists, women's health activists, representatives from the National Abortion Rights Action League (NARAL), NOW-NY, and the Socialist Workers Party (SWP) met in the basement of the Village Vanguard and formed CARASA. These women included Dr. Helen Rodriguez-Trias, who had been chief of pediatrics at Lincoln Hospital and actively opposed sterilization abuse for several years with the Committee to End Sterilization Abuse (CESA), Meredith Tax, who was involved with the anti-war movement and also founded Bread and Roses, a Boston-based socialist-feminist organization, and chaired CARASA for the first two years, Beth Bush, Harriet Cohen, Rhonda Copelon, Susan Davis, Atina Grossman, an activist who had been involved with the CESA, Rosalind Petchesky, a reproductive rights activist and historian of the reproductive rights movement, Karen Stamm, Anne Teicher, and Barbara Zeluck.

At first, CARASA represented a coalition of groups that ranged from liberal and mainstream to socialist feminist, including NARAL, NOW-NY, the National Women's Political Caucus, the Center for Constitutional Rights, the Committee to End Sterilization Abuse, Feminist Healthworks, Mass Party Organizing Committee, Medical Committee for Human Rights, Socialist Workers Party, and International Socialists. Soon after the founding, the organization adopted a committee system overseen by a 14- to 16-member Steering Committee that included representatives from several smaller working groups, including community outreach, trade union/workplace, fund raising, health/hospitals, legislative, press/media, research, newsletter, child-care, and sterilization.[4] The women who created CARASA wanted to secure reproductive control for the least-advantaged women—the poor, the young, and women of color; those women who would most likely lose their access to abortion and contraception when New Right and Right-to-Life legislation—such as Hyde—became law. CARASA's emphasis on establishing reproductive rights for women who had the least control over their reproduction marked a new stage in abortion politics.[5]

According to Karen Stamm and Meredith Tax, both founders of the group and activists who had experience in the feminist and civil rights movements, CARASA immediately had a class focus that set them apart from all other abortion rights groups. Many of the founding members had been involved in New Left organizations, which shaped their interest in addressing class oppression. They had connections to the student movements of the late 1960s such as Students for a Democratic Society (SDS) and to the anti–Vietnam War campaigns. Furthermore, many of the white and middle-class CARASA members had sharpened their political teeth in the civil rights movement of the 1960s, in the radical feminist movement of the late 1960s and early 1970s, and in Marxist/feminist groups in the early 1970s. A significant number of CARASA's founders had connections to the New American Movement (NAM), a group of leftist activists advocating a socialist politics in the United States. The socialist orientation of the majority of CARASA's early constituency encouraged them to emphasize economic access to reproductive freedom as the central focus of their politics. Another group of women joined CARASA later, including Maxine Wolfe, who had experience with the

Communist Party and International Socialists, and Stephanie Roth and Sarah Schulman, whose feminist backgrounds in high school and college made them less committed to a socialist program.[6]

CARASA also defined their politics in opposition to feminist and abortion rights groups that defended legal abortion as a single-issue campaign—such as NARAL—which quickly dropped out of the CARASA coalition after an agenda had been created. CARASA members applied the terms reproductive rights/reproductive freedom to a series of linked requirements that would provide a material context for reproductive decisions without coercion: they demanded welfare rights, subsidized childcare for low-income women, workplace safety, and an end to sterilization abuse. Without all these provisions, they argued, low-income and working-class women could not secure reproductive freedom, whereas middle-class women could still buy the means to control their reproduction. For example, at a December 1977 conference, Barbara Zeluck declared, "we defined all 'reproductive rights' as CARASA concerns, i.e., a woman's right to choose when or when not to bear children, the availability of good child-care, and a woman's ability to earn enough to support a family."[7]

The loose structure of the organization allowed each CARASA activist to focus on the reproductive rights issues that seemed most important to her. At the first meeting, the founders formed committees to address problems of abortion access, sterilization abuse, workplace safety, and childcare, among other topics. CARASA activists decided to invest primarily, however, in two issues—abortion access for low-income women and protection from sterilization abuse. For CARASA's founders, these two goals represented the two most basic elements of reproductive freedom: the right to limit fertility and the right to reproduce regardless of race or income.

The women who formed CARASA responded to criticisms of the feminist abortion rights and feminist movements made by black and Puerto Rican nationalists and black and Latina feminists organized in the Young Lords, the Black Panthers, and a number of Third World feminist groups across the country, alleging that feminists had ties to the population control establishment and failed to separate themselves from eugenicist or genocidal ideas. CARASA members wanted to refashion the feminist abortion rights movement into one for reproductive rights by adopting many of the same reproductive rights goals put forth by women of color. They had learned that some women did not place great importance on legal abortion and that many Black Nationalists had disparaged abortion and contraception provision in their neighborhoods as genocidal. Women and men of color also rejected arguments made for abortion rights that promoted the use of fertility control to end poverty. Rather than confine their demands to abortion rights and fertility limitation—a political goal that remained central to the movement—CARASA expanded their demands to include the means to bear and raise healthy children. To create an inclusive reproductive rights movement, CARASA members incorporated both the anti–population control criticisms of black women and Latinas—the right to bear and raise healthy children—and mainstream feminist demands for access to safe methods of abortion and contraception that would give women autonomy over their personal reproduction.

Although CARASA feminists understood that female reproduction did not affect all women in the same way—depending upon cultural or social contexts women had very different experiences of reproduction and reproductive control—many in CARASA wanted to unify women into a new multiracial, multiclass, gay positive feminist movement by rethinking the abortion and the feminist movements. They hoped that by campaigning for an inclusive reproductive rights agenda—that emphasized economic access to reproductive control—they could integrate political demands made by black women, Latinas, other women of color, the poor, and working-class women. These groups would then become part of a new movement that demanded reproductive rights. The success of this goal depended upon creating coalitions with women of color, the poor, and working women.

Political expediency was another important motive for creating a diverse reproductive rights agenda with economics at the center. CARASA members responded to the Right-to-Life onslaught on abortion rights and the conservative backlash against feminism. Anti-abortion forces linked abortion to issues such as sexual morality, a conservative family model, and opposition to women's increasing tendency to work outside of the home even when they had pre–school age children. According to CARASA's organizers, this strategy allowed the Right-to-Life movement to expand beyond an exclusive crusade against abortion. Anti-abortion became the cornerstone of a New Right movement that promoted a nostalgic vision of the family and women's role within it—a desire to return to the world of June Cleaver and "Leave It To Beaver," when female sexuality supposedly remained confined to the boundaries of the nuclear family. CARASA members argued that because the New Right understood the connections among issues such as sexuality, work, and family—and understood that the easiest targets for their conservative agenda were poor women—feminists needed to respond with a class-conscious sexual politics that addressed multiple issues of reproductive freedom. In this way they could build a mass movement that united women of all classes and races in a common fight against forces committed to restricting women's control over their reproductive lives, their work lives, and their sexuality. CARASA's research committee detailed these reasons for building a mass movement in the concluding chapter—"The Fight For Reproductive Freedom"—in their first pamphlet, "Women Under Attack," researched and written by Rosalind Petchesky and Rayna Rapp:

> One reason why the "Right-to-Life" Movement has been effective is that its leadership understands the interconnections between abortion and changes in the family, sexuality, and women's work—although its position on these issues is a reactionary one. We can no longer afford to separate abortion from other aspects of reproductive freedom, such as contraception, child-care, prenatal and maternal care, sexual freedom—particularly for homosexuals and lesbians—and sterilization abuse. An analysis of the interrelated aspects of reproductive freedom arms us to fight effectively against those who are attacking our rights and provides us with the basis for uniting the majority of people in this country around such issues. We have a common interest with all persons, of all economic, racial, ethnic, and religious groups, who do not want the U.S. government nor any church to decide for them when and under what conditions they may have children; and who wish to expand the existing possibilities of reproductive choice for themselves and all people.[8]

CARASA met with far more success in making their demands for economic access to reproductive control a part of the abortion and reproductive rights movement than they did in creating an all-inclusive feminist movement. In 1978, they became members of a national network of reproductive rights groups, the Reproductive Rights National Network (R2N2), founded by Meredith Tax, in which they influenced the growth of a nationwide campaign for economic guarantees of reproductive freedom. CARASA members participated in actions in other cities sponsored by R2N2 member organizations, although the core of R2N2's participants were in New York City. Unfortunately, by mid-1983, CARASA had all but dissolved as members of the group clashed over the priority that lesbian rights should be given in a reproductive rights movement. Several women felt lesbian rights and sexual politics should become CARASA's focus, while others insisted that CARASA remain committed to destroying economic barriers to reproductive freedom. This debate caused a rift in the organization that could not be repaired.[9]

CESA and the Battle for Sterilization Guidelines

CARASA members had followed in the footsteps of another reproductive rights organization—the Committee to End Sterilization Abuse (CESA)—when they connected the right to abortion with a campaign against sterilization abuse. In late 1974 and early 1975, a group of about 10 women, including Dr. Helen Rodriguez-Trias, Rosa Garcia, Maritza Arrastia, and Anna Maria Garcia, of the nationalist Puerto Rican Socialist Party, Nancy Stearns, who had colitigated *Abramowicz v. Lefkowitz*, and Karen Stamm, began meeting to form CESA to fight sterilization abuse in New York City. These women gained their political experience in other organizations that addressed women's reproductive and health care concerns such as the Center for Constitutional Rights, the Medical Committee for Human Rights, women's health movement groups, and radical feminist organizations.

In founding CESA, they responded to several prominent sterilization abuse scandals brought to popular attention by the national mainstream presses, including the Nixon administration's 1972 failure to implement a set of Health, Education, and Welfare (HEW) sterilization guidelines that would have protected women and girls from forced or coerced sterilization in federally subsidized clinics. For six months, boxes of 25,000 copies of federal guidelines languished on a shelf in a warehouse because the Nixon administration did not want to be associated with sterilization in an election year. The regulation bungle came to light in 1973, when the public learned that Minnie Lee Relf had been sterilized at a federally funded clinic. If the HEW had released the sterilization guidelines, she might not have been sterilized. In April 1974, after the National Welfare Rights Organization (NWRO) brought a suit against HEW in *NWRO v. Weinberger*, HEW implemented sterilization regulations. These prohibited the sterilization of anyone less than 21 years of age, required a 72-hour waiting period, and protected a woman from losing her Aid to Families with Dependent Children (AFDC) support if she did not agree to sterilization. Despite this decision, in the same year that the regulations were passed, HEW developed a program to reimburse states for the sterilization of poor women.[10]

CESA members had an anti-imperialist and feminist orientation that would also be adopted by CARASA. Their politics stemmed, in part, from their association with the Puerto Rican Socialist Party, which had had connections to the Young Lords. Several of the members also had backgrounds in civil rights and the New Left.[11] At first, CESA focused on sterilization abuse in Puerto Rico. As they became increasingly aware of the problems with coerced and forced sterilization in New York City they began to make links between reproductive abuses in the United States and those occurring in Third World countries as a result of U.S. development aid. They argued that both domestic and international population policy targeted people of color as surplus populations. By making these issues central, CESA succeeded in attracting a multiracial membership. According to Stamm, both black activists and Puerto Rican Nationalists allied with CESA to end forced sterilization in New York. She added that because CESA addressed problems associated with sterilization abuse and population control, women of color felt comfortable asking CESA members for information on other reproductive issues, such as voluntary abortion and contraception.[12]

CESA members also criticized the feminist abortion rights movement. They agreed with the arguments made by women of color and members of the Young Lords that abortion needed to be accompanied by access to comprehensive health care in order to be considered desirable for poor and Third World women. Helen Rodriguez-Trias was an outspoken advocate of this idea. She argued at the Women's Center Reid Lectureship at Barnard College in 1976 that it was important to place reproductive health care in a larger system of total health care: "I see this beginning to happen in the abortion movement, where more and more women, realizing the limitations of focusing on one isolated issue, are viewing abortions in the broader setting of total health care."[13]

Esta Armstrong, who worked at the New York City Health and Hospital's Corporation (HHC) and spearheaded the CESA campaign for sterilization regulations in New York City, recalled that she became aware of the problem of sterilization abuse in 1971, when employed at a city health center where "half the female patients who used the clinic had been sterilized." Sterilization was the only method these women knew of to prevent pregnancy. Furthermore, Armstrong observed that city-employed physicians encouraged sterilization for their minority patients. She responded particularly viscerally to a case in which a prison physician sterilized a black 18-year-old woman incarcerated on minor drug charges. The doctor justified the sterilization by claiming the young woman was retarded. Armstrong speculated that if there had been a regulation requiring informed consent and a waiting period, this woman would have kept her reproductive functioning.[14]

In January 1975, a coalition of groups formed an umbrella anti–sterilization abuse organization, called the Advisory Committee on Sterilization, to assist the New York City HHC in creating a set of regulations that would protect women who used municipal hospitals; this group included staff from HHC and representatives from organizations such as CESA, the Center for Constitutional Rights, the Health Policy Advisory Center (Health Pac), a clearinghouse for women's health movement information that also published a journal called *HealthRight*, the Harlem Hospital Community Board, the Puerto Rican Socialist Party, the National Black Feminist Organization, the Lower East Side Neighborhood Health Center, Gouverneur Hospital Community Board, Morrisania Hospital, Bellevue Hospital Community Board, and others.[15]

CESA and the Advisory Committee expressed dissatisfaction with the 1974 HEW federal sterilization guidelines as well. They argued that HEW guidelines were neither monitored nor enforced. To prove their point, they cited evidence from a 1973 study by the Health Research Group that reported on several instances of coerced sterilizations in Baltimore City Hospital; the patients were asked to sign consent forms for sterilization during labor, although none expressed interest in sterilization. The American Civil Liberties Union (ACLU) Reproductive Freedom Project published another survey on hospital adherence to the HEW sterilization regulations. They reported that in some cases consent had been obtained from patients at the time of an abortion or at childbirth. CESA and the Advisory Committee decried sterilization obtained in conjunction with any surgical or major medical procedure, particularly immediately prior to or following abortion or childbirth. At these moments, they declared, a woman was incapable of giving informed consent because she was in pain, under stress, and possibly anesthetized.[16]

CESA and the Advisory Committee drafted an alternative set of guidelines that included a 30-day waiting period and required the following:

that consent not be given at the time of abortion or childbirth; that there be counseling on other fertility control options; that information on sterilization be given in the patient's native language; that the idea for sterilization must originate with the patient; that women could bring a patient advocate and another person of their choosing to accompany them through the process; and that the patient present written understanding of sterilization with an emphasis on its permanence. These guidelines—implemented in New York City hospitals on November 1, 1975—became the model for the revised HEW regulations and other state regulations, restricting sterilization procedures in locally funded institutions.[17]

Anti–sterilization abuse activists immediately encountered opposition to the guidelines. First, "six professors of obstetrics and gynecology representing six major medical schools" responded by filing a suit—*Douglas v. Holloman*—"opposing the guidelines issued by HEW . . . and the New York City Municipal Hospital System." They argued that guidelines interfered with patients' rights to acquire sterilization and infringed on doctors' right to free speech. The City of New York Department of Health issued a statement against the guidelines: "the effect of the guidelines is discriminatory because of the waiting period imposed." The American College of Obstetricians and Gynecologists (ACOG) opposed any regulation of sterilization, claiming that it would violate the doctor-patient relationship and a doctors' ability to "practice medicine" or "choose" sterilization for his/her patients. In a letter to the HHC Board of Directors, ACOG fellows roundly criticized the guidelines as "prejudicial, inaccurate, and distorted" and argued that they "are so restrictive as to, in effect, make sterilization unavailable to the patients." Planned Parenthood, the Association for Voluntary Sterilization (AVS), and NARAL also opposed the regulations. They argued that the waiting period would prevent women from having a full range of reproductive options.[18]

The demand for a 30-day waiting period between the initial patient information session and the actual procedure proved the most divisive among feminists. Many feminists cautioned that a waiting period would discourage women from choosing sterilization when they really wanted to end their childbearing permanently. National NOW (NOW-NY actively supported regulation), in particular, fought the sterilization guidelines with the argument that any restrictions on contraceptive devices would unduly hinder women's reproductive autonomy. Furthermore, the AVS, National NOW, and NARAL opposed any state involvement in reproductive decisions; they believed that state involvement in sterilization could snowball into a pronatalist agenda that would limit all contraception. CESA members countered these arguments with evidence indicating that minority and poor women suffered from sterilization abuses and desperately needed some form of protection. They asserted that a 30-day waiting period would save women from being pressed into a hasty decision to end their childbearing capacity permanently. Because sterilization was an irreversible procedure, they argued, it merited tighter regulation than other methods of contraception. According to some in CESA, opposition to regulation by white and middle-class women betrayed their selfishness and inability to see past their own circumstances.[19]

Despite the intense debate, in 1975, HHC approved the sterilization regulations drawn up by CESA. These only covered municipal hospitals monitored by HHC, however. In 1976–1977, another regulation battle ensued over a City Council proposal—Public Law #37 announced by Councilman Carter Burden—intended to extend the HHC regulations to all of New York City. According to Dr. Rodriguez-Trias, "The [City Council] law embodies the principles of the guidelines on sterilization of the New York City Health and Hospitals Corporation, applying them to all New York City health facilities, *both public and private*. The law also regulates sterilization of *both women and men*." The City Council convened public hearings on the Burden sterilization law, which CESA stacked with supporters of regulation. New York NOW, the ACLU, and the National Black Feminist Organization lent their public support to the Burden proposal. Planned Parenthood opposed it because of the 30-day waiting period. Planned Parenthood executives intended to offer sterilization surgery at their clinics, so they had an interest in making the procedure easier to deliver. Planned Parenthood's efforts failed when the City Council passed the Burden law with a vote of 38 to 0 in April of 1977. CESA and members of the Advisory Committee continued to organize around the issue of sterilization abuse and women's health and reproduction after the Burden proposal became city policy. They gave healthcare referrals, offered information on patient rights and legal advocacy, and educated the public on the problem of sterilization abuse.[20]

CESA's last two legislative fights occurred in 1978. By this time, CARASA had formed in response to the Hyde Amendment and had joined CESA in their anti–sterilization abuse campaign. The first battle began when Assemblymen Mark Siegel and Allen Hevesi, chairman of the Health Committee, introduced a bill that would allow "medical" exceptions to the 30-day waiting period; doctors could advise that the surgery take place after only a 72-hour wait. CESA and CARASA members complained that because Siegel sat on the board of AVS, he did not act as an independent interest in proposing the bill. Like Planned Parenthood, AVS board members wanted to expand sterilization in New York City by opening their own outpatient clinics. Without the 30-day provision, they could streamline the sterilization process for their voluntary patients—many of whom would be white and middleclass. In the end, the Siegel/Hevesi bill failed because of CESA and CARASA's lobbying efforts and public forums about the dangers of forced and coerced sterilization for poor and minority women.[21]

Also in 1978, CESA and CARASA mounted a campaign for the Nadler bill—proposed by State Assemblyman Jerry Nadler—which included a set of sterilization regulations for New York State very similar to those passed in New York City and subsequently adopted by HEW in the same year.[22] This campaign required both lobbying and educational efforts. CARASA's Sterilization Committee spent much of their time educating other feminists, particularly those in National NOW, about the dangers of sterilization abuse for minority and poor women.[23]

After the New York State legislature passed the Nadler bill and HEW adopted new regulations modeled on those in New York City, CESA disbanded, but several CESA members, including Stamm and Dr. Rodriguez-Trias, became active in CARASA. According to Stamm, by 1978, with HEW regulations in place, sterilization abuse had become less urgent for most feminist activists, whereas abortion rights had again taken center stage as a result of the Hyde Amendment.[24]

A New Reproductive Rights Agenda

While CARASA's ideological focus remained relatively consistent until the early 1980s—members agreed that reproductive rights required the economic means to control fertility by choosing either to have or not to have a child—CARASA activists did not always agree on a political strategy for their organization. At the group's inception in 1977, they debated the advantages of focusing on abortion rights and the regulation of sterilization alone as opposed to broadening their agenda. One CARASA member who advocated concentrating on abortion and sterilization abuse rejected the "laundry-list" approach to securing reproductive freedom, which included demands for sexual freedom, contraception, legal abortion, freedom from forced sterilization, pregnancy disability payments, control of the birthing process, a safe workplace, free, quality child-care, free medical care, and a guaranteed adequate income. Rather, she believed a more strategic agenda would include "two main demands that put class, race, and sex into focus within the context of reproductive freedom." These demands were access to safe, legal, and affordable abortion for all women and an end to sterilization abuse among poor and minority women.[25]

Other early CARASA members maintained that abortion alone should remain the preeminent demand; a long list of reproductive rights requirements simply diluted the struggle for abortion. Ellen Willis, a member of Redstockings, CARASA, and a founder of the performance-oriented feminist abortion rights group No More Nice Girls (NMNG), criticized CARASA for its scattershot agenda. She and several other women split from CARASA and created NMNG in 1977 out of frustration with CARASA's broad strategy. Willis thought CARASA should concentrate exclusively on abortion as a sexual and political right. She recalled that CARASA's defense was to "craft an alliance that will work" with women of color and advocates for the poor to defend a woman's economic access to abortion. But, according to Willis, "their basic fallacy was thinking that you could make an end run around abortion as a sexual/political issue." She argued that without understanding the anti-abortion movement as an attack on women's sexuality and morality, CARASA failed to get at the core of abortion rights. Willis added that "CARASA gave up by talking about reproductive rights rather than abortion. They did not understand that abortion was not only about health and welfare, but about freedom and sex, about saying yes I have a moral right to kill this fetus in order to survive as a human being." By focusing on economics, Willis argued, CARASA members ceded moral ground to the Right-to-Life movement. According to Willis, they needed to counter the Right-to-Life by defining the right to abortion as a moral absolute.[26] Ros Baxandall, member of Redstockings, CARASA, and participant in No More Nice Girls, agreed with Willis that CARASA members watered down their feminist politics by devoting their attention to too many subjects other than abortion.[27] Theresa Horvath, CARASA member and cochair of the organization from 1978 to 1981, also remembered "CARASA felt less comfortable with that issue [abortion]." She reported that "there were debates over abortion, but abortion was more problematic. Everyone could say they were against sterilization abuse, however, we lacked the courage to follow that lead and we were not going to call ourselves socialist feminists. We needed to focus on abortion and still maintain a class analysis."[28]

Horvath recalled that at the beginning there was plenty of unacknowledged dissatisfaction in the ranks over "the economic analysis thing." This underlying dissension "provided a tension that couldn't be [easily] resolved" because "the economic analysis was never evaluated." A few powerful women in the group, particularly Tax—one of the founders, a "visionary" political organizer, and the chair of the Steering Committee—refused to allow CARASA's broad perspective to be a topic of debate. At the time, however, Horvath agreed with Tax's strategy. She was active in feminist politics as a college student in the 1970s and remembered becoming bogged down in personal and political disagreements over group focus and personal agenda items that made the organizations much less effective politically. She asserted, "I did not want to be in another consciousness raising group." She remembered thinking to herself after joining CARASA, "let's do some serious work." "There was satisfaction that we were in something that was in momentum," she added. Furthermore, "as we started to talk about sexuality and all of our feelings everything fell apart. We had tried to structure it so that everyone would be welcome."[29]

For the most part, as the organization developed, CARASA activists allowed each member the freedom to choose her own political focus; this policy resulted in some fragmentation of the group, although ideologically most members believed that an economic and class analysis should unify them, and abortion access and prevention of sterilization abuse should take priority. Women who disagreed with this ideology—such as those in NMNG—generally left the organization.

In its simplest form, CARASA defined reproductive rights as every "woman's right to choose when or when not to bear children." This required that women have access to inexpensive and safe abortions at all stages of pregnancy and without any restrictions, whether financial, or by laws designed to make abortion more difficult to obtain, such as parental consent, spousal consent, "informed" consent (which stipulated that the patient sit through a counseling session explaining the stages of embryonic and fetal development), or the risk of life or health. It also necessitated protection from sterilization abuse, forced or coerced fertility control, and an increase in the state's responsibilities for human health and welfare, particularly for the poor. Reproductive rights feminists in

CARASA believed that the state had an obligation to guarantee that every woman could have children regardless of her income, race, marital status, or sexual orientation. They also proclaimed that the state needed to commit to ensuring that when children were born, they were raised outside of poverty.[30]

The long list of demands CARASA expected to have fulfilled by the state before reproductive freedom could be achieved suggested their faith in the possibility of significant economic reforms. Their reproductive rights agenda grew from an ideological commitment to a socialist state and a Marxist/feminist perspective honed in the early 1970s. They emphasized the links between this broad political perspective and their reproductive rights demands. For example, they declared in their Principles of Unity, published in February 1979, "Reproductive freedom depends on equal wages for women, enough to support a family, alone or with others; welfare benefits for an adequate standard of living; decent housing to provide a comfortable, secure place to live and rest; reliable, skilled child-care and schools to enable our children to become healthy adults." None of these requirements could stand alone; for women to freely choose to bear a child, they needed state-supported social services to ensure that children would grow up healthy.[31]

As their definition of reproductive freedom suggested, CARASA did not want to limit themselves to the abortion issue, despite the concerted attacks on legal abortion by the religious right that would eventually force the movement in that direction. Many CARASA members had participated in the feminist abortion rights movement earlier in the decade and had learned that that effort had failed to include the reproductive needs of black, Latina, and poor women. In a *CARASA NEWS* commentary, Stamm suggested that the single-issue strategy for securing and defending abortion rights was not a good idea because many Americans did not support abortion in all circumstances. She believed that the reproductive rights movement needed to appeal to a broad array of views held by different groups of individuals. CARASA's work in coalition with other groups could help bring different constituencies together for common reproductive rights goals. Stamm wrote, "Many of us hold this limited . . . approach [focus on abortion rights] partly responsible for the decline in the pro-choice position between 1973–77. . . . [T]he pre-1973 support for abortion was not based on a broad social analysis but was limited in depth and scope to an individual choice among women seeking freedom from their traditional roles." She continued, describing a broad reproductive rights agenda that included much more than abortion rights:

> Reproductive rights includes abortion rights, freedom from sterilization abuse, available child-care, living wages or adequate public assistance, access to decent health care, safe, effective, cheap contraception, freedom to be a lesbian and live without discrimination, housing and anything else that gives real support to people to enable them to choose freely.[32]

Pairing the right to legal abortion with the demand that all women have access to the *means* to ensure reproductive control became a staple of CARASA rhetoric, if not always their focus in their political actions. They believed that women should not be prevented from having the children they want because of forced sterilization, an inadequate income, or discrimination based on race, gender, class, or sexual orientation.

CARASA members argued that single-issue abortion politics had been tainted by population control groups such as Zero Population Growth (ZPG), an organization that made an end to worldwide population increase their highest priority. Because these single-issue groups were pro-choice and made alliances with nominally feminist abortion rights groups—NARAL and Planned Parenthood, in particular—feminists who supported abortion rights often became implicated in rumors that population control meant genocide. In order to dispel this image, feminist reproductive rights activists believed they needed to campaign against restrictions on poor and minority women's ability to have the children they wanted. A CARASA member, writing critically of feminist abortion rights activists in the past, claimed that CARASA combated "a heritage from the women's liberation movement of failing to work hard to bridge this objective gap [with minority women] by fighting sterilization abuse or actively supporting struggles over day-care and public schooling." She demonstrated that population control arguments could cause traditionally pro-abortion groups to turn anti-abortion: "It came as no surprise to us that local welfare rights groups in Akron, OH came out supporting Right-to-Life after a pro-choice campaign advocated Medicaid abortion funding for fiscal reasons. These were the very women who were the targets of the Hyde Amendment." Welfare rights groups opposed any campaigns for abortion rights that recommended the reduction of the numbers of poor people in order to preserve public coffers.[33]

Thus, CARASA members actively distinguished themselves from the population control milieu by linking abortion and anti–sterilization abuse "with other economic, social and medical aspects of reproductive freedom." They created a new feminist reproductive rights agenda that could not be confused with population control. According to one CARASA member, by linking abortion and sterilization, CARASA could "prove—by what we do rather than by what we say—that we are as committed to defending the reproductive rights of working-class and minority women as we are to abortion rights, and that we see the relationship between the two."[34]

Abortion Rights

The Hyde Amendment and other attacks by the religious right afforded CARASA founders the impetus they needed to mobilize and redefine the feminist abortion rights movement to achieve what they termed "reproductive rights," which would guarantee abortion access to the poorest women. According to early CARASA members, the state had an obligation to provide abortion for women who did not have financial access to it. They surmised that the Hyde Amendment would prevent many poor women from having abortions and would promote sterilization. In *Women Under Attack*, CARASA reported that

> some 300,000 women a year who seek abortions are entirely dependent on Medicaid and other public funds for medical care; the average cost of a private abortion in 1976 was $280, which is higher than the average monthly welfare payment for an entire family; the federal government continues to pay 90% of the costs of sterilization, so that denying abortion funds puts women who cannot afford more children under increased pressure to become sterilized.[35]

CARASA members believed the Hyde Amendment restrictions were the greatest threat to abortion rights (and a threat to women's lives) since the Supreme Court found abortion to be constitutionally protected in 1973.

Reproductive rights activists from the Center for Constitutional Rights, the ACLU, and Planned Parenthood rallied forces to fight Hyde by joining *McRae v. Califano* (filed in 1976)—the suit challenging it.[36]

Lawyers for the pro-choice ranks—Rhonda Copelon of CARASA argued the case in front of the Supreme Court—contended that the law violated an individual's constitutional right to freedom of religion and the First Amendment's guarantee of separation of church and state.[37] They deemed that it "interferes with free exercise of religion for many whose religions counsel or support the right to choose." They also argued that Hyde violated "the Equal Protection of the laws by singling out abortion as the only form of medical care which will not be provided by Medicaid even where medically necessary." The state ought to "remain neutral and reimburse for abortion as well as childbirth, thus allowing each indigent pregnant woman to make her own conscientious choice." [38] Expert witnesses who testified against Hyde in hearings for *McRae* predicted "that the denial of reimbursement for abortion will increase the pressure on poor women to be sterilized so as to avoid unwanted pregnancy, particularly since 90% of the cost of sterilization is reimbursed under Medicaid."[39]

In 1978, the same year the Supreme Court upheld Hyde as constitutional, HEW began tightening the rules under which federal funds could pay for abortions; a Medicaid patient needed two doctors' recommendations, testifying that the abortion was medically necessary to protect her life or her health. The federal government would not finance elective abortion, although it continued to fund sterilization, prenatal care, and childbirth. CARASA members viewed this policy as a punitive and anti-natalist measure for the poor; indigent women were financially pressured to "choose" a permanent method of controlling their fertility if they wanted to limit their childbearing.

CARASA published statistics on the effects that Hyde had on poor women's access to abortion. They revealed that in 1978 "only 31 abortions were certified as reimbursable in Arkansas, Mississippi, Oklahoma, South Carolina, and Texas. No Medicaid-funded abortions were performed in Alabama, Maine, Montana or Nevada." In 1977, before the Supreme Court had decided *McRae* in favor of Hyde, these states had authorized the performance of 2,366 Medicaid abortions. In one year, there had been a 99 percent decrease in Medicaid-funded abortions. These figures indicated that Hyde had had a very real effect on poor women's ability to control their fertility. Many women, who in the past would have chosen to terminate a pregnancy using Medicaid, now carried it to term, terminated a pregnancy illegally, or scraped together the money for a legal abortion by borrowing and forgoing other necessities.[40]

As a result of Hyde, CARASA members placed safe, legal, and affordable abortion at the forefront of their political ideology. In their 1978 Principles of Unity, CARASA members stated: "All women should have the right to safe abortions, regardless of income." They continued, "We want to end the Medicaid cutbacks which force poor, minority and working women into unwanted childbirth, back street abortions and unwanted sterilizations." With the end of federally supported Medicaid, they insisted that the State of New York "bears an obligation to ensure unimpeded access to abortion and medical services for women who cannot afford private care." New York State preserved state Medicaid funding, although with an annual legislative battle.[41]

In October 1979, CARASA members held a week of events to address abortion rights issues. They reported that reproductive rights activists in 80 cities organized over 200 activities to coincide with CARASA's week. CARASA's Abortion Rights Action Week Steering Committee decided to focus their program on four constituencies of women who they believed had difficulty gaining access to abortions: minority women, working-class women, teenagers, and housewives. In their flyers for the event, they encouraged women to participate in the week by inviting speakers and organizing discussion groups in their unions, church organizations, and women's clubs on abortion and contraceptive rights, health insurance coverage for abortion, parental consent restrictions on abortion, and public school sex education. CARASA members believed that the majority of women in New York State and elsewhere in the United States wanted access to abortion but did not have a forum to show their support. A conference on abortion rights would educate women on the topic and encourage them to begin to participate in a movement to keep abortion legal and accessible to all women. CARASA hoped the Abortion Rights Action Week would allow them to take an offensive position in the battle with the Right-to-Life movement over access to legal abortion. Since passage of the Hyde Amendment, Tax argued in her *CARASA NEWS* article announcing the event, the feminist reproductive rights movement had been on the defensive as the New Right succeeded in its efforts to restrict abortion access among mostly poor women.[42]

During the week CARASA held forums on abortion rights topics, although "other issues of reproductive rights, including sterilization abuse, birth control, sex education, welfare and the health care system" were also addressed. They gathered signatures from participants at the event for a petition calling for protection of reproductive rights to be hand delivered to Congress. The petition concluded: "WE BELIEVE that women's reproductive freedom and the right to choose when and if to have children can only be secured when our society provides support for women whatever choice they make." The week's events culminated in a rally at Battery Park in New York City (in view of the Statue of Liberty), at which the petition signatures were presented to representatives to bring to Washington. CARASA gained support for their week from "the ACLU, . . . the New Hampshire Feminist Health Center (representing women-controlled clinics), the National Alliance of Black Feminists, MANWA (the Mexican-American National Woman's Association), the Commission Feminin Nacional Mexicana, the National Lawyers' Guild, Catholics for a Free Choice, 1199, CLUW (Coalition of Labor Union Women), Planned Parenthood, Americans United to Save Legal Abortion, Health Pac, the National Women's Political Caucus of SUNY, and R2N2 (Reproductive Rights National Network)."[43]

Despite efforts to stay on the offensive with their Abortion Rights Action Week, CARASA members continued to combat the "Right-to-Life" movement's attempts to roll back legal abortion. By 1978, the religious right had successfully lobbied 17 state legislatures to call for a National Constitutional Convention to ratify a constitutional amendment—the Human Life Amendment—that would protect the life of an embryo from the moment of conception. If passed, women would risk manslaughter charges for aborting a pregnancy, and it would make contraceptive devices such as the pill and the IUD illegal because both occasionally caused the uterus to expel a fertilized egg. In the fall of 1979, Rhonda Copelon, CARASA member and the abortion rights lawyer who argued the unsuccessful constitutional challenge to the Hyde Amendment in *McRae*, commented that the Human Life Amendment (HLA) "has the potential of investing the state with more thoroughgoing and destructive control over women's bodies and lives than has ever been imagined."[44]

By 1981, the abortion battle was concentrated in the Senate, which held hearings on a bill almost identical to the Right-to-Life's Human Life Amendment, called the Human Life Statute (HLS), which declared "that a fetus is a 'person' from the moment of conception." A CARASA press release argued that "this law would put women having abortions in danger of being prosecuted for murder. Many women will face dangerous illegal abortions or forced motherhood." Several CARASA members, including Maxine Wolfe, Sarah Schulman, and Stephanie Roth, with the Women's Liberation Zap Action Brigade (ZAP), disrupted the Senate

Subcommittee on Separation of Powers hearings on the statute in April 1981, stating that "we are angry and determined that women's voices . . . be heard at these hearings. Giving a fertilized egg the rights of a person is a new chapter in the old story of men controlling women's lives. The question of when human life begins is being framed at the expense of women's lives."[45]

CARASA's Abortion Rights Action Week and campaigns against Hyde, HLA, HLS, and other pro-life attacks kept abortion rights at the center of reproductive politics in the late 1970s and early 1980s. While CARASA linked abortion and sterilization abuse in their ideological rhetoric, Right-to-Life and New Right backlash against victories won by the previous decades' abortion rights movement—such as *Roe v. Wade*—motivated CARASA members to mobilize the bulk of their often scarce political forces in favor of abortion rights. For reproductive rights activists, it seemed that guarantees protected by *Roe* might very soon be extinguished. Even if abortion remained legal, the Right-to-Life movement had begun to erode poor and young women's access to abortion and contraception. Many middle-class women, who had stayed neutral in the political battle to end sterilization abuse waged by CESA, felt compelled to join a movement protecting abortion rights when these seemed threatened. For example, the CARASA members who disrupted the Senate hearings on the HLA recalled their adamant defense of abortion as a woman's right, "We went to the hearings and heard anti-abortionists claim that a zygote is a human life, that a fertilized egg is a citizen; and we grew angrier and angrier. No one ever said the word 'abortion' and no one ever mentioned women—our bodies, our decisions, our lives."[46]

At the same time, those CARASA members who disrupted the Senate hearings on the HLA voiced opposition to population control and sterilization abuse, even if these issues were not their primary political focus. They wanted to bring attention to the linked reproductive needs of Third World women, women of color, and poor women because they recognized that the New Right strategy of attacking women's reproductive rights consisted of whittling away at the most vulnerable women's access to fertility control. They further conjectured that if the New Right succeeded in dispensing with the reproductive rights of poor, minority, and young women, they would soon attack more advantaged women's abortion access. The protesters at the Senate hearing recounted their attempt to speak to a broad reproductive rights agenda that encompassed both abortion rights and an anti–population control stance:

So we stood up in that hearing room in Washington D.C. and stated the obvious: "A Woman's Life is a Human Life." We said it to the Senators, to the president of Right-to-Life, to the representatives of population control organizations who sterilize poor and Third World women, and we said it to representatives of the media so that everyone watching national television and reading the newspapers could hear us.[47]

Anti-Sterilization Abuse

The federal government coupled abortion with sterilization by terminating funding for the former and continuing funding for the latter through the Medicaid program. The Sterilization Committee members of CARASA, including Karen Stamm, Dr. Rodriguez-Trias, Ros Petchesky, and Anne Teicher, pointed out that HEW paid for 15,000 sterilizations a year, covering 90 percent of the cost of the operation for Medicaid recipients. This policy made sterilization more accessible than abortion and increased the potential for its abuse. For this reason, CARASA decided to make an end to sterilization abuse one of their two highest agenda items. CARASA members explained:

> The abortion cutbacks will mean increased sterilization abuse because federally funded abortions are no longer an option for poor women. Since birth control is never 100% effective, sterilizations become the only funded alternative to bearing unwanted children. Even now the federal government continues to pay for Medicaid sterilizations; many medical institutions are pushing this procedure as a form of birth control for poor women. Both the Hyde Amendment and forced sterilization are illegitimate interferences with a woman's right to choose whether or not to bear children. To limit a woman's reproductive choices is sexist; to promote sterilizations in Black, Hispanic and Native American communities is racist.[48]

This statement encapsulated CARASA's reasoning behind bringing abortion rights and protection from sterilization abuse under one banner. The two issues together represented the two sides of the reproductive rights politics advocated by CARASA. A woman not only required the means to control her fertility by preventing or terminating a pregnancy at any time, but she also required the means to have children. At its most basic level, the right to bear children required that a woman retain her reproductive capacity. Forced or coerced sterilization violated this right more explicitly than any other restriction on reproduction. CARASA members asserted that

> no government or population agency should be able to force a woman to be sterilized by such tactics as: threatening welfare cutoff, denying her other medical services, making it the condition for an abortion, getting her to sign a consent form when she is in labor or having an abortion, or lying about the irreversible character of the operation. We believe it is critical to combine the issues of abortion rights and sterilization abuse. We want safe and fully available health care for everyone.[49]

A dual commitment to ending sterilization abuse and maintaining abortion rights remained important to CARASA's sense of their own successes. In reviewing their achievements of 1978, a CARASA member from the Sterilization Committee reported, "We played our part in keeping abortion funding in New York [state Medicaid]. We fought attempts to cut the heart out of the sterilization regulations in New York and actively worked to get them extended nationally." She added that despite some difficulties, CARASA had also begun to create a national coalition (particularly with the campaign to institute sterilization regulations in California) to end sterilization abuse. Finally, the Sterilization Committee argued that the problem of sterilization abuse remained associated with that of abortion rights because poor women still risked forced sterilization after an abortion in private clinics not covered by federal HEW regulations. The regulations still needed to be extended to private facilities, particularly as outpatient clinics became the primary providers of abortion in the 1970s.[50]

Activists in the group also hoped that by putting an emphasis on an anti–sterilization abuse campaign in their drive for reproductive freedom they could begin to build an inclusive feminist movement, one that took into account the different needs of poor women and women of color, as well as white and middle-class women. They conjectured that their inclusiveness would attract black women and Latinas to work in coalition with them.

In late 1978, after HEW instituted the new sterilization regulations, CARASA's Sterilization Committee members devoted their collective energies to monitoring enforcement. Although they were satisfied with the sterilization regulations passed at the city, state, and federal levels, there was no official mechanism through which the regulations would be enforced. In order to solve the problem of enforcement, the Sterilization Committee developed a hospital monitoring project, in which CARASA members would act as experts on sterilization and its abuses. They envisioned creating a type of "grand rounds" that would educate the hospital administration and medical staff about the incidence and circumstances of sterilization abuse among New York City's low-income population. The committee had acquired statistics from HHC, indicating that hospitals serving poor New Yorkers performed a large number of sterilizations. This statistic suggested the possibility of coerced sterilization among poor women. According to Petchesky, the New York City General Accounting Office had polled hospital executives about compliance with the HEW regulations, but CARASA members found that they were not very effective in gathering accurate results. As Petchesky explained, any regulatory legislation needs to be backed up by consumer or health groups in order to force compliance, even if there are no official agencies. Unfortunately, CARASA's Sterilization Committee never succeeded in making sufficient contacts with the hospital administrations to successfully implement their plan. Dr. Rodriguez-Trias left CARASA for California and others in the committee lacked the connections to effectively educate and monitor city hospitals. Petchesky recalled that the group could have been more successful if they had been able to devote themselves full time to the project, but they all had families and careers to juggle in addition to grassroots activism.[51]

In another effort to enforce the federal regulations, CARASA's Sterilization Committee allied with the Legal Aid Society. This attempt met with a little more success. The Sterilization Committee discovered that rampant sterilization abuses occurred outside of New York in areas without health activists organized to monitor compliance with the new federal regulations. Meredith Tax reported on a class-action suit that CARASA joined on behalf of a group of women from Pinal County in Phoenix, Arizona. These women had been denied "maternity care, and instead [offered] abortions and sterilizations." The lawyers in the suit charged, "the county has required plaintiffs to practice birth control in order to receive medical care, and that it has offered them free abortions and free sterilization in place of medical care." For example, one patient/plaintiff reported, "she went to the county medical investigator before her pregnancy and was told she would not be eligible for care unless she took birth control pills." After refusing the pills and becoming pregnant, "she returned to a medical investigator to apply for delivery of her child under that county welfare program. She was then told . . . that the county would not pay for the birth of her child, but that it would pay for an abortion, and that following the abortion, she would automatically be sterilized." The suit filed by the Legal Aid Society and joined by CARASA, on behalf of this woman and others with similar stories, charged "that Pinal County's welfare policies are unconstitutional because they deny poor women the right to equal protection under the laws and the right to procreate."[52]

CARASA's Sterilization Committee also opposed Planned Parenthood's design for quick and easy sterilizations in outpatient centers. In December 1978, Planned Parenthood's executive board announced they intended to use the minilaparotomy procedure—a technique for tubal ligation that required a very small incision in the abdominal wall and was colloquially known as "band-aid" surgery—to facilitate easy sterilization. They claimed that the New York City regulations made sterilization difficult to obtain for women who had voluntarily chosen the procedure, and that the city needed another clinic to satisfy the large demand they expected, now that this simple procedure had become available. They also asserted that New York City exempted outpatient clinics from regulation. Stamm reported that in violation of the regulations, Planned Parenthood wanted to avoid informing their patients of the possible risks associated with the "minilap" procedure by publicizing it as low-risk surgery—akin to a scratch that required a band-aid. She declared, "We support the right of people to choose when and whether to have children; but we oppose efforts to present sterilization as a substitute for lousy, unsafe contraceptions, and pushing it on the population by making it more conveniently available and cheaper than abortion procedures." By publicizing the risks associated with minilaparotomy, CARASA could help prevent abuses by reproductive health providers not prioritizing the protection of women's voluntary choice to bear children.[53]

CARASA's Sterilization Committee brought attention to other loopholes in the city's sterilization law. Stamm provided evidence that women were "pressured to get sterilized if they suffered from heart, circulatory, kidney, diabetic, etc. conditions without being informed that sterilization is not therapeutic and that choices can still be made." Furthermore, she noted that doctors often recommended sterilization for women with social conditions such as alcoholism, emotional disturbance, or retardation—none of which were medical indicators for sterilization. According to Stamm, physicians often let their biases about who should reproduce influence their ideas of who needed sterilization. There was an assumption among some physicians that certain women could not handle the responsibility of controlling their reproduction. They justified their recommendations for sterilization by arguing that women with these problems could not manage a pregnancy or children. But other methods of contraception—such as the pill, barrier methods, or condoms, with abortion as a backup—would prevent pregnancy without permanently terminating a woman's ability to reproduce. As a result of these arguments, CARASA helped to pass an extension to the New York City regulations that prohibited sterilization for any medically therapeutic indications.[54] CARASA feminists also opposed eugenic justifications for sterilization by educating their readers and the public about a Connecticut law that allowed the sterilization of mentally retarded minor patients without their parents' or their own consent. They joined the Connecticut Civil Liberties Union in a suit that opposed the Connecticut eugenics law.[55]

Occupational Health and Safety

Another reproductive rights issue that several CARASA feminists chose to address was workplace safety, particularly around the mandatory sterilization of working women of reproductive age exposed to hazardous materials on the job. This topic fit very well with CARASA's overall ideological goal of ensuring real reproductive choice to low-income and poor women. In 1978, American Cyanimid required female employees of childbearing age in jobs that exposed them to toxic substances to be sterilized or lose their positions at the company. Officials argued that the policy was instituted to "protect" female employees. CARASA members active in the Trade Union/Workplace Committee characterized the American Cyanamid regulation as a straightforward example of the way that economics often determined reproductive access and control.[56]

In the 1970s, the long history of gendered labor protectionism based on assumptions about working women's sex-related needs merged with an interest in protecting fetal life.[57] The American Cyanamid sterilizations occurred at a paint factory (of that name) in Willow Island, West Virginia, that manufactured lead chromate, which caused birth defects in the children of pregnant women exposed to it. American Cyanamid gave

female workers who risked exposure to lead chromate a "choice" between keeping their jobs or transferring to lower-paying jobs that were
safe from toxic materials. To keep their better-paying jobs, however,
women would have to undergo sterilization or prove they were already
sterile. Two women employed in the lead chromate department opted for
less lucrative janitorial positions, while five of the others decided on sterilization. Their sterilizations remained uncontroversial until the union
representing the plant—the Oil, Chemical and Atomic Workers Union
(OCAW)—discovered the agreement. The OCAW filed a complaint with
the Federal Occupational Safety and Health Administration (OSHA).[58] A
year later American Cyanamid closed the paint production factory and
fired the women who had been sterilized. The five women sued the company for gender discrimination and won.[59]

With public attention focused on the American Cyanamid incident in
1979, CARASA members began to hold forums on the problem of coerced sterilization in the workplace. CARASA activists involved in this
campaign believed that the *American Cyanamid* case raised a major reproductive rights issue that needed to be addressed by feminists. It also
provided CARASA members with the opportunity to expand their coalition-building efforts to working-class women by addressing a reproductive rights issue that directly affected them. As one CARASA member reported after the American Cyanamid sterilizations became headline news,
"the increasing evidence of widespread sterilization abuse in industry,
such as at American Cyanamid, will help us link our work at the work-
places and in the unions with community work." Netsy Firestein, a CESA
member commenting in *CARASA NEWS*, affirmed that coerced workplace sterilization was the new issue reproductive rights groups needed to
confront: "This is an example of sterilization abuse groups like CESA
have not dealt with before. . . . Up until now we have been concerned
mainly with women on welfare and minority women who have been coerced into sterilization. We now have the chance to focus on women who
are being sterilized because they don't want to lose their jobs or take jobs
with less pay."[60]

CARASA joined a coalition of groups, including labor representatives,
environmentalists, consumer groups, and women's groups, demanding
reproductive rights in the workplace; in early 1979, they formed a national coalition called the Committee for the Reproductive Rights of
Workers (CRRW). CARASA, in conjunction with CRRW, the New York

Committee for Occupational Safety and Health (NYCOSH), Health Pac, and the Coalition of Labor Union Women (CLUW), organized an April 1979 conference on occupational health and reproductive rights in response to the *American Cyanamid* case.[61] Participants at the conference agreed that American Cyanamid and other companies who maintained these sorts of sexually discriminatory labor policies had no interest in protecting female workers from the effects of hazardous chemicals. The women were sterilized to prevent harm to a "potential fetus," even if they said they had no plans to become pregnant, were using birth control, and planned to abort any unplanned conception. According to one member of the coalition group, Dr. Wendy Chavkin of NYCOSH (organized around issues of occupational safety), both Dow Chemical and General Motors in Canada used the threat of sterilization to keep women out of higher paying and skilled jobs that might expose them to hazardous chemicals. In her speech at the conference, Dr. Helen Rodriguez-Trias made connections between the American Cyanamid reproductive abuses and sterilization abuse in Puerto Rico. In both situations, she argued, economic mandates took precedence over women's personal health. The conference encouraged the Coalition of Labor Union Women to pass a resolution on reproductive rights that mirrored CARASA's Principles of Unity and included the absolute right to bear or not to bear children, the right to safe and effective birth control, the right to legal abortion regardless of income, the right to freedom from sterilization abuse, and the right to a workplace free of hazards to workers or their children.[62]

CARASA activists, Fran Sugarman and Ruthann Evanoff, who was cochair of CARASA with Horvath, believed that CARASA should pursue the connections made at the conference among reproductive rights groups and organizations representing working women by continuing to build links between occupational health and other reproductive rights issues:

> Continuing and strengthening the connections made at the conference between occupational health and reproductive rights should be a priority for CARASA members. Working with trade unions allows us to directly address women workers on many areas of health care and reproductive rights. Establishing working relationships with occupational health and safety groups broadens and strengthens our struggle for reproductive freedom.[63]

CARASA members hoped that the inclusion of workplace safety issues on the reproductive rights agenda would help to build a mass feminist movement that spoke publicly about the reproductive health needs of all women.

In November 1982, CARASA continued to demonstrate their commitment to building links with working-class activists by holding another forum on reproductive rights and the workplace titled "Women's Rights in the Workplace and the Home: A Dialogue Among Trade Union Women." The forum was cosponsored by CARASA, the DC 37 Women's Committee, the DC 37 Educational Fund, and the New York Council for the Humanities. It was held at the DC 37 headquarters and drew over 200 participants. Speakers included Louise DeBow from the DC 37 Women's Committee, Rayna Rapp from CARASA and a professor of Anthropology at the New School, Hunter College Professor Ebun Adelona, and Dr. Wendy Chavkin. Barbara Omolade, a counselor and instructor at the Center for Worker Education at City College, and one of the speakers at the conference, was a feminist organizer in black women's community struggles, particularly around education.[64] Other participants were from the National Congress for Puerto Rican Rights. Conference participants urged unions to do more to integrate women's political demands— specifically around reproductive rights, access to health care, and child-care—into their agendas.[65]

Child-Care

CARASA's Child-Care Committee believed that few feminist abortion rights activists had made child-care central to their politics in the past, despite the fact that the vast majority of working women would benefit from access to improved child-care. Thus, members of CARASA's Child-Care Committee, largely directed by Meredith Tax and Beth Bush Greenstein, declared they needed to do as much as possible to establish it as a priority on their political agenda.[66] As Greenstein put it: "The right to have an abortion is understood as a reproductive right but supportive alternatives for child-care are rarely thought of as part of reproductive freedom." She continued, explaining that child-care options "should be considered the other side of the 'right to choose': not to have an abortion, but to have a child without being forced to sacrifice one's economic independence."[67]

CARASA's Child-Care Committee understood that poor women, working-class women, and women of color all needed child-care as much as they needed access to abortion. Thus, the issue had the potential to unify women politically across race and class lines that had sometimes proved intractable. Greenstein explained her perspective on poor and minority women's need for the social services that would allow them to care for their children: "As women from Black and other minority communities know, the 'right to decide' to have children is limited by racial and economic class membership as well as by sexist laws and customs" that limit the public provision of child-care. CARASA activists listed demands for federal and state subsidized day-care and employment for the poor as two essential and complimentary requirements for ending female poverty and creating a context for women to make autonomous reproductive choices that included having children regardless of race or class.[68]

CARASA members also realized that publicly funded child-care had become a cross-class political goal because in recent years, many middle-class women with children had also begun to work outside of the home. Like working-class women, many middle-class women now depended on child-care as a fundamental necessity for their survival. Greenstein explained that while the feminist movement had neglected the issue of child-care over the past 10 years, "there has been an unprecedented increase in the workforce participation of women with children: from 40% in 1970 to 50% only eight years later." These women confronted a terrible scarcity of child-care facilities: there were only 1.6 million licensed day-care spaces for 7 million children. Greenstein also noted that, during the same period, female-headed households increased substantially—by 44 percent over an 8-year period. Half of these women's households fell below the poverty line in the mid-1980s, indicating that women's wages were not adequate to support a family. On average for full-time work they earned only 64 percent of salaries retained by men. All these factors forced feminist reproductive rights activists to put publicly supported child-care at the top of their list of reproductive rights demands.[69]

Despite the enormity of the problem, CARASA complained that the federal government refused to support women who desperately needed both work income for their families and day-care in order to keep working. In 1971, President Nixon vetoed the Comprehensive Child-Care Act, arguing that the deprivatization of child-care would cost too much and that families should take responsibility for caring for their own children. Greenstein reported that an anti–child-care subsidy attitude prevailed in

Washington, D.C. She argued that the "U.S. government has repeatedly stated that parents prefer to make their own private arrangements for the care of their children. And for lack of publicly funded facilities, they have been forced to do so." CARASA activists involved in fighting for subsidized child-care disagreed with the government's assumption; women wanted reasonably priced and easily accessible child-care, even if that meant relying on the government. The important issue to most women was good care for their children; they didn't care who provided it.[70]

CARASA believed that feminists needed to take the moral high ground in terms of promoting the importance of women's economic role in the family; the religious right could not be allowed to corner the market on pro-family rhetoric, particularly when that rhetoric threatened to make life more difficult for single mothers and women who worked. Greenstein defined the issue: "All of us are acutely aware that protecting 'the family' has become a focus for the anti-abortion movement and the New Right." According to Greenstein, New Right rhetoric, shored up by Reagan administration policy, was an "attempt to force women back into traditional nuclear family roles which have neither been possible nor desirable for a long time." She concluded that "we must raise a positive vision of family relationships which are less oppressive to women and work to include it in our political movement for reproductive rights." CARASA's strategy to fulfill this goal included "a national grassroots campaign to win federal funding for comprehensive, high-quality child-care, available to all who need it and want it."[71]

The CARASA Child-Care Conference, "Child-Care: What We Want and How to Get It," held in the spring of 1980, connected demands for publicly funded child-care to the larger reproductive rights movement. Conference speaker Nancy Romer "pointed out that while people usually think only of birth control, abortion and protection from sterilization abuse as reproductive rights issues, child-care is one of the most important aspects of reproductive freedom because without it many people feel that they cannot choose to have children." Romer explained that women's position in the family had changed so that they were more often heads of households and primary or dual earners; these situations required affordable day-care. She added that other countries provided subsidies for child-care in order to facilitate women's work: "The U.S. is the only western industrialized country without a policy for support of parents in the workforce—maternity benefits, health care, or provisions for child-care." Because child-care had become such an economic necessity,

CARASA activists demanded that the U.S. government look toward Europe's social democratic systems to create a national child-care program. Romer thought that these goals could be achieved "through the combined efforts of those in the reproductive rights movement, women in trade unions and local community groups," all of whom wanted to make subsidized quality child-care a political priority. Greenstein added that the conference resulted in "general agreement on the absolute necessity of federal legislation to provide subsidies for child-care facilities which would be locally controlled by parents and caregivers."[72]

In one flyer distributed by CARASA at their Child-Care Conference, the Child-Care Committee listed their reasons for requiring subsidized child-care as an essential ingredient for ending sterilization abuse and establishing reproductive freedom for all women—particularly low-income and women of color who had the least control over their reproduction. They believed that without the resources to care for children and earn a living, poor women would opt for sterilization. A decision for sterilization could not be considered voluntary as long as women lacked resources such as child-care to facilitate childbearing in addition to voluntary measures to prevent or terminate pregnancy in the form of contraception and abortion. Yet, the federal government would not pay for abortion and "pushed" sterilization "as a 'solution' to social problems." CARASA activists argued, "Little is done to correct poor living conditions or provide important social service programs like day-care. It is realistic to say that sterilization abuse happens when someone is forced to have the operation because of these social and economic conditions."[73]

CARASA activists hoped that concrete campaigns for measures that would expand poor and minority women's capacity to control their individual reproduction would attract minority and low-income women to the movement. For example, in 1980, CARASA members joined other activists lobbying for affordable day-care centers by sponsoring a mass demonstration aimed at New York State Governor Carey's administration. CARASA wanted Carey to route federal funds intended for public child-care to New York City, arguing that these had been used to cover administrative costs in Albany. Greenstein alleged that "at least 50 day-care centers which are threatened with closing early next year, for lack of funds" would be affected by the Carey administration's failure to deliver federal monies to New York City. CARASA's Child-Care Committee also met to draft a "program for comprehensive child-care legislation" that would give low-income women access to affordable day-care.[74]

Coalition Building: Toward an All-Inclusive Feminist Politics

CARASA activists also attempted to establish political coalitions with low-income women of color by participating in events sponsored by poor and minority women. Recalling the criticism leveled at feminists active in the 1970s for being limited by their race and class perspectives, they wanted to demonstrate their commitment to building an inclusive feminism. With their coalition-building efforts peaking in the early 1980s, white middle-class feminists in CARASA tested the limits of their capacity to create an all-inclusive feminist politics. Not all CARASA feminists felt comfortable organizing with women different from themselves; their difficulties revealed the extent to which CARASA members still lived in a community segregated by race and class. Differences fostered by racism and classism and nurtured by segregation proved difficult to bridge, even temporarily. Some CARASA members recalled that CARASA's concern for integrating the reproductive rights movement reflected an elitist attitude that ultimately worked to their detriment because, despite their emphasis on the concerns of minority and poor women, they created a political agenda without really consulting the women they claimed they most wanted to help. Theresa Horvath, in particular, remembered that often women of color were very unsure of CARASA's political program. Through coalition work, she "realized how problematic our program was." She added, "people couldn't figure out if we were for abortion rights and against sterilization abuse or for sterilization and against abortion. Many women of color thought we were a community organization telling them not to be sterilized." For Horvath, this confusion suggested that CARASA members sometimes had difficulty defining their political priorities. She remembered that CARASA couldn't say exactly what they wanted groups working in coalition with them to do.[75]

Despite these difficulties, coalition building remained a very central, if controversial, aspect of CARASA's political work. For example, the Upper West Side Committee of CARASA, of which Horvath was a member, reported that "we feel that, in doing outreach work, we should make connections between the issues we are specifically committed to and a broader range of health care issues (such as day-care), so that women we speak with do not feel that we have isolated the two issues of abortion rights and sterilization abuse from other, equally basic needs." The Upper West Side Committee consistently made contacts with organizations of Latinas and other groups representing the interests of women of color such as the Latin Women's Collective, the Escolar Day Care Center, El Comite, the Godard Riverside Community Center, and the William R. Ryan Clinic (also called the Neighborhood Health Services Program). They attended community coalition meetings and tabled at community fairs.[76] Horvath recalled "we worked with community coalitions and church meetings, mostly with people of color."[77]

The Upper West Side Committee confronted other difficulties in their attempts to organize in conjunction with groups of Latinas. They admitted that connections with these women were sometimes tenuous, in part, because they needed more people who spoke Spanish and had experience within the community. For example, at a health fair held in East Harlem, CARASA tablers felt uncomfortable with their inability to speak directly to many Puerto Rican and Dominican women who did not speak English. They commented that "this experience only reinforces our sense that a really thorough knowledge of community politics is essential for successfully building a community-based movement around CARASA's issues." Still, one of their most successful coalition-building efforts occurred when they cosponsored a street fiesta in East Harlem with "some housing groups, a church, a day care center, the Puerto Rican Socialist Party, El Comite and the Puerto Rico Solidarity Committee." Despite divisions of language and culture, their organizing efforts around day-care remained some of their most fruitful in the nonwhite communities of New York, because adequate and affordable subsidized child-care was a reproductive rights demand that many minority and low-income women could understand very well.[78]

CARASA feminists put their coalition-building strategy into action by joining the 1983 Medgar Evers College (CUNY) Student-Faculty protest. One of the primary demands among the Medgar Evers students and faculty was the creation of a child-care center. Because 73 percent of the students at Medgar Evers were black women and many of these were low-income women with children, subsidized day-care stood at the top of their list of requirements. CARASA member Sally Avery Bermanzohn reported that "with a majority of Medgar Evers College students parenting dependent children, child-care has been a major demand." She described the unsatisfactory situation at CUNY: "Child-care is a growing problem for many CUNY faculty, staff, and students. Over 20% of CUNY students have young children, yet the Board of Trustees requested no funds for child-care in their 1982 budget. Some CUNY buildings have been deemed completely off-limits to children." Trevor Belmosa, a male organizer for the protest added, "The demand for day-care facilities is not a privilege. For a woman to stay home and take care of children and be denied the right to an education, is a reflection of the backwardness and sexism of society." The Medgar Evers group, with CARASA support, organized a drop-in center for children of students, particularly necessary for evening classes and on Saturdays; they argued that every CUNY campus required a day-care facility. The protesters also demanded a women's center, an end to sexual harassment, and a search for a black woman to become the college's president.[79]

During their weeks of protest, politically active black and white women at Medgar Evers met to discuss "the necessity—and difficulty—of supporting each others' struggles." They discovered similarities in their definition of feminism, "including demands for reproductive rights, lesbian rights, and an end to violence against women. All these are fundamental concerns for women to control their bodies." At the same time, "black women pointed out that feminist issues must be more inclusive because women are also concerned about their children, families, and communities. Fights for education, housing, unionization must be recognized as feminist concerns and supported by the women's movement." Medgar Evers activists made an argument for a feminist movement broadly defined that paralleled CARASA's reproductive rights agenda. Because CARASA members had listened to the criticisms of mainstream feminism made by women of color, they had already integrated into their political agenda many of the demands made by the Medgar Evers students.[80]

While the Medgar Evers protests unified black and white women around establishing child-care services and addressing racism on campus, other attempts to build coalitions with women of color around reproductive rights issues met with less success. CARASA feminists discovered that working women and women of color often had little interest in making reproductive rights a high political priority. For example, in 1980, CARASA joined the City-Wide Coalition to Save Our Hospitals—a group formed to prevent the closing of municipal hospitals such as Metropolitan and Sydenham—in which they organized with hospital workers, many of whom were minority women. CARASA members believed that because health workers provided abortions, sterilizations, and contraception, they would have interest in the reproductive rights movement. But the health workers at Metropolitan and Sydenham resisted CARASA organizers' efforts to add reproductive rights issues to their agenda. They had already made keeping the hospitals open and maintaining jobs their top priority. Furthermore, according to one CARASA participant in the City-Wide Coalition, there was minimal involvement by CARASA members in liaison work with hospital workers. Many in CARASA found coalition work too overwhelming and time consuming. It demanded tremendous patience and a capacity to accommodate to other people's political perspectives that proved difficult.[81]

CARASA also encountered problems when building coalitions around the issue of sterilization abuse, particularly after the New York City guidelines became law and activists found themselves without a concrete political goal to address. In 1980, Helen Wood of the Sterilization Committee, described some of these difficulties; she noted that one of CARASA's primary goals in continuing their work to eradicate sterilization abuse had been to "overcome our isolation from Third World women by working with them." Despite these efforts, however, "we haven't been using the issue the way we hoped to—to put us in league with minority women, fighting the government's efforts at population control." Wood continued, noting that regardless of the evidence that "sterilization abuse is one of those issues, which has shown us we can overcome our isolation," many of these efforts "met with mixed success." She suggested that CARASA's coalition-building attempts were often more rhetorical than concrete. She "encouraged existing feminist groups to take up the issue in a more tangible way than before" rather than backing away from the problem of sterilization abuse altogether because the regulations appeared to solve the problem. CARASA and other feminist groups could monitor the New York City regulations and help to combat reproductive health cutbacks affecting poor black women and Latinas by "participating in coalitions to save the hospitals [and] fighting welfare cuts." According to Wood, CARASA activists needed to continue the fight against reproductive problems that affected poor and minority women, while, at the same time, they allowed them to define their own battles. Many in CARASA found this a difficult balance to maintain.[82]

CARASA discussed their intent to build coalitions with women of color and low-income women in feminist-activist forums such as the R2N2 conference held in Boston in April 1982. Interracial coalition-building was a popular and controversial topic at the R2N2 conference, drawing reproductive rights and feminist activists from around the country. The tremendous interest generated for this topic by participants suggested that CARASA members were part of a political trend that placed

coalition-building near the top of feminist agendas. It also confirms rec-
ollections by CARASA members, notably Petchesky and Horvath, that
R2N2 integrated women of color more effectively than did CARASA.[83]
At the conference, Jean Hunt from the Philadelphia Reproductive Rights
Organization (PRRO) spoke on "how white women in a predominantly
white network can and must take up anti-racist work." She detailed the
activities of PRRO in this arena: They "set up information tables in all
neighborhoods, focusing on issues of access to abortion" and discovered
that "abortion is not a ghettoized issue; white and black women were
concerned with attacks on their rights." Dr. Vicki Alexander of CARASA
and the Alliance Against Women's Oppression, a multiracial feminist
group, pointed to the "historical racism of the eugenics movement as the
basis for people of color's suspicions of the Reproductive Rights movement, and the need to be clear about our critique of population control.
She exhorted the women's movement to 'become as intolerant to racism
as to sexism.'"[84]

Although CARASA members made economic access to abortion, freedom from sterilization abuse, workplace safety, and rights to child-care
priority agenda items, they still found that many black women and Latinas avoided the reproductive rights movement for some of the same reasons they gave earlier in the decade. Black women at the R2N2 conference accused "white feminist women of say[ing] they want to deal with
racism, but [they] are not really willing to relinquish their power."[85]
Bermanzohn articulated her understanding of poor and minority
women's lack of interest in reproductive rights: "For some, the right to
abortion means freedom from motherhood, freedom to pursue careers,
and this is important. But you can't assume that this is where all women
are coming from. You must strive to understand the pain of poverty.
There is nothing more painful than not being able to feed your children."
Bermanzohn suggested that for poor women, many of whom were
women of color, reproductive rights politics weren't important because
being poor exhausted all of their energies. Until their poverty ended, poor
and minority women would have little interest in any organization that
did not directly and concretely address and relieve their economic problems. Many CARASA feminists struggled to meet these demands but
found that creating an all-inclusive feminism would take more than a
rhetorical commitment to addressing poor women's needs; they would
have to make issues such as welfare rights, state subsidies for public hous-

ing, and Medicaid coverage for all health care needs (including abortion) top priorities.[86]

Some CARASA members believed they had trouble attracting working-class, poor, and women of color to their organization because the reproductive rights movement was responding to attacks by the religious right in the early 1980s. Mainstream white activists again made protecting legal abortion top priority. The Hyde Amendment and sterilization abuse had given CARASA members impetus to embrace issues of economic access to reproductive freedom, but in the early 1980s they began to experience an onslaught of right-wing terror against abortion rights, never experienced by reproductive rights feminists in the 1970s. The Right to Life had mobilized an army of conservative Christians to attack abortion clinics (sometimes violently), which sapped political energy from reproductive rights mobilization in other areas. Efforts at political all-inclusiveness, including attempts at building a movement that prioritized poor women's interests, fell away as reproductive rights feminists organized into clinic defense groups across the country. Suddenly, they needed to mobilize forces to help patients enter abortion clinics safely. Also, with a Supreme Court that appeared increasingly hostile to women's rights, they feared that *Roe v. Wade* would soon be overturned, and all women were on the brink of returning to a shadowy world of unwanted pregnancy and back-alley abortion. As protecting legal abortion became the priority issue for many feminists nationwide, CARASA members found it increasingly difficult to sell their broad economic agenda as part of mainstream feminist politics.

Lesbian Rights

By 1980, a new wave of younger women had joined CARASA who wanted to make lesbian rights and sexuality a higher priority. They argued that the same New Right mobilization that had begun chipping away at reproductive freedom was now attacking the rights of gay men and lesbians. With this new influx, members found themselves frequently disagreeing over questions of homophobia and the place of lesbianism in the group. The primary conflict around lesbianism and homophobia hinged not only on the relative attention to be accorded reproductive problems experienced by lesbians, but also on how CARASA's politics should be defined. Up to this point, CARASA members had largely agreed to focus on economic access to reproductive rights. Some of the new members wanted to change this political focus to put sexuality at the center of CARASA's politics. Other members disagreed with this suggestion, arguing that CARASA could not make sexuality a political priority when so many economically based reproductive freedom issues required equal attention.

As they became involved in conversations about lesbianism, CARASA members focused more and more on the internal differences of the women within the group rather than on the external reproductive rights campaigns. Stamm recalled it took only a few members to shift the attention of the entire group. Stamm also remembered that some CARASA members felt they were put on the defensive by accusations of homophobia, preventing them from considering the problem productively.[87] Horvath confirmed Stamm's contention that "the last major split concerned just three women," but that was enough to cripple CARASA. She described her own sense that "much of what they were saying was true—sexual politics were ignored by CARASA. No one knew who was gay or straight and as the lesbian movement began to gather steam it seemed strange to be so out of it in terms of lesbian rights." Horvath commented further that "the tone had been set to come together around this particular project (reproductive rights). Although we took a stand for lesbian rights, these were not central."[88]

Several activists, including Stephanie Roth, Sarah Schulman, and Maxine Wolfe, founded the Lesbian Action Committee to address heterosexism and homophobia in CARASA. Questions about homophobia and lesbianism generated such heated debate that most of the members of this group became alienated from CARASA and resigned between December 1981 and March 1982. A Lesbian Rights Committee formed in 1983, but this postdated CARASA's most active period.

Other feminist organizations preceding CARASA also experienced discord when discussing how to integrate lesbian rights into a feminist agenda. Both radical and mainstream feminist organizations of the early 1970s struggled with internal disagreements over lesbianism. Some feminists believed that lesbianism represented the highest form of feminist political expression, whereas others disagreed with the notion that a woman could choose to be a lesbian as a political statement. Several groups floundered and fragmented over internal accusations of homophobia, including NOW-NY. Some lesbians felt that their political priorities were being ignored in favor of those championed by a majority of heterosexual women.[89]

At their founding, CARASA largely ignored lesbian rights. Because CARASA members had created their organization to combat the Hyde Amendment and other restrictions on poor women's reproductive autonomy, including sterilization abuse, they were less attentive to the connections between gay and reproductive rights. Janet Price, of the Lesbian Action Committee, recalled: "Back in the early days . . . we tended to draw the line at things that make the decision to have a child or not a free choice. These tended to be economic entitlements."[90]

Despite their initial neglect of the issue, CARASA feminists established political links between lesbian and reproductive rights issues relatively quickly. The campaigns for reproductive and gay rights had common roots in the feminist movement of the late 1960s and early 1970s. Both issues were central to feminism throughout the decade. Furthermore, unlike women of color and poor women, lesbians were already a fundamental part of CARASA at the outset and lesbian politics were at least familiar to many nonlesbian members. This history facilitated theoretical and political connections between the right to reproductive control and the right to freely express sexual identity.

Before the end of their first year, women in CARASA extended their reproductive rights agenda to include lesbian civil rights and lesbians' right to bear and raise children. CARASA members realized that because the New Right targeted poor women, women of color, working women, and lesbians equally in their campaign to strip women of reproductive and sexual autonomy, feminists needed to combat an all-encompassing conservatism with their own understanding of the political connections among these groups. For example, in one 1979 flyer for the International Campaign for Reproductive Rights, which would include demonstrations in Kenya, Puerto Rico, and Italy, CARASA organizers connected the economic needs of low-income women with the reproductive needs of lesbians: "Of course, safe, available and effective birth control and abortion, and an end to sterilization abuse, important as they are, are not sufficient to allow women to have and raise children if and when they want to. We also need paid maternity and paternity leaves, better health care for everyone, a guaranteed income, and an equal right to custody of their children for lesbian mothers."[91]

CARASA feminists integrated sexual autonomy into their reproductive rights politics by characterizing the freedom to express sexual identity as essential to reproductive freedom. For example, in 1978, at a series of gay rights hearings before the New York City Council on an ordinance protecting gay rights, a CARASA member testified: "While we are immediately concerned with the two issues of defending abortion rights and ending sterilization abuse, in a larger sense we are concerned with all issues relating to women's reproductive freedom. We believe in the right of all women to make their own choices about their bodies; their sexuality; about whether or not to bear children." With this statement, CARASA feminists suggested that lesbian rights were a necessary part of guarantees of reproductive freedom. The speaker continued, explaining the connections among reproductive rights, the right to a sexual preference for a same sex partner, and a lesbian's right to raise children: "Our view of women's reproductive rights includes a belief in each woman's right to exercise her sexual preference without penalty. It also includes the right of lesbians to be parents, to involve themselves in the lives of children without fear that their lesbianism may be used as a pretext to snatch those children from them." The same speaker concluded by connecting lesbian rights to the struggle against racism and classism. She announced that "we in CARASA see the fight for reproductive freedom for women as being linked to an end to all forms of oppression, including racism, class divisions, age discrimination, and the persecution of gay men as well as lesbians."[92]

Despite their commitment to ensuring lesbians' reproductive and civil rights, CARASA members had difficulty agreeing on the political emphasis lesbian rights should be given in relation to other reproductive rights issues. Toward the end of CARASA's existence, the debates over where lesbian rights fit on the agenda became divisive and ultimately destructive to the group's sense of cohesiveness. Some CARASA members felt that their sexual identities were marginalized because CARASA made reproductive issues such as abortion, birth control, and sterilization abuse central to the organization and excluded issues that directly affected lesbians. In 1980, Alison Colbert, a member of the Lesbian Rights Committee, wrote "An Open Letter to CARASA" in which she revealed her perspective on lesbian participation in the reproductive rights movement. She argued that because lesbians were central to the movement, lesbian rights needed greater attention, but few lesbians had interest in abortion as a political priority: "Lesbians . . . undoubtedly experience the threat from the Right to our right to work and live out of the closet, but we may not live with abortion as a gut/personal issue, any more than a heterosexual woman will experience the threat to Lesbian survival rights in this way." Colbert recalled that many heterosexual members made assumptions about other women's sexual identity, causing them to neglect political issues that affected lesbians differently or specifically: "CARASA women sometimes seem to assume all members are heterosexual unless told otherwise." While some CARASA members shifted their political priorities away from abortion rights to focus more intently on issues pertaining to sexual orientation and gay liberation, others maintained that abortion still needed to be the central political focus. These two groups found themselves on opposite sides of a debate that eventually fractured CARASA.[93]

Several of the younger CARASA members, including Colbert, Wolfe, Schulman, and Roth wanted to make sexuality, rather than reproduction and economic access, the defining political issue for CARASA. This shift in political perspective was a radical departure from CARASA's socialist feminist roots.[94] For instance, Roth refused to see lesbianism as just one issue of many: "It should be clear that lesbian rights is an integral part of our definition of reproductive rights. As such, we don't perceive of this as simply another separate issue to add to our long list, but also as a way of understanding and analyzing all of the issues we address." She described reproductive freedom as women's right to enjoy their sexuality, with other women if they chose. Just as abortion allowed women greater freedom to be sexual without worrying about an unwanted pregnancy, lesbians needed a society without homophobia in order to have sexual and reproductive freedom. Roth also drew a parallel between the challenge lesbianism posed to a patriarchal family model and that posed by a woman who prevented or terminated a pregnancy—in both cases, a woman's sexuality was not tied to her reproductive system; both gave her sexual autonomy. She argued that women who did not conform to norms of heterosexual sexuality—because they were sexual with women or chose not to have children—threatened both patriarchy and a homogenizing heterosexual society.[95]

Several members of the Lesbian Action Committee chose to resign from CARASA because they believed that members of the organization had failed to address their own homophobia and the discrimination faced by lesbians in their daily lives.[96] For example, Schulman resigned from CARASA over homophobia in the group; she expressed resentment that

CARASA members had accused her of being a separatist when she had been intimately involved in all aspects of the reproductive rights movement and worked on a variety of political issues. Schulman felt accusations of separatism negated her work as a reproductive rights activist:

> In a classic use of homophobia as a means to achieve political ends, one co-chair has been telling figures in the gay left and other political communities that we are "separatists" who don't want to work with men. This erases the fact that we have made long commitments to abortion rights. This ignores and erases any work that we have done in CARASA and makes us only into "lesbians". This erases my years of work in the Bronx Coalition Against Sterilization Abuse (a mixed left coalition). It plies on people's stereotypes and fears about lesbians.[97]

The resignations were signs of CARASA's dissolution as their focus on group identity intensified. Members of the organization became increasingly frustrated with accusations and counteraccusations of homophobia or separatism, leaving them with very little energy to devote to other issues. While questions of homophobia and heterosexism within the organization most likely needed attention, CARASA members had reached a point of stasis in their internal discussions.

In the end, CARASA never resolved the schism generated by disagreement over a political emphasis focused on economics and one devoted to sexuality and personal identity. Karen Stamm suggested that CARASA members did not have a sufficient sense of their own importance and strength as a political organization to stay together after the infighting began. Instead, differences around how to establish a politics that made sexual identity fundamental to reproductive freedom fragmented the group until it became ineffective. This is not to say that CARASA's economic analysis could not have encompassed the reproductive rights of lesbians. I believe it could have done so, and many women in the group tried to do just that. But most CARASA members felt it was easier to walk away from the political fray than to remain involved in an organization that spent more time discussing internal differences than organizing.[98] For the most part, CARASA activists decided to go back to school, focus on their careers, have children, or direct their feminist political energies elsewhere.[99]

With hindsight, however, we should not be surprised that CARASA's economic focus was challenged in the early 1980s. CARASA existed during a decade of left-wing retreat. The ideas that they championed were be-coming less and less popular as the Reagan administration gradually whittled away at the economic entitlements created during the New Deal and the Johnson presidency. It was becoming easier to focus on issues such as sexual freedom and sexual expression rather than economic rights to bear children. America had entered an era that frowned on Aid to Fam-ilies with Dependent Children (AFDC), worried that women in receipt of welfare were purposefully having more children to increase their monthly payments, and characterized poor black women as "welfare queens."

Despite their stormy clashes, CARASA members made important strides toward expanding at least the rhetoric of reproductive freedom to include as many women as possible and to link issues of sexuality, social welfare, and reproduction. No other U.S. abortion rights group had con-ceived of reproductive politics in exactly that fashion. For the first time in second wave feminist history, CARASA gave economic issues and coali-tion-building with working-class, poor, and minority women political precedence in order to achieve their ideal of a multirace and class-con-scious feminist movement that could help secure reproductive freedom for all women.[100]

Conclusion

I want to conclude this history of the feminist reproductive rights movement by emphasizing how essential women of color were to the transformation of the abortion rights movement of the late 1960s and early 1970s into a more inclusive movement for reproductive freedom by the early 1980s. Despite their importance, the contributions of women of color to mainstream feminism, in general, and the abortion and reproductive rights movement, in particular, have not been properly acknowledged. It is almost a cliché in women's studies circles to say that women of color and white women have made different demands of feminism. But how exactly women of color have shaped mainstream feminism has not been explored in much detail. I hope that this book begins to correct this gap in the scholarship on second wave feminism and the reproductive rights movement.

Now that we better understand how feminists of the 1970s transformed their ideas on reproductive rights, we need to ask what we can learn from the past in order to build a better reproductive rights movement for the twenty-first century. It is vital to note the parallels between attacks on reproductive freedom in the 1970s and more recent coercive measures that restrict the reproductive freedom of women in the 1990s, particularly of women of color. By comparing the two, we see that women—mostly poor women of color—are still not free of coerced fertility control. We also see that there is still a great need for a feminist movement that addresses reproductive freedom broadly—in terms of claiming the right *both* to limit fertility and to bear wanted children. We must also consider parallels between how the feminist reproductive rights movement of the 1970s addressed reproductive freedom for poor women of color and how feminists addressed the same issue in the 1990s. Did 1990s feminists, as part of what some call the third wave of feminism, draw on reproductive rights discourse developed in the late 1970s or did they experience some of the same blind spots of second wave feminists who did not consistently make race or class analysis central to the abortion rights movement? Or, a third alternative, did they do both—incorporate some of the lessons of the reproductive rights movement while also repeating some of the lapses. My final purpose here is to sketch what I think are the lessons that contemporary feminist abortion and reproductive rights movement activists need to learn from their predecessors to build an inclusive movement for reproductive freedom for all women.

Reproductive Abuses: Past and Present

Just as many people did not recognize that coerced sterilization was a reproductive rights abuse in the past, many are not aware that reproductive abuses continue in the United States. Unfortunately, many of the same attitudes that prevailed in the 1960s and 1970s about who has the right to reproduce have also inspired contemporary campaigns to limit the fertility of certain women. With this in mind, it should not be surprising that the women most vulnerable to abuse are minorities, the poor, and, often, drug-addicted women or women recovering from drug addiction.

Indeed, there are several examples of coercive fertility control campaigns from the 1990s that have predominantly targeted poor women of color. One of these is CRACK (Children Requiring a Caring Community), a private organization founded in Anaheim, California. CRACK currently offers drug-addicted and recovering female addicts with at least two children $200 if they agree to be sterilized or use long-term hormonal contraceptives such as Depo Provera or Norplant. Orange County, California homemaker Barbara Harris founded the organization in 1997. In 1999, it expanded to Chicago, Florida, New Hampshire, and Washington State. Since 1997, CRACK has paid at least 366 women to become sterilized or use long-term contraceptives. Harris argued that she was motivated to begin this program because of the large numbers of drug-addicted babies born to poor women. She pointed to one case—the mother of "Zachary"—who gave birth to six drug-addicted babies. Harris also adopted four children born to another drug-addicted mother. She said that her personal experience raising "crack babies" was the inspiration for her program.[1]

Advisory Board members of CRACK have denied employing any coercive methods to attract women to their program. Many of the women who opted for sterilization, however, had their children placed in foster care programs and hoped to regain custody; for women in these straightened circumstances, $200 could look like a lot of money.[2]

Other women who participated in the CRACK program found out about it through the criminal justice system—often while in jail for buying or selling illegal drugs—before they received any treatment for their addictions. These women were extremely vulnerable when offered cash for permanent contraception; some of them wanted money to satisfy their drug habit. No doubt few of them considered how they would feel if their circumstances changed, and they wanted more children, or how they would feel about their decision after the money had been spent. Even women who had completed a drug rehab program and expressed interest in CRACK's offer were at a disadvantage, because they often needed money for very basic needs, to buy food or pay rent. In a *Los Angeles Times* article on CRACK, 20-year-old Stacey Davis—a recovered speed addict and mother of three children all in foster care—told reporter Lynn Smith, "I'm not going to lie . . . I mean, I need the money right now." CRACK openly targets susceptible poor and minority women for its sterilization program. Beginning in May 1998, CRACK began advertising on bus benches, at welfare offices, and at hospitals serving the poorer districts in Los Angeles and Orange counties.[3]

Harris offered her motivation for paying poor women to be sterilized: "My focus is just going to have to be on the poor babies. That's the bottom line." The fact that Harris is paying women to become sterilized suggests something different, however. Her tacit assumption is that it is better that poor babies are not born if their mothers use crack cocaine or other illegal substances. One must ask, is this the best way to "help" these children? Is it best that they are not born at all?[4]

The CRACK campaign is a private program; it receives no state funding. In that sense, CRACK-sponsored sterilizations differ from the coerced and forced sterilizations that occurred in federal clinics in the 1960s and 1970s. In the 1960s and 1970s, many of the sterilizations of poor women were directly funded, administered, and regulated by the federal government's Health, Education and Welfare (HEW) department. In the case of the CRACK campaign, Medicaid and state insurance programs pay for many of the participants' tubal ligations or Norplant insertions. Thus, state funds do pay for at least some of the sterilizations, but the state has nothing to do with the promotion or administration of the CRACK program. Reproductive rights activists have pointed out, however, that sterilization is funded by the federal Medicaid program, while abortion, a nonpermanent method of fertility limitation, is not. They suggest that poor women who want to limit their fertility temporarily might choose to be sterilized because they anticipate not being able to afford an abortion if other forms of nonpermanent contraceptives fail.

In evaluating the level of coercion used by the CRACK campaign, we need to assess the notion of "choice" employed by those who support or sponsor the program. Harris argues that the women involved "chose" to become sterilized, so the program does not violate women's constitutional right to procreate voluntarily. Unlike federal clinics in the 1960s and 1970s, when, in many cases, women were sterilized without their knowledge, told that their welfare payments would be cut off if they were not sterilized, or told by a physician that he would not deliver their babies if they were not sterilized postpartum, the CRACK campaign operates on a voluntary basis. But one must ask, what does "choice" mean to a poor drug-addicted woman, who cannot get into a drug-treatment program because she is pregnant and because the wait list is too long, who cannot afford health care or groceries because she is poor? Rather than offering to restrict their fertility, a campaign that addressed the foundations of the problems these women face might offer, for example, prenatal care, nutrition counseling, treatment for addiction to illegal substances such as crack, and counseling or treatment for addiction to *legal* substances that can also be harmful to the fetus such as cigarettes and alcohol. This kind of program would help facilitate a poor woman's "choice" to bear healthy children.[5]

Another example of reproductive coercion that disproportionately affected poor women and women of color in the 1990s was the arrest and prosecution of drug-addicted women for delivery of illegal substances to their fetuses. Many of the same issues that arise in a discussion of the CRACK campaign also apply to the incarceration of pregnant drug addicts. In the mid-1980s, as the media picked up on reports that large numbers of crack-addicted babies were being born in inner-city hospitals, it became increasingly popular to target poor, crack-addicted, pregnant women for punishment. The most common goal of state authorities was permanent or temporary removal of the child from the drug-addicted mother. Some states also began incarcerating poor pregnant women, sometimes for the duration of their pregnancies, and charging them with delivery of illegal substances to minors. These women were often incarcerated for far longer periods than were their nonpregnant counterparts. Between 1985 and 1995, at least 200 women in 30 states were accused of some crime related to their drug use while pregnant. Legal scholar Dorothy Roberts reports that 75 percent of these women were black.[6]

Some may argue that these women broke the law and therefore deserve to be punished through incarceration. If the state had an interest in punishing women for drug use, however, it would not target pregnant women. Rather, it would target women who abuse drugs more generally. States who incarcerate pregnant drug-abusers respond to this assertion with the argument that they are protecting the fetus by focusing on pregnant women.

The state's claim to be protecting the fetuses of black women drug users by incarcerating their mothers becomes suspect, however, when one looks at the high rates of infant mortality in poor black neighborhoods, the lack of prenatal care available to the poor, and the dearth of treatment programs available to poor pregnant women. If the state wanted to protect the fetus, wouldn't it address these problems as well? Roberts records that "in 1987 the mortality rate for Black infants in the United States was 17.9 deaths per 1,000 births—more than twice that for white infants (8.6)." High black infant mortality rates are directly attributable to the lack of prenatal care among poor black women. There is a wealth of evidence suggesting that drug use disproportionately harms the fetus when the mother lacks prenatal health care, is malnourished, and is using other legal drugs such as cigarettes or alcohol. There is also no prenatal care for women in prison, so her fetus may very well suffer more in prison than if the mother was on the outside. In addition to lacking prenatal care, most drug-addicted pregnant women can't access treatment for their drug habits either. Treatment programs *exclude* pregnant women. Finally, pregnant women who fear incarceration for drug use may choose abortion over the possibility of a prison stay. When the state opts for incarceration of pregnant women over the provision of prenatal care and drug treatment, it is difficult to understand how authorities can claim to be protecting the fetus.[7]

On the face of it, it may appear as if all poor women potentially suffer from drug use–related reproductive abuses regardless of racial identification. There is overwhelming evidence that black and white women have equal incidence of drug use (and abuse). Despite this data, the means by which women were identified for prosecution reveals that black women are the prime targets for prosecution and incarceration during pregnancy. The vast majority of women caught up in the criminal justice system for drug use during pregnancy were identified because of their close contact with state and federal health care and welfare facilities that serve poor people who are disproportionately black. Public hospitals serving poor and minority populations are far more likely to screen newborn babies for the presence of drugs in their systems than are private hospitals serving more affluent white patients. Furthermore, women who fail to get prenatal care are often specifically targeted for toxicological screening. These women are overwhelmingly poor and disproportionately black. Finally, most hospitals leave the decision for screening up to a staff (physicians included) that carries ideological baggage with them about who is most likely to be a drug abuser. In one study of pregnant women in Pinellas County, Florida, black women were ten times more likely to be reported for drug use than white women, although both groups abused drugs at an approximately equal rate. In South Carolina, a state that strongly advocated the incarceration of drug-addicted pregnant women, all of the women but one arrested for drug use during pregnancy were black. This inequity occurred despite records of comparable drug abuse among whites and blacks in that state.[8]

With this material before us, we need to ask why the state has an interest in punishing poor pregnant black women for drug use rather than providing them with prenatal care and treatment for drug addiction. There are two explanations for the state's behavior. First, punishing black women for bearing drug-addicted babies diverts attention from a medical system that overwhelmingly neglects the needs of minority and poor women and their children. Roberts writes, "Making criminals of Black mothers apparently helps to relieve the nation of the burden of creating a health care system that ensures healthy babies for all its citizens." The second reason is ideological. We live in a society that has historically denigrated black women as mothers. Black women are stereotyped as bad mothers. From the black matriarch of the 1960s, to the welfare queen of the 1980s, to the crack-addicted pregnant black woman of the 1990s, stereotypes of black women consistently portray them as dangerous mothers—dangerous to their children and dangerous to society.[9]

The efforts to control the reproduction of poor women of color in the 1990s have historical roots in the 1960s and 1970s and parallel the involuntary sterilization of poor women and women of color in those decades. In the 1960s and 1970s, poor women of color were the targets of coercive and punitive sterilization efforts in federally funded birth control clinics and in state legislatures. As we saw in chapter 2, physicians who took it upon themselves to end women's childbearing capacity without their knowledge coercively sterilized black women. Minnie Lee Relf was only the most well-known case among what were most likely hundreds, if not thousands, of coerced and forced sterilizations of women of color.[10] As was also revealed in chapter 2, numerous state legislatures, including California, Connecticut, Delaware, Georgia, Illinois, Iowa, Louisiana, Maryland, Mississippi, Ohio, South Carolina, Tennessee, and Virginia, considered institutionalizing sterilization as a method to control the welfare roles with punitive sterilization legislation in the 1960s. Although none of these laws were passed, the serious consideration of legislation that would force poor women to end their childbearing permanently, after they had two children, indicates the attitude of those in power toward poor women of color who chose to become mothers.

I believe that a similar sentiment motivated state legislators to consider punitive sterilization legislation in the 1960s, physicians to involuntarily sterilize poor women of color in HEW clinics or through the federal Medicaid program in the 1960s and 1970s, and state officials to incarcerate poor pregnant women of color in the 1990s. It is the same attitude that motivated the anti-welfare campaigns of the 1980s and 1990s. There is a belief in the United States that poor women of color should not reproduce in large numbers because they and their children are considered dangerous and burdensome to society. This belief is the eugenic force behind population control—both domestic and international. It is an attitude that informs the sentiment that only a heterosexual couple who can afford to raise their children independently of the state should have children. This perspective opens up a host of questions about the relationship between groups of individuals and the state, how these relationships evolved historically, and how they should change. To answer all these questions would be to wander far beyond the scope of this conclusion. It is sufficient to say at this point that it should not be within the power of the state to decide who should reproduce and who should have their ability to reproduce terminated or constrained. This viewpoint shaped the politics of black feminist organizations like NWRO, the Black Women's Liberation Group of Mount Vernon, the Black Women's Liberation Committee, and the Third World Women's Alliance and also CARASA. All women, these reproductive rights activists argued, should be able to bear children if they want to, and the state should facilitate this choice by providing minimum economic means. That, and only that, is real reproductive freedom.

Reproductive Freedom Today: Lessons Learned

Now we need to ask if the present reproductive rights movement still makes the rights of poor women of color in relation to their fertility a central focus. I think the answer is mixed—in part, yes, in part, no.

There is a tendency among feminists, both contemporary and historical, to suggest that by defending the rights of white middle-class women to bodily integrity and sovereignty, women of color and poor women's rights will also be defended. As will be clearer by now, this logic is problematic. It has been demonstrated that both the state and reproductive providers treat poor women of color and white middle-class women differently. For instance, when white middle-class women were fighting for greater access to contraceptives, including voluntary sterilization, poor and minority women were still forced or coerced into sterilization. To counter measures directed at poor women of color with the argument that we need to protect women's bodily integrity and sovereignty, in general, does not address the specific problems encountered by poor women of color.[11]

As we learned from reproductive rights activists in groups such as CARASA and feminists of color active in the 1970s, reproductive freedom requires more than bodily integrity and sovereignty. To guarantee reproductive freedom for all women, we need to focus on the reproductive rights of the most vulnerable women in society—these are poor women and disproportionately women of color. Poor women of color require economic guarantees that they can bear healthy children in order to know that they have real choices about their reproductive bodies. Feminists fail in their ultimate goal—to ensure the rights of *all* women—if they do not make a first priority the needs of those who have the least access to reproductive freedom.[12]

On the brighter side, there is also evidence that reproductive rights activists of the twenty-first century have begun to be aware of the specific reproductive experiences of poor women of color. For example, the Ms. Foundation for Women's Reproductive Rights Coalition and Organizing Fund (RRCOF) addresses reproductive rights issues in relation to welfare reform. They have made it a goal to fund organizations committed to addressing how the 1996 Personal Responsibility and Work Opportunities Reconciliation Act has negatively impacted poor women's access to reproductive control. RRCOF is opposed to the 1996 legislation's provision of funds to states that promote "abstinence only" education and to "family cap" initiatives, which deny increased benefits to women who have additional children while on welfare. In the case of the latter initiative, the Ms. Foundation views the welfare reform legislation as a direct infringement on a poor woman's right to have children. To combat the current campaign by state legislators to limit poor women's reproductive freedom, "the Ms. Foundation hopes to foster new partnerships between economic justice/welfare rights groups and reproductive rights groups." Patricia Jerido, program officer for the Ms. Foundation for Women, has argued that her organization defines reproductive rights broadly. They believe that reproductive freedom means the right to have children as well as limit fertility. This position seems to be a direct legacy of the feminist reproductive rights movement of the 1970s.[13]

Reproductive rights activist with the Campaign for Access and Reproductive Equity (CARE) and philosophy professor, Marlene Gerber Fried, agrees that the feminist reproductive rights movement has been influenced by black feminist groups to be more conscious of the economic context that needs to exist before poor women of color can claim reproductive freedom. She also believes that the mainstream reproductive rights movement is more effective at linking issues than it was in the 1970s and the early 1980s. Fried explained, "People in mainstream organizations have a broader consciousness beyond abortion that includes contraceptive equity (pushing state health insurance providers to cover contraceptives), HIV and AIDS awareness, emergency contraception, and welfare issues." At the same time, she believes that the movement has not entirely embraced the idea that reproductive freedom encompasses the right to the economic means that would allow poor women to bear wanted children. Fried continued to explain that some of the neglect of economic "bread and butter" issues, such as access to housing, jobs, health care, and child-care as part of the reproductive rights movement, "has to do with the broadside attacks on abortion over the last twenty years. How many fronts can you fight?" she asked. She added, however, "some of it is a narrow world view—not thinking about welfare reform as population control."[14]

By contrast, women of color organizations are currently addressing reproductive freedom issues broadly at the grassroots level. For example, the organization SisterSong: Women of Color Reproductive Health Project, founded at the 1997 and 1998 Latina Roundtable on Health and Reproductive Rights meetings for women of color organizations, uses a human rights framework to address reproductive rights issues that concern women of color. They argue that their "human rights-based reproductive health agenda challenges the traditional American liberal human rights framework, by giving economic, social, and cultural rights the same consideration given to civil and political rights." By rearticulating reproductive rights and health care as human rights issues, SisterSong activists argue that they critique the American political rights–based system that ignores the fundamental importance of basic human needs for the poor such as access to quality health care and freedom from disease. Issues of concern to SisterSong revolve primarily around the pervasive incidence of reproductive tract infections (RTIs), which kill thousands of women every year and disproportionately affect women of color. Organizers argue that by addressing RTIs as they affect groups of women of color, SisterSong can work to improve general reproductive health care among women of color without limiting themselves to issues of reproductive control such as abortion or contraceptive rights.[15]

Despite these efforts, poor women, who are disproportionately women of color, are still at risk for abuse and lack basic reproductive freedoms. Some mainstream feminist organizations, like the Ms. Foundation, recognize this fact. At the same time, abortion rights take center stage for most mainstream reproductive rights organizations. The most recent reproductive rights attacks listed by Planned Parenthood include attempts by President Bush to eliminate contraceptive coverage in health plans for federal employees, proposed legislation designed to restrict RU486 (the abortion pill), proposed legislation that would make it a criminal act for anyone other than a parent to bring a teenager across state borders for an abortion, attempts to establish fetal personhood with "The Unborn Victims of Violence Act," which makes it a separate crime to cause injury or death to a fetus or an embryo, and finally, the global gag rule, which bars U.S. funding to any nongovernmental organization that provides abortion services or information on abortion. Everything on this list concerns abortion rights centrally. Nowhere is it mentioned that poor women and women of color are more vulnerable than middle-class or white women to reproductive abuses and have less access to personal reproductive control and health care.

It is time for reproductive rights feminists to take stock of the movement and whom it serves. Women's liberationists of the 1970s learned through complex alliances with women (and some men) of color that different women had very different reproductive experiences, depending on their race and economic class. These experiences often determined the extent to which women were satisfied with a movement that centered on abortion rights and a politics of "choice." Feminist organizations such as CARASA decided that the only way they could legitimately represent the reproductive needs of all women was to fight for the reproductive rights of women with the least access to reproductive freedom. In order to make "choice" a reality for all, the agenda needed to incorporate the right of poor women and women of color to choose to have children. Contemporary feminists need to ask themselves: Are we still fighting for the rights of the women with the least? If we don't fight the battle from the bottom up, we betray the best sentiments of feminism—to give all women access to the freedom to make real reproductive choices for themselves and their families without coercion.

Notes

INTRODUCTION

1. Accosta's story comes from Claudia Dreifus, "Sterilizing the Poor," *The Progressive* 39 (December 1975): 13–19.

2. Ibid., 15.

3. For more on second wave feminism see Sara Evans, *Personal Politics: The Roots of Women's Liberation in the Civil Rights Movement and the New Left* (New York: Alfred A. Knopf, 1979); Alice Echols, *Daring to Be Bad: Radical Feminism in America, 1967–1975* (Minneapolis: University of Minnesota Press, 1989); Ruth Rosen, *The World Split Open: How the Modern Women's Movement Changed America* (New York: Viking, 2000); Estelle Freedman, *No Turning Back: The History of Feminism and the Future of Women* (New York: Ballantine Books, 2002). Brownmiller, Susan. Interview by author. New York, NY. 30 September 1996.

4. Estimates of illegal abortion in the 1960s range from 200,000 to 1.3 million a year. Estimated deaths were from 5,000 to 10,000 a year. See Leslie Reagan, *When Abortion Was a Crime: Women, Medicine, and the Law in the United States, 1867–1973* (Berkeley: University of California Press, 1997), 76–79; Linda Gordon, *Woman's Body, Woman's Right: Birth Control in America* (New York: Penguin Books, revised edition, 1990), 420; Carole Joffe, "Portraits of 'Three Physicians of Conscience': Abortion before Legalization in the United States," *Journal of the History of Sexuality* 2, no.1 (1991): 46–67; Lawrence Lader, *Abortion II: Making the Revolution* (Boston: Beacon Press, 1973), 21–22; and James Mohr, *Abortion in America: The Origins and Evolution of National Policy* (Oxford: Oxford University Press, 1978), 254.

5. Willis, Ellen. Interview by Author. New York, NY. October 1, 1996.

6. Gordon, 332; Dorothy Roberts, "Punishing Drug Addicts with Babies," in *Abortion Wars: A Half Century of Struggle, 1950–2000*, edited by Rickie Solinger, 132 (Berkeley: University of California Press, 1998); Dorothy Roberts, *Killing the Black Body: Race, Reproduction, and the Meaning of Liberty* (New York: Pantheon, 1997), 76–79.

7. Philip R. Reilly, *The Surgical Solution: A History of Involuntary Sterilization in the United States* (Baltimore: Johns Hopkins University Press, 1991), 41–55; Donald T. Critchlow, *Intended Consequences: Birth Control, Abortion, and the Federal Government in Modern America* (New York: Oxford University Press, 1999), 72–81, 142–144.

8. See Jessie M. Rodrique, "The Black Community and the Birth Control Movement," in *Passion and Power: Sexuality in History*, edited by Kathy Peiss and Christina Simmons, 138–156 (Philadelphia: Temple University Press, 1989), for evidence that African-American women made conscious choices to control their fertility earlier in the twentieth century.

9. "The National Organization for Women Statement of Purpose," in *Feminism in Our Time: The Essential Writings, World War II to the Present*, edited by Miriam Schneir, 95–102 (New York: Vintage Books, 1994).

10. Reagan, 6–7, 14–15, 44–45, 109, 133.

11. Ibid., 173–179, 207–208.

12. Rickie Solinger, "'A Complete Disaster': Abortion and the Politics of Abortion Committees, 1950–1970," *Feminist Studies* 19, no.2 (1993): 241–268; Reagan, 173–174, 191, 207–212; Nanette Davis, *From Crime to Choice: The Transformation of Abortion in America* (Westport, CT: Greenwood Press, 1985), 21–22.

13. Rickie Solinger, *The Abortionist: Woman against the Law* (New York: Free Press, 1994); Reagan, 193–200; Nancy Howell Lee, *The Search for an Abortionist* (Chicago: University of Chicago Press, 1969).

14. Self-induced abortions were more dangerous than assisted ones; black women's reliance on self-induced abortions contributed to their higher morbidity during abortion. Reagan, 42–44, 137–138.

15. Reagan, 207–212.

16. Mohr, 253–254; Davis, 129–155; Reagan, 216–222.

17. Lawrence Lader, *Abortion* (New York: Bobbs-Merrill, 1966), 12, 148–149.

18. Ibid., 10–16; Eva Rubin, *Abortion, Politics, and the Courts: Roe v. Wade and Its Aftermath* (Westport, CT: Greenwood Press, 1982), 34; Marian Faux, *Roe v. Wade: The Untold Story of the Landmark Supreme Court Decision That Made Abortion Legal* (New York: New American Library, 1988), 45–50.

19. Lader, *Abortion II*, 43, 57–58.

20. Judith Hole and Ellen Levine, *Rebirth of Feminism* (New York: Quadrangle Books, 1971), 283.

21. Lader, *Abortion II*, 12, 26, 45, 93–95. NARAL was founded in 1969 by Lawrence Lader, Ruth P. Smith (former executive director of ASA), and Dr. Lonny Meyers. NARAL became the National Abortion Rights Action League in 1973.

22. Ibid., 42. Lader gave private referrals from 1965 onward, after his first book on abortion was published.

23. For more see David Garrow, *Liberty and Sexuality: The Right to Privacy and the Making of* Roe v. Wade (Berkeley: University of California Press, 1988).

24. Lader, *Abortion II*, 175.

25. Ibid., 13.

26. Reagan, 222–228.

27. Rubin, 42–43.

28. Lader, *Abortion II*, 1–3, 12–16.

29. Ibid., 170–173. In Washington State there was a popular feminist movement to change the old abortion law through referendum, which culminated in a successful bid for legal abortion in 1970.

30. James Reed, *From Private Vice to Public Virtue: The Birth Control Movement and American Society* (Princeton: Princeton University Press), 1978, 284–288, 377–381; Gordon, 391–401; Critchlow, 50–111, 145–147.

31. Ellen Willis, "Up From Radicalism: A Feminist Journal," *US Magazine* (October 1969): n.p.

CHAPTER 1

1. Brian Barrett and Lewis Grossberger, "Women Invade Abortion Hearing," *New York Newsday*, 14 February 1969.

2. Shulamith Firestone, *The Dialectic of Sex: The Case for Feminist Revolution* (New York: Morrow Quill Paperbacks, 1980).

3. Alice Echols, *Daring to Be Bad: Radical Feminism in America* (Minneapolis: University of Minnesota Press, 1989), 23–50.

4. In 1965, SNCC ejected whites from the organization, arguing that blacks needed to organize around their own oppression as leaders in the movement. This idea inspired early second wave feminists to begin organizing around women's experiences of sexism in the civil rights and New Left movements. See Sara Evans, *Personal Politics: The Roots of Women's Liberation in the Civil Rights Movement and the New Left* (New York: Alfred A. Knopf, 1979); Echols, *Daring to Be Bad*.

5. See Evans, particularly chapters 2, 3, and 4. For brief biographies of individual feminists, see Echols, 379–385.

6. For more, see Judith Hole and Ellen Levine, *Rebirth of Feminism* (New York: Quadrangle Books, 1971) and Echols, 72–82.

7. Echols, 51–103.

8. At the time Barbara Susan used her mother's name as her surname. She now goes by the name she was born with, Barbara Kaminsky.

9. Echols, 114–120; Ellen Willis, "Women and the Left," *Notes From the Second Year: Women's Liberation*, 1970, 55–56.

10. Willis, quoted in Echols, 117; Willis, 55–56.

11. Echols, 139–140

12. Willis, 55.

13. Pat Manardi, "The Politics of Housework," in *Voices From Women's Liberation* (New York: Signet, 1971), 336–341; Barbara Susan, "About My Consciousness Raising," *Woman's World* (December 1969): 1–4.

14. Echols, 144–145.

15. Willis, Ellen. Interview by author. New York, NY. 1 October 1996.

16. David J. Garrow, *Liberty and Sexuality: The Right to Privacy and the Making of* Row v. Wade (New York: Macmillan, 1998), 60–61.

17. Lucinda Cisler, "Unfinished Business: Birth Control and Women's Liberation," in *Sisterhood Is Powerful: An Anthology of the Writings of the Women's Liberation Movement*, edited by Robin Morgan, 245–288 (New York: Random House, 1970).

18. Cisler, 245–288; Leslie Reagan, "Crossing the Border for Abortions: California activists, Mexican Clinics, and the Creation of a Feminist Health Agency," *Feminist Studies* 26, no. 2 (2000): 326–352.; Ellen Willis, "Abortion: Is a Woman a Person?", in *Powers of Desire: The Politics of Sexuality*, edited by Ann Snitow, Christine Stansell, and Sharon Thompson, 471–476 (New York: Monthly Review Press, 1983).

19. The New York abortion law codified the common law to make abortion a crime after quickening or about 20 weeks. The revised statute of 1829 made the killing of any unborn fetus manslaughter, regardless of its gestational age. (N.Y. Rev. Stat. (1829), Pt. IV, ch. 1, tit. 2, & 9.) See Cyril C. Means, Jr., "The Law of New York Concerning Abortion and the Status of the Foetus, 1664–1968: A Case of Cessation of Constitutionality," *New York Law Forum* 14, no.3 (Fall 1968): 411–515.

20. Lader, *Abortion II*, 56–60. Assemblyman Anthony Beilenson had introduced a similar abortion reform bill in California in 1961.

21. Abby Goodnough, "His Last Harangue," *New York Times*, 17 June 1998, B1, B4; Lader, *Abortion II*, 129–144. In 1970, the New York State legislature passed a slightly altered version of Cook's bill by a margin of one vote, changed in favor of repeal at the last minute by Assemblyman George Michaels of Auburn, making abortion legal in New York.

22. Quoted from Edith Evans Ashbury, "Women Break Up Abortion Hearing," *New York Times*, 14 February 1969, 42. Also see Cisler, 272; Ellen Willis, "Talk of the Town: Hearing," *New Yorker* (March 1969): 30.

23. Speakers' list from "Hearing on Possible Changes in the Abortion Law," 13 February 1969, Redstockings Women's Liberation Archives for Action, Gainesville, FL.

24. Ashbury, "Women Break Up Abortion Hearing," 42.

25. Willis, "Talk of the Town: Hearing."

26. Hole and Levine, 296; Ashbury, "Women Break Up Abortion Hearing"; Barrett and Grossberger, "Women Invade Abortion Hearing."

27. See Lucinda Cisler, "Abortion Law Repeal (sort of): A Warning to Women," in *Radical Feminism*, edited by Anne Koedt, Ellen Levine, Anita Rapone, 151–64 (New York: Quadrangle Books, 1973); Willis, Ellen. Interview by author. 1 November 1992; Ellen Willis, "Up From Radicalism: A Feminist Journal"; "Congress to Unite Women: Report from the New York City Meeting of November 21, 22, 23, 1969," in Koedt et. al., 302–317.

28. Cisler, 153.

29. Willis, "Talk of the Town," 30.

30. Barrett and Grossberger.

31. Redstockings Flyer, "Who Are the Experts?—Women's Liberation Movement," 13 February 1969.

32. *The Choices We Made*, edited by Angela Bonavoglia (New York: Random House, 1991), 30.

33. Redstockings Abortion Speakout (audiotape), Washington Square Methodist Church, 21 March 1969, Redstockings Women's Liberation Archives; Irene Peslikis, "Moderator Notes for Redstockings Abortion Speakout," 21 March 1969, Redstockings Women's Liberation Archives; Hole and Levine, 296–297.

34. Redstockings Abortion Speakout (audiotape), Redstockings Women's Liberation Archives.

35. Rosalyn Baxandall, *Women and Abortion: The Body As Battleground* (Westfield, N.J.: Open Press, 1992), 3.

36. Susan Brownmiller, "Redstocking's Rap," Redstockings Women's Liberation Archives.

37. Peslikis, "Moderator Notes for Redstockings Abortion Speakout."

38. Redstockings Abortion Speakout (audiotape).

39. Brownmiller, Susan. Interview by author. New York, NY. 1 October 1996.

40. Willis, "Up from Radicalism," 5.

41. Baxandall, Rosalyn. Interview by author. New York, NY. 22 January 1996.

42. Susan Brownmiller, "Sisterhood Is Powerful," *New York Times*, 15 March 1970, 27.

43. Willis, "Up From Radicalism," 109.

44. *United States v. Vuitch*, 305 F.Supp. 1032 (DC 1969); *People v. Belous*, 71 Cal.2d 954, 458 P.2d 194, 80 Cal.Rptr. 354 (1969).

45. In the early 1970s, WHC changed its name to Health-Pac and led the women's health movement in pressing for greater female patient control over personal health care.

46. See Amy Kesselman, "Women versus Connecticut: Conducting a Statewide Hearing on Abortion," in *Abortion Wars: A Half Century of Struggle, 1950–2000*, edited by Rickie Solinger, 42–68 (Berkeley: University of California Press, 1998); *Abele v. Markle*, 342 F. Supp. 800, 801, n.4 (D. Conn. 1972).

47. Gerald B. Lefcourt, also of the Lawyers Commune, had done much of the original footwork for the case but stepped aside when it became clear that the primary strategy would be to organize on behalf of women. David Bird, "Women and Doctors Sue to Upset Abortion Laws," *New York Times*, 8 October 1969, 53.

48. "Changing the Abortion Law," *New York Times*, 10 November 1969, 10; Stearns, Nancy. Interview by author. New York, NY. 3 June 1998.

49. Nancy Stearns, "*Roe v. Wade*: Our Struggle Continues," *Berkeley Women's Law Journal* 4 (1988–1989): 1–11; Diane Schulder and Florynce Kennedy, *Abortion Rap*. New York: McGraw-Hill Book, 1971, xvi; Eva Rubin, *Abortion, Politics, and the Courts:* Roe v. Wade *and Its Aftermath* (Westport, CT: Greenwood Press, 1982); Stearns, interview, 1998; *Roe v. Wade*, 410 U.S. 113 (1973).

50. Stearns, interview, 1998; Stearns, 5.

51. Stearns, 3–4; For a detailed discussion of the development of *Doe v. Bolton* and *Roe v. Wade*, see Marian Faux, Roe v. Wade: *The Untold Story of the Landmark Supreme Court Decision That Made Abortion Legal* (New York: New American Library, 1988); David Garrow, *Liberty and Sexuality: The Right to Privacy and the Making of* Roe v. Wade (New York: Macmillan, 1994).

52. Stearns, interview, 1998; Echols, 167, 219; Mary King, *Freedom Song: A Personal Story of the 1960s Civil Rights Movement* (New York: Morrow, 1987), 175–180.

53. *Abromowicz v. Lefkowitz*, Plaintiffs' Brief, The Center for Constitutional Rights.

54. Stearns, interview, 1998; Weinfeld and Kennedy quoted in Schulder, 93; Edward Ranzal, "U.S. Court to Hear Challenge of State Abortion Laws," *New York Times*, 6 November 1969, 28; "Abortion Court Named," *New York Times*, 7 November 1969, 14.

55. Schulder, 5.

56. Schulder, 166, 172, and Plaintiffs' Brief, 3–4.

57. Schulder, 4.

58. Ibid., 97.

59. Nancy S. Erickson, "*Muller v. Oregon* Reconsidered: The Origins of a Sex-Based Doctrine of Liberty Contract," *Labor* History 30 (1989): 241.

60. John W. Johnson, *American Legal Culture, 1908–1940* (Westport, CT: Greenwood Press: 1981), 29–30.

61. Mark Tushnet, *The NAACP's Legal Strategy against Segregated Education, 1925–1950* (Chapel Hill: University of North Carolina Press, 1987). Diane

Schulder and Florynce Kennedy compare the civil rights movement and women's rights: "The 1970s for women could very well be a replay of the phase of Black people's struggle for civil rights beginning in 1954 with the school desegregation decision (*Brown vs. Board of Education*)." Schulder, 95.

62. Ibid., viii, 1–3, 12; Rubin, 31.

63. Tushnet, 118–119.

64. Schulder, 97. Thomas Ford quoted in Schulder, 100.

65. Ibid., 100.

66. Ibid., 95–102.

67. Stearns, 3; Stearns, interview, 1998.

68. This story is summarized from the deposition transcript, which appears in Schulder, 36–43. Barbara (Susan) Kaminsky. Interview by author. New York, NY. 15 May 1993. Susan wrote for RAT in 1970 after it had been taken over by the women in the organization and began to be published as *Women's LibeRATion*.

69. Schulder, 33.

70. Ibid., 38.

71. Ibid., 39.

72. Garrow, 395; Faux, 35.

73. Brett Harvey, "No More Nice Girls," in *Pleasure and Danger*, edited by Carole Vance, 204 (Boston: Routledge and Kegan Paul, 1984).

74. In 1970, Hawaii was the first state to make abortion legal under most circumstances. Both New York and Alaska reformed their abortion laws in the same year. Soon after these, Washington State legalized abortion by popular referendum. See Laurence H. Tribe, *Abortion: The Clash of Absolutes* (New York: W.W. Norton, 1990), 49.

75. Lader, *Abortion II*, 154–157.

76. Cisler, "Abortion Law Repeal (sort of)," 151–164.

77. Laura Kaplan, *The Story of Jane: The Legendary Underground Feminist Abortion Service* (New York: Pantheon Books, 1995); Pauline Bart, "Seizing the Means of Reproduction: An Illegal Feminist Abortion Collective—How and Why It Worked," in *Women, Health and Reproduction*, edited by Helen Roberts, 109–128 (London: Routledge and Kegan Paul, 1981).

78. Cisler, "Abortion Law Repeal (sort of)," 160.

79. Lader, *Abortion II*, 149–152.

80. Cisler, "Abortion Law Repeal (sort of)," 151–164.

81. Kathie Sarachild, "The Myth of Abortion Law Repeal," *Woman's World* 1, no.1 (15 April 1971): 9–10.

82. "Abortion Action," *Off Our Backs*, 11 April 1970, 13.

83. Untitled article, *RAT* (7–21 March 1970):13.

84. Echols, 145. Echols makes this argument in her assessment of the "prowoman" line.

85. Peslikis, "Moderator Notes for Redstockings Abortion Speakout."

86. Willis, "Up From Radicalism: A Feminist Journal," n.p.

87. Willis, interview, 1996. In 1972, the Supreme Court ruled in *Eisenstadt v. Baird,* 405 U.S. 438 (1972) that all individuals, married and unmarried, had a constitutional right to access to contraceptives.

88. Firestone, 142.

89. Federal Medicaid covered abortion until 1976, so even indigent women, without the means to pay for it, could choose abortion.

90. Hanisch, Carol. E-mail correspondence with author. New Paltz, NY. March 2002.

91. Author's interviews with Ellen Willis, Rosalyn Baxandall, Susan Brownmiller, and Nancy Stearns.

CHAPTER 2

1. This chapter focuses on the reproductive rights views of black women who were vocal about and often active in the women's liberation movement of the early 1970s. Most of these women supported aspects of mainstream feminism, although their agenda diverged in important ways.

2. Ross, Loretta. Interview by author. New York, NY. 1 August 2001; Loretta Ross, "African American Women and Abortion," in *Abortion Wars: A Half Century of Struggle, 1950–2000,* edited by Rickie Solinger, 161–207 (Berkeley: University of California Press, 1998).

3. See Jessie Rodrique, "The Black Community and the Birth Control Movement," in *Unequal Sisters,* edited by Ellen DuBois and Vicki Ruiz, 333–344 (New York: Routledge, 1990), for discussion of African-American support for birth control earlier in the twentieth century.

4. Barbara Omalade, "Hearts of Darkness" in *Powers of Desire,* edited by Ann Snitow, Christine Stansell, and Sharon Thomson, 350–370. (New York: Monthly Review Press, 1983). Omalade discusses some of the reasons black women felt they could not join mainstream (white) feminist efforts.

5. Mary Smith, "Birth Control and the Negro Woman." *Ebony* (March 1968): 29–36.

6. E. Frances White, "Africa On My Mind: Gender, Counter Discourse and African-American Nationalism," *Journal of Women's History,* 2, no.1 (Spring 1990): 73–97. White discusses the conservative nature of Black Nationalist views on gender relations.

7. Claybourne Carson, *In Struggle: SNCC and the Black Awakening of the 1960s* (Cambridge, MA: Harvard University Press, 1981), 96–119, 149, and 164–166.

8. Hugh Pearson, *The Shadow of the Panther* (Reading, MA: Addison-Wesley, 1994, 129–133).

9. Testimony by former Panther members suggest that the Panthers on the east coast were more accepting of female leadership and gave women combat roles in the most militant wings of the party. Silvers, Cleo. Interview by author. New York, NY. 27 October 1997. McCreary, Thomas. Interview by author. New York, NY. 14 May 1997. Also see Tracye Matthews, "'No One Ever Asks, What a Man's Place in the Revolution Is': Gender and the Politics of the Black Panther Party, 1966–1971," in *The Black Panther Party (Reconsidered)*, edited by Charles E. Jones, 267–304 (Baltimore: Black Classic Press, 1998).

10. Kay Lindsey, "Poem," in *The Black Woman*, edited by Toni Cade Bambara, 17 (New York: Signet, 1970).

11. Others in the movement had made the connection between sexism and racism. See Sara Evans in *The Personal is Political: The Roots of Women's Liberation in the Civil Rights Movement and the New Left* (New York: Alfred A. Knopf, 1979).

12. M. Rivka Polatnick, "Poor Black Sisters Decided for Themselves: A Case Study of 1960s Women's Liberation Activism," in *Sixties Women's Liberation Activism*, edited by Kim Marie Vaz, 110–130 (Thousand Oaks, CA: Sage Publications, 1995); M. Rivka Polatnick, "Diversity in Women's Liberation Ideology: How a Black and a White Group of the 1960s Viewed Motherhood," *Signs* 21, no.3 (Spring 1996): 679–706; see Ula Y. Taylor, "'Negro women are great thinkers as well as doers': Amy Jacques-Garvey and community feminism in the United States, 1924–1927," *Journal of Women's History* 12, no.2 (Summer 2000): 104–127, for a discussion of the connections between black women's feminist and community activism earlier in the twentieth century.

13. Black Women's Liberation Group, Mount Vernon, New York, "Statement on Birth Control." In *Sisterhood Is Powerful: An Anthology of Writings from the Women's Liberation Movement*, edited by Robin Morgan, 360–361 (New York: Random House, 1970).

14. Kristen Anderson-Bricker, "'Triple Jeopardy': Black Women and the Growth of Feminist Consciousness in SNCC, 1964–1975," in *Still Lifting, Still Climbing: African American Women's Contemporary Activism*, edited by Kimberly Springer, 49–69 (New York: New York University Press, 1999).

15. Ibid., 60–61.

16. "Puerto Rican Women Sterilized: An Interview with Dr. Helen Rodriguez," *Triple Jeopardy* 4, no.2 (Jan.–Feb. 1975): 3–4; Ishi Houmah, "Indian Women Sterilized," *Triple Jeopardy* (Summer 1975): 16.

17. Cellestine Ware, *Woman Power* (New York: Tower Publications, 1970), 78.

18. Linda La Rue, "The Black Movement and Women's Liberation," in *Words of Fire: An Anthology of African-American Feminist Thought*, edited by Beverly Guy-Sheftall, 164–173 (New York: The New Press, 1995).

19. Toni Cade Bambara, "The Pill: Genocide or Liberation." In Bambara, ed., 162–169.

20. Ibid, 164.

21. Ibid, 167–168.

22. Population research provides evidence that black women wanted birth control. See Donald Bogue, "Family Planning in the Negro Ghettos of Chicago," *Millbank Memorial Fund Quarterly* 48, no.2 (1970): 283–307; Joseph Goldman and Leonard Kogan, "Ghetto Poor Favor Birth Control," *Public Welfare and Family Planning* 3, no.1 (January 1971): 3; Gerald Lipson and Dianne Wolman, "Polling Americans on Birth Control and Population," *Family Planning Perspectives* 4, no.1 (January 1972): 39–42.

23. "Third World Sisters," *The Militant*, 30 July 1971, 21. The Third World Women's Workshop released a pro-abortion/anti–sterilization abuse statement at the national abortion conference and came out against punitive sterilization laws.

24. Philip R. Reilly, *The Surgical Solution: A History of Involuntary Sterilization in the United States* (Baltimore: Johns Hopkins University Press, 1991, 15); Dorothy Roberts, *Killing the Black Body: Race, Reproduction, and the Meaning of Liberty* (New York: Pantheon Books, 1997), 93.

25. Jack Slater, "Sterilization: Newest Threat to the Poor," *Ebony* (October 1973): 150; B. Drummond Ayres, "Racism, Ethics and Rights at Issue in Sterilization Case," *New York Times*, 2 July 1973, 10; B. Drummond Ayres, "Sterilizing the Poor: Exploring Motives and Methods," *New York Times, "The Week in Review"* 8 July 1973, 4; "Sterilized: Why?" *Time: The Weekly News Magazine* 102 (23 July 1973) (Laura X, Women's Liberation Archive, Women and Health, Reel #8); Henry Woodhead, "Legal Aid: Sterilization Draws Suit," *The Atlanta Constitution*, 28 June 1973.

26. *Relf v. Weinberger*, 372 F. Supp. 1196, 1199 (D.D.C. 1974), vacated, 565 F.2d 722 (D.C. Cir. 1977).

27. *National Welfare Rights Organization v. Caspar W. Weinberger*, C. A. No. 74–243, "Plaintiff's Proposed Findings of Fact and Conclusions of Law," 2–3; Thomas M. Shapiro, *Population Control Politics: Women, Sterilization, and Reproductive Choice* (Philadelphia: Temple University Press, 1985), 90–92. For more detailed background on NWRO, see Deborah White, *Too Heavy a Load: Black Women in Defense of Themselves, 1890–1980* (New York: W.W. Norton, 1998); Guida West, *The National Welfare Rights Movement: The Social Protest of Poor Women* (New York: Praeger, 1981).

28. "Sterilization: Coercing Consent," *The Nation*, 30 March 1974, 388; Reilly, 150–151.

29. Stephen Trombley, *The Right To Reproduce* (London: George Weidenfeld and Nicholson, 1988), 177. In New York, before 1970, 80 percent of abortion deaths were among black and Puerto Rican women. See Linda Gordon,

Woman's Body, Woman's Right: Birth Control in America, revised edition. New York: Penguin Books, 1990, 420. See Leslie Reagan, *When Abortion Was a Crime: Women, Medicine, and Law in the United States, 1867–1973* (Berkeley: University of California Press, 1997), 206–214.

30. Helen Rodriguez-Trias, "Women and the Health Care System: Sterilization Abuse," The Women's Center, Barnard College, 1978 (lecture given at the Women's Center Reid Lectureship, 10–11 November 1976); Rosalind Pollack Petchesky, "'Reproductive Choice' in the United States" in *And the Poor Get Children*, edited by Karen L. Michaelson, 50–88 (New York: Monthly Review Press, 1981).

31. Petchesky, "'Reproductive Choice.'"

32. Denton Vaughan and Gerald Spearer, "Ethnic Group and Welfare Status of Women Sterilized in Federally Funded Family Planning Programs, 1972," *Family Planning Perspectives* 6, no.4 (Fall 1974): 224–229.

33. Petchesky, "'Reproductive Choice.'"

34. "Genocide in Mississippi," SNCC Papers, microfilm reel 19, 3–4, Martin Luther King Jr. Library and Archives, Martin Luther King Jr. Center for Nonviolent Social Change, Atlanta; "Illegitimacy Bill," 21 May 1964, SNCC Papers, box 32; Julius Paul, "The Return of Punitive Sterilization Proposals: Current Attacks on Illegitimacy and the AFDC Program," *Law and Society Review* 3, no.1 (1968–69): 77–106.

35. Ellen Key Blunt, "Still to Overcome: She Found No Freedom," *Washington Post*, 27 January 1965, C1; Thomas B. Littlewood, *The Politics of Population Control* (Notre Dame, IN: University of Notre Dame Press, 1977), 74–75; Paul, 78, 90; Chana Kai Lee, *For Freedom's Sake: The Life of Fannie Lou Hamer* (Urbana: The University of Illinois Press, 1999), 80–81.

36. Robert G. Weisbord, *Genocide? Birth Control and the Black American* (Westport, CT: Greenwood Press, 1975) 141–146; Damschroder quoted in *Cincinnati Post and Times Star*, 25 April 1973; Littlewood, 79–80.

37. Letter to Dr. Rosenfeld from Ann Carson, Research Department of NWRO (19 December 1973); "Sterilization: Coercing Consent," *The Nation*, 30 March 1974, 388, NWRO Papers, Box 2189, Moreland Springarn Research Center, Howard University Library; Program Planning Proposal—Family Planning (Draft)—[Title X funds], Introduction (n.d., 1969?), NWRO Papers, Box 2032; Mrs. Bobby McMahan, Health Committee, National Welfare Rights Organization, Before the Subcommittee on Health, Committee on Labor and Public Welfare, U.S. Senate, Thursday, Feb. 19, 1970 [S.2108]—Family Planning and Population Act of 1969 [Senator Tydings, D-Maryland, 1969], NWRO Papers, Box 2050.

38. Doris Bland, "Tell It Like It Is," *NOW! National Welfare Leaders Newsletter (NWRO)*," 2 February 1968; Elsie Carper, "Mother's Day Parade Open's Drive By Poor," *Washington Post*, 13 May 1968, 1, 10.

39. "Welfare Women Fight Tenn. Sterilization Bill," *Southern Patriot*, April 1971, 1; "Sterilizing the poor in Tennessee," *Great Speckled Bird*, April 1971 (Laura X, Women's Liberation Archive, Women and Health Collection, Reel #11); "Sterilize welfare mothers?" *Guardian*, 10 April 1971 (Laura X, Women's Liberation Archive, Women and Health Collection, Reel #11).

40. Letter to Charles C. Edwards from the Rural Coalition of Mississippi, Jackson Mississippi, 31 August 1973, re: HEW Guidelines for Sterilization of Mentally Incompetents, NWRO Papers, Box 2189; Letter to Dr. Rosenfeld from Ann Carson, Research Department of NWRO, 19 December 1973, NWRO Papers, Box 2189.

41. Littlewood, 109; Ayres, "Sterilizing the Poor."

42. Shapiro, 90–91; Claudia Dreifus, "Sterilizing the Poor," *The Progressive* 39 (December 1975): 13–19; Bernard Rosenfeld, Sidney Wolfe, and Robert Mc-Garrah, Public Citizen Health Research Group, "Study on Surgical Sterilization: Present Abuses and Proposed Regulations," 29 October 1973.

43. Rosenfeld et al.

44. "Sterilization," *Civil Liberties Newspaper*, March 1974.

45. For more see Reilly, *The Surgical Solution*.

46. Different versions of Nial Ruth Cox's story have appeared in various sources. See Weisbord, *Genocide?*; Jack Slater, "Sterilization: Newest Threat to the Poor," *Ebony*, October 1973; and "Sterilization," *ACLU News*, September 1973 (Laura X, Women's Liberation Archive, Women and Health Collection, Reel # 11).

47. *ACLU News*, press release, 21 January 1974 (Laura X, Women's Liberation Archive, Women and Health Collection, Reel #11).

48. "3 Carolina Doctors Are Under Inquiry in Sterilization of Welfare Mothers," *New York Times*, 22 July 1973, 30; Nancy Hicks, "Sterilization of Black Mother of 3 Stirs Aiken, S.C.," *New York Times*, 1 August 1973, 27.

49. Trombley, 190–191; Littlewood, 109; "Doctor in Sterilization Dispute Barred From Medicaid Births," *New York Times*, 29 September 1973, 21.

50. Angela Davis, "Racism, Birth Control, and Reproductive Rights," in *From Abortion to Reproductive Freedom: Transforming a Movement*, edited by Marlene Gerber Fried, 15–25 (Boston: South End Press, 1990).

51. Gordon, 258–259, 281–288. Gordon argues that Margaret Sanger made alliances with eugenicists in her promotion of the American Birth Control League. In the early years of her birth control activism, however, she allied herself with members of the working class and the labor movement.

52. Miriam Stone, "Tubal Ligation: Why and Why Not," *New York Magazine*, 25 September 1972 (Laura X, Women's Liberation Archive, Women and Health Collection, Reel #8); Jane E. Brody, "More Than 100,000 Persons a Year Are Reported Seeking Sterilization as Method of Contraception," *New York Times*, 22 March 1970; "Sterilization Gains Favor As Birth Control Method,"

San Francisco Chronicle, 14 February 1971 (Laura X, Women's Liberation Archive, Women and Health Collection, Reel #8); "Those Who Choose To Be Sterilized," *San Francisco Chronicle,* 3 August 1972 (Laura X, Women's Liberation Archive, Women and Health Collection, Reel #8).

53. Letter from Mary McDermott to *Boston Female Liberation Newsletter,* 2 August 1971.

54. *Griswold v. Connecticut* made contraception legal for married couples. Privacy would be invoked again to establish a constitutional right to abortion in 1973.

55. "Mother of 3 to Fight Sterilization Ban," *New York Times,* 29 August 1971 (Laura X, Women's Liberation Archive, Women and Health Collection, Reel #8).

56. "Third World Sisters: No forced sterilization," *The Militant,* 30 July 1971, 21 (Laura X, Women's Liberation Archive, Women and Health Collection, Reel #11).

57. Reagan, 210–215; Marion K. Sanders, "The Right Not To Be Born," *Harper's Magazine* (April 1970): 92–99; Shirley Chisolm, *Unbought and Unbossed* (Boston: Houghton Mifflin Company, 1970), 113–122; Willard Cates, Jr., M.D., M.P.H., "Abortion Attitudes of Black Women," *Women & Health* 2, no.3 (November/December 1977): 3–9.

58. By 1991, black women induced 65.9 abortions per 1,000 pregnancies; Latinas induced 36.2 abortions per 1,000 pregnancies; and white women induced 17.9 abortions per 1,000 pregnancies. Rosalind Pollack Petchesky, *Abortion and Woman's Choice: The State, Sexuality, and Reproductive Freedom,* revised edition (Boston: Northeastern University Press, 1990), 156–157; Reagan, 206–214.

59. "Black Women Leaders Assail Medicaid Anti-Abortion Ban," Planned Parenthood Press Release, 20 December 1973. Planned Parenthood Federation of America Records, Sophia Smith Collection, Box 66, Smith College, Northampton, MA.

60. Chisolm, 114.

61. Ibid., 116.

62. Ibid., 114.

63. Idem.

64. Gordon, 95–116.

65. Chisolm, 122.

66. Frances Beal, "Double Jeopardy: To Be Black and Female," in *The Black Woman,* ed. Toni Cade Bambara (New York: Signet, 1970), 93–99.

67. Mary Treadwell, "Is Abortion Black Genocide?" *Family Planning* Perspectives 4, no.1 (January 1972): 4–5.

68. Beal, 97–98.

69. Ibid. In a salpingectomy, a surgeon cauterizes the fallopian tubes,

whereas a hysterectomy is the removal of the uterus. Hysterectomy is a much more invasive surgery, putting the patient at much greater risk for complications.

70. For more on black women's reproductive experiences during slavery in the antebellum American South, see Deborah White, *Ar'n't I a Woman* (New York: W.W. Norton, 1985).

71. Ross, 184–185; Smith, Barbara. Interview by author. 19 May 1995.

72. Naomi Gray, "Blacks Question Zero Population Growth as Goal," Planned Parenthood World Population Collection, n.d. (1971), Box 197, Sophia Smith Collection, Smith College.

73. Loretta Horrell, "Gray Denounces 'Black Genocide,'" *Pittsburgh News*, 31 March 1971, Planned Parenthood Federation of America, Box 107.

74. Gray, "Blacks Question Zero Population."

75. Treadwell, "Is Abortion Black Genocide?", 4.

76. Lucinda Cisler, "Unfinished Business: Birth Control and Women's Liberation," in *Sisterhood Is Powerful: An Anthology of the Writings of the Women's Liberation Movement*, edited by Robin Morgan, 245–288 (New York: Random House, 1970).

CHAPTER 3

1. "More Involuntary Sterilizations Disclosed," *The Black Panther* 10, no.9 (14 July 1973): 7.

2. Harold 4X, "Welfare Dupes Black Teenagers: Alabama sisters 'sterile for life' father suing gov't'," *Muhammad Speaks*, 13 July 1973, 4, 10; "OEO, HEW Funds Were Used—Center Brings Suit to Ban Imposed Sterilization and Medical Experimentation on Poor People," *Poverty Law Report: A Publication of the Southern Poverty Law Center* 1, no.3 (September 1973): 1, 4.

3. Gerald Lipson and Dianne Wolman, "Polling Americans on Birth Control and Population," *Family Planning Perspectives* 4, no. 1 (January 1972): 39–42; Castellano Turner and William A. Darity, "Fears of Genocide among Black Americans as Related to Age, Sex, and Region," *American Journal of Public Health* 63, no.12 (December 1973): 1029–1034; Willard Cates, Jr., M.D., M.P.H., "Abortion Attitudes of Black Women," *Women & Health* 2, no.3 (November/December 1977): 3–9; Kenyon C. Burke (Planned Parenthood–World Population Community Affairs Director), "Black Organizations and Population Policy," *Miami Times*, 11 December 1973.

4. "Birth Control. The relevant question is not, 'If you have all those babies, how will you care for them?' But 'Why can't we all get enough to care for our children?'" *The Black Panther* 4, no.9 (7 February 1970): 7.

5. Frances Ruffin, "Birth Control, A Choice: Genocide or Survival?"

Reprinted from *Essence*, September 1972, Planned Parenthood World Population, Box 9, Sophia Smith Collection, Smith College.

6. Cleaver, Kathleen. Interview by author. New York, NY. 8 October 1996. Cleaver was involved with both the Student Non-Violent Coordinating Committee and the Black Panther Party.

7. Robert G. Weisbord, *Genocide? Birth Control and the Black American* (Westport: Greenwood Press, 1975), 34–37.

8. Thomas Littlewood, *The Politics of Population Control* (Notre Dame, Indiana: University of Notre Dame Press, 1977), 118.

9. Statistics back up the Panther's position: By providing Harlem women with better contraceptive services, Harlem Hospital was able to reduce abortion deaths from 6 per year to 0 between 1962 and 1968. See Donald P. Schwartz, "The Harlem Hospital Center Experience," in *The Abortion Experience: Psychological & Medical Impact*, edited by Howard J. Osofsky and Joy D. Osofsky, 94–121 (New York: Harper and Row, 1973), 94–121.

10. Ronald Walters, "Population Control and the Black Community: Part II," *The Black Scholar*, June 1974, 29.

11. Ibid., 31.

12. Roy Innis, "Speaking Out: The Zero Population Growth Game," *Ebony*, November 1974, Planned Parenthood World Population, Box 197, Sophia Smith Collection.

13. Planned Parenthood Memorandum, re: Southern Christian Leadership Conference Workshop on Family Planning, 4 April 1966, Planned Parenthood World Population, Box 197, Sophia Smith Collection.

14. Julius Lester, "From the Other Side of the Tracks," *The Guardian*, 17 August 1968, Planned Parenthood World Population, Box 197, Sophia Smith Collection.

15. Weisbord, 42–46, 48, 88.

16. For more on population control in the United States, see Linda Gordon, *Woman's Body, Woman's Right*, revised edition (New York: Penguin, 1990); Rosalind Pollack Petchesky, *Abortion and Woman's Choice*, revised edition (Boston: Northeastern University Press, 1990).

17. Gordon, 303.

18. Paul Ehrlich, *The Population Bomb* (New York: Ballantine Books, 1969). Dr. Paul Ehrlich, Stanford University biologist and author of the controversial *The Population Bomb*, warned that world starvation could ensue without population control. He advocated the use of voluntary methods of birth control under ideal circumstances, but if these failed he recommended the use of involuntary methods too.

19. Littlewood, 9.

20. James Reed, *From Private Vice to Public Virtue* (Princeton: Princeton

University Press, 1984), 371–380; Rickie Solinger, *Wake Up Little Susie: Single Pregnancy and Race Before* Roe v. Wade (New York: Routledge, 1992), 208–209; Martha Ward, *Poor Women, Powerful Men: America's Great Experiment in Family Planning* (Boulder, CO: Westview Press, 1986), 45; Donald T. Critchlow, "Birth Control, Population Control, and Family Planning: An Overview," *Journal of Policy History* 7, no.1 (1995): 1–21; Donald T. Critchlow, *Intended Consequences: Birth Control, Abortion, and the Federal Government in Modern America* (New York: Oxford University Press, 1999).

21. Critchlow, "Birth Control, Population Control," 14–15.

22. Reed, 54–56.

23. Littlewood, 9–10.

24. Petchesky, 118–120.

25. Elijah Muhammad, "The Birth Control Death Plan: Muhammad's Prophetic Warning," *Muhammad Speaks*, 27 October 1967, 7–8. For more on the Black Muslims see C. Eric Lincoln, *The Black Muslims in America*, third edition (Grand Rapids: William B. Eerdmans, 1994), and Claude Andrew Clegg III, *An Original Man: The Life and Times of Elijah Muhammad* (New York: St. Martin's Griffin, 1997).

26. Muhammad, 7.

27. "Mr. *Muhammad Speaks*," *Muhammad Speaks*, 4 July 1959, Planned Parenthood World Population, Box 197, Sophia Smith Collection.

28. Turner and Darity, 1029–1034.

29. "Black Population, 1 Billion!" *Muhammad Speaks*, 6 October 1967, 5, 24.

30. Muhammad, "The Birth Control Death Plan," 7–8.

31. Ibid., 7.

35. Ibid.

36. Steven Trombley, *The Right to Reproduce: History of Coercive Sterilization* (London: Weinfeld & Nicolson, 1988), 219; Betsy Hartmann, *Reproductive Rights and Wrongs: The Global Politics of Population Control* (Boston: South End Press, 1995), particularly chapters 12 and 13; Nilanjana Chatterjee and Nancy E Riley, "Planning an Indian Modernity: The Gendered Politics of Fertility Control," *Signs* 26, no. 3 (Spring 2001): 812–845.

34. Muhammad, "The Birth Control Death Plan," 6–7.

35. Lonnie 2X, "Murder of the Black Unborn: Massive Birth, Sterilization Program Aimed at Reducing Black Population," *Muhammad Speaks*, 6 October 1967, 5–6.

36. Ruth Dixon-Mueller, *Population Policy & Women's Rights: Transforming Reproductive Choice* (Westport: Praeger, 1993); Hartmann, 251–254.

37. The Population Council was influential in shaping population control policy in developing nations in the 1960s. See Hartmann, 85, 251.

38. "U.S. Behind Plot for 'Birth Control' of African-Asian Population," *Muhammad Speaks,* 20 June 1969, 7.

39. Lonnie 2X, 5.

40. Charles Greenlee, "Quiet Drive for Black Genocide," *Muhammad Speaks,* 2 May 1969, 27–28, 33, 38.

41. "Negro Infant Deaths Still 90% Higher Than Whites," *Muhammad Speaks,* 29 September 1967, 6.

42. "How Poverty Kills Black Babies at Appalling Rate," *Muhammad Speaks,* 15 December 1967, 22.

43. "Nutrition Expert Surveys Pre-Natal U.S.A.: Pigs Get Better Care Than Pregnant Women," *Muhammad Speaks,* 25 April 1969, 35, 38.

44. "Poverty and Ill Health Go Hand-in-Hand, Doctor Says," *Muhammad Speaks,* 29 December 1967, 2.

45. Statistics back up the Black Muslim assertion that African Americans have consistently received inadequate health care compared to that received by white Americans. See Petchesky, 151–152; Teri Randall, "Infant Mortality Receiving Increasing Attention," *JAMA, The Journal of the American Medical Association* 263, no. 19 (16 May 1990): 2604–2605; "Black-White Disparities in Health Care," *JAMA, The Journal of the American Medical Association* 263, no.17 (2 May 1990): 2344–2347.

69. Ogun Kokanfo, "Why Blacks Must Resist Govt.'s Genocidal Birth Control Programs: Budget for Welfare Delayed: Birth Control Budget Zooms Up," *Muhammad Speaks,* 25 July 1969, 7.

47. McCreary, Thomas. Interview by author. New York, NY. 14 May 1997.

48. Ibid.

49. Historian Angela Brown argues that women were influential in the Black Panther Party, particularly after 1974. Karl Knapper, "Women and the Black Panther Party: an interview with Angela Brown," *Socialist Review* 26, no.1-2 (1996): 33–67.

50. Knapper (interview with Brown), 52–53. Brown found that there were coalitions of black and white women that formed around feminist topics. She also argues that there were some black women who left the Black Panther Party because gender issues were becoming more important to them. Other black women remained in the party but influenced its politics in a more feminist direction.

51. Hugh Pearson, *The Shadow of the Panther* (Reading: Addison-Wesley, 1994), 109–111; Knapper, 40. For more on the history of the Black Panthers, see *The Black Panther Party [Reconsidered]* , edited by Charles Jones (Baltimore: Black Classic Press, 1998).

52. Both Susan Brownmiller and Rosalind Baxandall recalled alliances made between Black Panthers and anti-war protesters (many of whom were involved

in women's liberation as well). Brownmiller, Susan. Interview by author. New York, NY. 30 September 1996; Baxandall, Rosalind. Interview by author. New York, NY. 22 January 1997.

53. Elaine Brown, *Taste of Power: A Black Woman's Story* (New York: Pantheon Books, 1992), 234–235. Newton quoted in Brown, 249; Knapper, 38, 50.

54. Brown, 357, 362–376, 401–429.

55. Ibid., 357.

56. Ibid., 362.

57. Ibid., 447–450.

58. "Birth Control. The relevant question is not, 'If you have all those babies, how will you care for them?'," 7.

59. "Health Care—Pig Style," *The Black Panther* 4, no.9 (7 February 1970): 7.

60. "NYC Passed New Abortion Law Effective July 1, 1970," *The Black Panther* 5, no.1 (4 July 1970): 2.

61. "Sterilization—Another Part of Black Genocide," *The Black Panther* 6, no.15 (8 May 1971): 2.

65. "Welfare Women Fight Tenn. Sterilization Bill," *Southern Patriot*, April 1971 (Laura X, Women's Liberation Archive, Women and Health Collection, Reel #11); "Sterilize Welfare Mothers?" *The Guardian*, 10 April 1971 (Laura X, Women's Liberation Archive, Women and Health Collection, Reel #11).

63. "Doctors Defend Sterilizations," *The Black Panther* 10, no.13 (11 August 1973): 5, 13.

64. "Puerto Rican Women's Leader Discusses Sterilization Abuse," *The Black Panther* 15, no.7 (29 May 1976): 5, 22.

65. Brown, 368.

66. "Our Health: Breast Cancer Check-Up," *The Black Panther* 12, no.20 (7 December 1974): 8.

67. "People's Free Clinic Helps Meet Community's Nutritional Needs," *The Black Panther* 12, no.17 (16 November 1974): 4, 20.

68. "Boston Abortion Witchhunt Convicts Black Doctor," *The Black Panther*, 13, no.3 (8 March 1975): 10, 24.

69. "Women's Rights Set Back By Supreme Court Rulings," *The Black Panther* 17, no.5 (16 July 1977): 14.

70. "Carter to Poor Women Seeking Abortions: Tough Luck!" *The Black Panther* 17, no.7 (30 July 1977): 9.

71. "Black Mother Victim of Decadent Welfare System," *The Black Panther* 5, no.15 (10 October 1970): 9; "Family Assistance Plan and Welfare—Racist Institutions," *The Black Panther* 6, no.7 (13 March 1971): 4; "Work or Starve: Carter Plan to Cut Millions Off Welfare," *The Black Panther* 16, no.29 (4 June 1977): 1, 6; "Milwaukee Welfare Mother Left Homeless," *The Black Panther* 16, no.29 (4 June 1977): 3, 12; "Supreme Court: Welfare Cutoffs For Not Cooperating," 16: no. 30 (11 June 1977): 5.

72. "Interview with Margaret Sloan: National Black Feminist Organization Seeks Solutions to Problems of Black Women," *The Black Panther* 14, no.3 (6 October 1975): 11, 20.

73. "Supreme Court Rulings Attack Women's Rights," *The Black Panther* 16, no.8 (1 January 1977): 7, 25.

CHAPTER 4

1. New York and Hawaii were the first states to legalize abortion in 1970.

2. Gloria Cruz (Health Captain), "Murder at Lincoln," *Palante* 2 (July 1970): 3.

3. The Young Lords' incorporation of feminism as an integral part of their party platform made them unique among nationalist organizations. Although the Black Panthers eventually accepted some feminist demands, at least rhetorically, the Nation of Islam found feminism to be antithetical to their idea of appropriate gender roles.

4. Iris Morales Luciano, "Puerto Rican Genocide," *Palante* 2 (May 1970): 8–9.

5. Background material on the Young Lords appears in the following: Iris Morales, *Palante Siempre Palante: The Young Lords Point of View*, PBS, 18 October 1996; The Young Lords Party and Michael Abramson, *Palante: Young Lords Party* (New York: McGraw-Hill, 1971); Augustin Lao, "Resources of Hope: Imagining the Young Lords and the Politics of Memory," *Centro: Journal of the Center for Puerto Rican Studies* 7 (Winter 94–95/Spring 95): 34–39; Roberto P. Rodriguez-Morazzani, "Puerto Rican Political Generations in New York: Pioneros, Young Turks and Radicals," *Centro: Journal of the Center for Puerto Rican Studies* 4 (Winter 1991–92): 96–117; Oliver, Denise. Interview by author. New York, 1 August 1999.

For more general information on the Young Lords, see: Hiram Maristany, *The Young Lords Party, 1969–1975* (New York: Visual Arts Research Center Relating to the Carribean, 1983); National Council of the Churches of Christ in the United States of America, *Young Lords Organization* (New York: 1970); *Ideology of the Young Lords Party* (New York: Young Lords Party, 1972).

6. Oliver, interview, 1999.

7. Ibid. The Young Lords Party and Abramson, *Palante*, 1–3; Lao, "Resources of Hope," 36; Morales, *Palante Siempre Palante*.

8. According to Minerva Solla, there were about 25–30 Young Lords in each of their branches—East Harlem, the founding branch, Lower East Side, Bronx, and Brooklyn. The rallies were considerably larger. The church takeover, for example, brought at least 500 people. Perez, Richie. Interview by author. New York, 23 January 1997; Jose Yglesias, "Right On With the Young Lords," *New*

York Times, 7 June 1970, 32; "2 Young Lords Accused of Harlem Arson Attempt," *New York Times*, 15 October 1970, 51; Judy Klemesrud, "Young Women Find a Place in High Command of Young Lords," *New York Times*, 11 November 1970, 52.

9. The Young Lords Party and Abramson, *Palante*, 3; Lao, "Resources of Hope," 38.

10. Silvers, Cleo. Interview by author. New York, 20 October 1997; Klemesrud, "Young Women Find a Place," 52.

11. Oliver, interview, 1999.

12. Ibid.

13. Ibid.

14. Ibid.

15. Of course, the feminist movement of the late 1960s and early 1970s was a large and diverse group of people who did not agree on any single agenda. Some radical feminists who organized in the late 1960s were concerned about the rights of minority women. A few—notably those organized into the Committee to End Sterilization Abuse (CESA) and the Committee for Abortion Rights and Against Sterilization Abuse (CARASA)—were aware of the problem of coerced sterilization among American women of color.

16. The Young Lords Party and Abramson, 52.

17. Ibid., 46–47.

18. Ibid., 50.

19. Sanabria, Angie. Interview by author. New York, 8 November 1996.

20. "Position Paper on Women," *NACLA Newsletter* 4, no. 6 (1970):14–17.

21. The Young Lords Party and Abramson, *Palante*, 50–51.

22. Ibid., 51.

23. Annette B. Ramirez de Arellano and Conrad Seipp, *Colonialism, Catholicism, and Contraception: A History of Birth Control in Puerto Rico* (Chapel Hill: University of North Carolina Press, 1983), 87–88, 159.

24. Sterilization is currently the most popular method of birth control among both men and women. The choice of sterilization is made across race and class lines. It is difficult, however, to measure the extent to which women (white or women of color) choose this method voluntarily because at this point there are no institutions in place to monitor the delivery of the procedure. Petchesky, Rosalind. Interview by author. New York, 4 December 1997.

25. de Arellano and Seipp, *Colonialism, Catholicism, and Contraception*, 16–17; Laura Briggs, "Discourses of Forced Sterilization: The Problem with the Speaking Subaltern," *Differences: A Journal of Feminist Cultural Studies* 10, no.2 (Summer 1998): 44–45.

26. de Arellano and Seipp, *Colonialism, Catholicism, and Contraception*, 19–23.

27. Briggs, "Discourses of Forced Sterilization," 40.

28. Nineteenth-century Comstock laws made any dissemination of information about birth control a felony in the United States.

29. Donald T. Critchlow, "Birth Control, Population Control, and Family Planning: An Overview," *Journal of Policy History* 7 (1995): 38; de Arellano and Seipp, *Colonialism, Catholicism, and Contraception*, 45–49; Briggs, "Discourses of Forced Sterilization," 42–43. Briggs points out that the 97 involuntary sterilizations ordered by Puerto Rico's eugenics board were relatively few compared to high sterilization states such as California or North Carolina.

30. de Arellano and Seipp, *Colonialism, Catholicism, and Contraception*, 141.

31. Betsy Hartmann, *Reproductive Rights and Wrongs: The Global Politics of Population Control* (Boston: South End Press, 1995), 190–191; de Arellano and Seipp, *Colonialism, Catholicism, and Contraception*, 139; see Briggs, "Discourses of Forced Sterilization," for convincing evidence that Puerto Rican women wanted to control their fertility. Briggs argues that Puerto Rican feminists were vehement about their demands for legal methods of birth control and sometimes advocated the use of sterilization as a contraceptive. They opposed pronatalist arguments made by Puerto Rican nationalists that all birth control equaled genocide. The Young Lords, on the other hand, identified themselves with the Puerto Rican nationalist movement and their anti-sterilization position. Women in the Young Lords complicated this position, however, by demanding access to safe and legal contraception and abortion.

32. Hartmann, *Reproductive Rights and Wrongs*, 190–191; Bonnie Mass, "Puerto Rico: A Case Study of Population Control," *Latin American Perspectives* 4 (Fall 1977): 66–81; Jay Katz, *Experimentation with Human Beings* (New York: Russell Sage Foundation, 1972), 739, 741; de Arellano and Seipp, *Colonialism, Catholicism, and Contraception*, 137–138.

33. Paul Vaughan, *The Pill on Trial* (New York: Coward–McCann, 1970), 39.

34. Elizabeth Siegel Watkins, *On the Pill: A Social History of Oral Contraceptives, 1950–1970* (Baltimore: The Johns Hopkins University Press, 1998), 32.

35. At the same time that the YLP raised the issue of genocide and reproductive coercion and abuse among women of color, feminist activists (mostly white) in the initial stages of creating a women's health movement began to speak out about the dangers of the birth control pill to all women who took it. They argued that for the entire decade of the 1960s, physicians and pharmaceutical companies kept vital information from women about the risks of the pill. These feminists (most notably those active in D.C. Women's Liberation) demanded that the Food and Drug Administration provide detailed and unbiased information about all the possible risks associated with pill usage in the form of an insert enclosed within pill packages. The correlation of the emergence of the early women's health movement and their criticism of the pill with outcries by women

of color against reproductive abuses suggests an important ideological link between white feminists and activist women of color. See Watkins, *On the Pill*, chapter 5.

36. Of course, white women also had very limited control over their fertility until the appearance of the birth control pill in 1960. *Griswold v. Connecticut*, 381 U.S. 479 (1965), the Supreme Court decision that legalized the use of birth control among married couples in all 50 states, further contributed to the broad acceptance of the use of birth control for all married women. It wasn't until 1972 that the Supreme Court—in *Eisenstadt v. Baird*, 405 U.S. 438—extended the right to contraceptive use to unmarried people.

37. de Arellano and Seipp, *Colonialism, Catholicism, and Contraception*, 26–27; Critchlow, "Birth Control, Population Control, and Family Planning," 36.

38. Gloria Colon, "Abortions," *Palante* 3 (March/April 1971): 12.

39. Morales Luciano, "Puerto Rican Genocide," 8–9.

40. Critchlow, "Birth Control, Population Control, and Family Planning," 13, 16–17, 27.

41. de Arellano and Seipp, *Colonialism, Catholicism, and Contraception*, 137.

42. Ibid.; Morales Luciano, "Puerto Rican Genocide," 8–9.

43. Iris Lopez, "Genocide for the Poor," *Palante* 5 (February 1974): 3.

44. Ibid.

45. Oliver, Denise. Interview by author. New York, 18 April 2000; Robles, Olgie. Interview by author. New York, 18 April 2000.

46. The Young Lords Party and Abramson, *Palante*, 71; "Position Paper on Women," 14–17; Cruz, "Murder at Lincoln," 3.

47. John Sibley, "Dr. Smith Is Back in Lincoln Post," *New York Times*, 2 September 1970, 75.

48. Harry Schwartz, "Hospital Target for a Test by Radicals," *New York Times*, 6 September 1970, 12.

49. Smith, Michael. Interview by author. New York, 12 July 1997.

50. "Position Paper on Women," 16.

51. "Lincoln Hospital Must Serve the People," *Palante* (September 1970): 3.

52. Willard Cates, Jr., "Legal Abortion: The Public Health Record," *Science* 215 (March 1982): 1586–1590; Petchesky, *Abortion and Woman's Choice: The State, Sexuality, and Reproductive Freedom*, revised edition (Boston: Northeastern University Press, 1990), 156–157.

53. "Position Paper on Women," 17.

54. Colon, "Abortions," 12.

55. Ibid.

56. The Young Lords Party and Abramson, *Palante*, 51.

57. Denise Oliver believed that the parallel development of feminism and the

Young Lords nationalist political ideology was essential to the adaptation of a feminist political discourse by the YLP in 1970. Oliver, interview, 1999.

58. Senator Daniel Patrick Moynihan's 1965 *Negro Family* embodied these stereotypical attitudes toward black masculinity and femininity. See Daniel Patrick Moynihan, *The Negro Family: The Case for National Action* (Washington, D.C.: United States Department of Labor, 1965).

59. There is an extensive literature on women and feminism in nationalist movements. A detailed discussion, however, lies outside the scope of this chapter. For more information see: Stephanie Urdang, *Fighting Two Colonialisms: Women in Guinea–Bissau* (New York: Monthly Review Press, 1980); Stephanie Urdang, *And Still They Dance: Women, War, and the Struggle for Change in Mozambique* (New York: Monthly Review Press, 1989); Richard Fagan, Carmen Diana Deere, Jose Luis Corragio, eds., *Transition and Development: Problems of Third World Socialism* (New York: Monthly Review Press, 1986); Andrew Parker, Mary Russo, Doris Sommer, and Patricia Yaeger, eds., *Nationalisms and Sexualities* (New York: Routledge, 1991); Barbara Laslett, Johanna Brenner, and Yesim Arat, eds., *Rethinking the Political: Gender, Resistance, and the State* (Chicago: University of Chicago Press, 1995); Caren Kaplan, Norma Alarcon, and Minoo Moallem, *Between Woman and Nation: Nationalisms, Transnational Feminisms, and the State* (Durham, NC: Duke University Press, 1999).

60. See Norma Alarcon, "The Theoretical Subject(s) of *This Bridge Called My Back* and *Anglo–American Feminism,"* in *Making Face, Making Soul/Hacienda Caras: Creative and Critical Perspectives by Women of Color*, ed. Gloria Anzuldua (San Francisco: Aunt Lute Books, 1997) for a discussion of how subjectivity is constituted across multiple discourses.

61. Radical feminists active in the movement to legalize abortion between 1969 and 1973 also occasionally linked abortion rights to sterilization abuse. Their primary focus, however, was legal abortion. Black feminists were much more outspoken about the importance of linking abortion and contraceptive rights with an end to sterilization abuse during this period. See Frances Beal, "Double Jeopardy: To Be Black and Female," in *The Black Woman*, ed. Toni Cade Bambara (New York: Signet, 1970), 97–98; Black Women's Liberation Group, Mount Vernon, New York, "Statement on Birth Control," in *Sisterhood Is Powerful: An Anthology of Writings From the Women's Liberation Movement*, ed. Robin Morgan (New York: Random House, 1970), 360–361; and "Third World Sisters," *The Militant* (July 1971): 21, for examples of black feminist positions on sterilization abuse, birth control, and legal abortion.

CHAPTER 5

1. Smith, Barbara. Interview by author. 19 May 1993.

2. The National Welfare Rights Organization (NWRO) argued that all women were just a man away from poverty. Samuel, Patricia. Interview by author. April 21, 2002.

3. CARASA, *Women Under Attack: Abortion, Sterilization Abuse, and Reproductive Freedom* (revised), edited by Sue Davis (Boston: South End Press, 1988), 21. The Hyde amendment forced poor women back into a situation much like that all women had lived with before abortion legalization in the early 1970s. The United States Supreme Court declared the Hyde Amendment constitutional in *Harris v. McRae*, 448 U.S. 297 (1980).

4. The Newsletter Committee created *CARASA NEWS*, which maintained a circulation of about 1,000.

5. Grossman, Atina. Interview by author. New York, NY. 19 September 1997.

6. Stamm, Karen. Interview by author. New York, NY. 24 August 1997; Tax, Meredith. Interview by author. New York, NY. 1 August 1994.

7. Barbara Zeluck, "Special Report: Know Your Rights—Pregnancy Disability Benefits," *CARASA NEWS* 2, no.2 (9 March 1978): 12.

8. *Women Under Attack*, 1979, 58.

9. Horvath, Theresa. Interview by author. New York, NY. 27 January 1998.

10. "Sterilization Guidelines: 22 Months on the Shelf," *Medical World News*, 9 November 1973, 53–61; Stamm, interview, 1997; "Why Sterilization Guidelines Are Needed," *CESA Notes*, 1974, 1, 10 (private collection); Rickie Solinger, *Beggars and Choosers: How the Politics of Choice Shapes Adoption, Abortion, and Welfare in the United States* (New York: Hill and Wang, 2001), 10–11.

11. Both Nancy Stearns and Karen Stamm had backgrounds in civil rights, New Left, and feminist organizations.

12. Thomas M. Shapiro, *Population Control Politics* (Philadelphia: Temple University Press, 1985), 138–139; Stamm, interview, 1997.

13. Helen Rodriguez-Trias, "Women and the Health Care System: Sterilization Abuse," The Women's Center, Barnard College, 1978 (lecture given at the Women's Center Reid Lectureship, 10–11 November 1976), 9.

14. Armstrong, Esta. Interview by author. New York, NY. 19 May 1995.

15. Shapiro, 137; "Why Sterilization Guidelines Are Needed," 1, 3; For more information on the women's health movement see Carole Weisman, *Women's Health Care: Activist Traditions and Institutional Change* (Baltimore: Johns Hopkins University Press, 1998); *Reforming Medicine: Lessons of the Last Quarter Century*, edited by Victor W. Sidel and Ruth Sidel (New York: Pantheon Books, 1984); Sheryl Burt Ruzek, *The Women's Health Movement: Femi-*

nist *Alternatives to Medical Control* (New York: Praeger, 1978); Gena Corea, *The Hidden Malpractice: How American Medicine Treats Women as Patients and Professionals*. New York: William Morrow, 1977; Ellen Frankfort, *Vaginal Politics* (New York: Quadrangle Books, 1972); Barbara and John Ehrenreich, *The American Health Empire: Power, Profits, and Politics* (New York: Random House, 1970).

16. Elissa Krauss, "Hospital Survey on Sterilization Policies," Reproductive Freedom Project, ACLU, 1975; Public Citizen's Health Research Group, "Study on Surgical Sterilization: Present Abuses and Proposed Regulations," 29 October 1973; "Why Sterilization Guidelines Are Needed," 3.

17. Rodriguez-Trias, 20; Shapiro, 146–148, 161–165.

18. Rodriguez-Trias, 21–22; Letter from Esta Armstrong to the Sterilization Advisory Committee, 19 April 1974, private collection; Letter from Norman Herzig, M.D., Director of Obstetrics and Gynecology, to Esta Armstrong, 31 July 1975, private collection; Letter from Myron Gordon, M.D. and Vincent Tricomi, M.D. to Lowell Bellin, M.D., Chairman and Board of Directors/Health and Hospitals Corporation of the City of New York, 30 April 1975 (private collection); Shapiro, 146–148, 161–165.

19. Shapiro, 146–148, 161–165.

20. Ibid.; Rodriguez–Triaz, Epilogue.

21. Anne Teicher, "Legislative Report: Sterilization Bill," *CARASA NEWS*, 2, no.2 (9 March 1978): 13.

22. Petchesky, Rosalind. Interview by author. New York, NY. 4 December 1997.

23. Meredith Tax, "CARASA's Steering Committee: What It Does, How It Works," *CARASA NEWS* 2, no. 2 (7 December 1978): 4.

24. Stamm, interview, 1997.

26. "National Committee Report," *CARASA NEWS*, 2, no.6 (1 July 1978): 10.

26. Willis, Ellen. Interview by author. New York. 1 October 1996.

27. Rosalyn Baxandall, Interview by author. New York, N4, 1997.

28. Horvath, interview, 1998.

29. Ibid.

30. *CARASA NEWS* 2, no.2 (9 March 1978): 12.

31. "CARASA Principles of Unity," *CARASA NEWS* 3, no.1 (1 February 1979): 28–29.

32. Karen Stamm, "Strategies for Reproductive Rights," *CARASA NEWS* 6, no.2 (March 1982): 8.

33. Ibid.; "Learning from the Past," *CARASA NEWS* 2, no.7 (3 August 1978): 1, 4.

34. "Learning from the Past," 9–10.

35. *Women Under Attack*, 1979, 21.

36. *McRae v. Califano*, 491 F. Supp. 630, 690–702 (E.D.N.Y. 1980). The lawsuit became *Harris v. McRae* in an appeal to the United States Supreme Court.

37. *CARASA NEWS* 2, no.2 (9 March 1978): 2.

38. Ibid., 3.

39. Rhonda Copelon, "*McRae vs. Califano*: 'Hyde' Hides Church–State Issue," *CARASA NEWS* 2, no.5 (1 June 1978): 2.

40. "Learning From the Past," 9–10.

41. "CARASA Principles of Unity (Proposed)," *CARASA NEWS* 2, no.5 (1 June 1978): 20–21.

42. Meredith Tax, "Abortion Rights Action Week," *CARASA NEWS* 3, no.6 (July–August 1979): 4–5; *Women Under Attack*, 1988, 56; CARASA Abortion Rights Action Week flyer, Boston Women's Health Book Collective Archive, Abortion: Pro–Choice Campaigns file.

43. "A Call To Action," *CARASA NEWS* 3, no.7 (September 1979): 1; Tax, "Abortion Rights Action Week," 5.

44. Rhonda Copelon, "The Truth About HLA," *CARASA NEWS* 3, no.8 (October 1979): 16.

45. "Women Are Not Criminals for Defending Their Rights," *CARASA NEWS* 5, no.9 (November 1981): 4–5.

46. Ibid.; Stamm, interview, 1997.

47. "Women Are Not Criminals," 4–5.

48. CARASA announcement for "March 31 International Day of Action—A Woman's Right to Safe Contraception and Abortion—No Forced Sterilization" (pamphlet, early 1979), private collection.

49. "CARASA Principles of Unity," 28–29.

50. "Learning From the Past," 9–10.

51. Petchesky, interview, 1997. In 1979, the Public Citizen's Health Research Group conducted a second study on compliance with the federal HEW regulations. They discovered "failure to obtain fully voluntary and informed consent from poor young women considering sterilization. . . . The 100,000 persons who receive Medicaid sterilizations each year continue to be subject to physicians and hospitals which are ignorant of or insensitive to the most basic requirements for informed and voluntary consent." Public Citizen's Health Research Group, 1.

52. Meredith Tax, "CARASA's Steering Committee".

53. Karen Stamm, "News," *CARASA NEWS* 2, no.11 (7 December 1978): 7.

54. Karen Stamm, "City Releases Sterilization Data," *CARASA NEWS* 2, no.11 (7 December 1978): 11.

55. Ann Teicher, "Eugenics Law vs. Right of Informed Consent," *CARASA NEWS* 2, no.11 (7 December 1978): 11.

56. For more on corporate regulation of women's reproduction, see Cynthia Daniels, *At Women's Expense: State Power and the Politics of Fetal Rights* (Cambridge: Harvard University Press, 1993); Alice Kessler-Harris, *Out to Work: A History of Wage–Earning Women in the United States* (New York: Oxford University Press, 1982), chapter 7, and "The Debate over Equality for Women in the Work Place: Recognizing Differences," *Women and Work: Annual Review* 1 (1985): 141–61; Lise Vogel, "Debating Difference: Feminism, Pregnancy, and the Workplace," *Feminist Studies* 16, no.1 (Spring 1990): 9–32.

57. Feminists and labor unions were embroiled in more than a half–century of debate over the relative benefits of protective labor legislation for women. See Kessler-Harris, chapter 7.

58. Fran Sugarman, "Jobs or Children: A Choice?" *CARASA NEWS* 3, no.2 (22 March 1979): 13.

59. Daniels, 63–64.

61. Netsy Firestein quoted in Sugarman, 13.

62. Fran Sugarman and Ruthann Evanoff, "Reproductive Hazards of Your Job," *CARASA NEWS* 3, no.4 (June 1979): 1, 3.

62. "Resolution on Reproductive Rights" *CARASA NEWS* 3, no.8 (October 1979): 9.

63. Sugarman and Evanoff, 3.

64. Barbara Omolade has continued to be active in black feminist politics and as an intellectual.

65. "Women's Rights in the Workplace and the Home: A Conference," 20 November 1982, Rayna Rapp Collection, Box 2, Folder 28, Wisconsin Historical Society; Sean MacDonald, vice president, Local 2054, "Forum Explores Rights of Women," *Public Employee Press* 9 (10 December 1982), Rayna Rapp Collection, Box 2, Folder 37.

66. Petchesky, interview, 1997.

67. Beth Bush Greenstein, "Child Care and the Right to Choose," CARASA NEWS 5, no.3 (April 1981): 5, 7.

68. Ibid.

69. Greenstein, 5; Sara Evans, *Born For Liberty: A History of Women in America* (New York: The Free Press, 1989), 301–304.

70. Greenstein, 7.

71. Ibid.

72. Beth Bush Greenstein, "Child Care Conference," *CARASA NEWS* 4, no.4 (May 1980): 12–13, 20.

73. CARASA announcement for "March 31 International Day of Action—A Woman's Right to Safe Contraception and Abortion—No Forced Sterilization."

74. Beth Bush Greenstein, "Raising Children: Continuing the Struggle," *CARASA NEWS* 4, no.10 (December 1980): 14.

75. Horvath, interview, 1998.

76. "Upper West Side," *CARASA NEWS* 2, no.12/3, no.1 (1 February 1979): 39; Horvath, interview, 1998.

77. Horvath, interview, 1998.

78. "Westside Community Outreach," *CARASA NEWS* 2, no.8 (7 September 1978): 18.

79. Sally Avery Bermanzohn, "Support for Medgar Evers in Women's Movement," *CARASA NEWS* 7, no.1 (January-February 1983): 8, 20.

80. Ibid.

81. "CARASA Action in Review," *CARASA NEWS* n.d. (Spring? 1980): 3–6, 18.

82. Helen Wood, "Sterilization Abuse," *CARASA NEWS* 4, no.9 (November 1980): 6–7.

83. Horvath, interview, 1998. Petchesky, interview, 1997.

84. Jill Benderly, "Report on the R2N2 Conference," *CARASA NEWS* 6, no.5 (June 1982): 7–9.

85. Ibid, 9.

86. Sally Avery Bermanzohn, "Speaking Out," *CARASA NEWS* 6, no.6 (July 1982): 22–23.

87. Stamm, interview, 1997.

88. Horvath, interview, 1998.

89. See Alice Echols, *Daring To Be Bad*, (Minneapolis: University of Minnesota Press, 1989), chapter 5, and Ruth Rosen, *The World Split Open: How the Modern Women's Movement Changed America* (New York: Viking, 2000), 164–175.

90. Janet Price, "Lesbian Rights and Reproductive Rights," *CARASA NEWS* 6, no.6 (July 1982): 6–7, 30.

91. "March 31 International Day of Action—A Woman's Right to Safe Contraception and Abortion—No Forced Sterilization."

92. "CARASA Speaks at Gay Rights Hearings," *CARASA NEWS* 2, no.11 (7 December 1978): 5–6.

93. Alison Colbert, "An Open Letter to CARASA," *CARASA NEWS* 4, no.1 (January 1980): 20.

94. Stamm, interview, 1997.

95. Stephanie Roth, "Lesbianism and the Politics of Women's Sexuality," *CARASA NEWS* 4, no.9 (November 1980): 11.

96. "Letters to CARASA," *CARASA NEWS* 6, no.4 (May 1982): 12–14.

97. "Letters to CARASA," *CARASA NEWS* 6, no.5 (June 1982): 18.

98. Stamm, interview, 1997.

99. Grossman, interview, 1997.

100. Petchesky, interview, 1997.

CONCLUSION

1. Robert Ourlian, "Woman Offers Payment if Addicts Get Sterilization," *Los Angeles Times*, 24 October 1997, A3; Lynn Smith, "The $200 Question; Concerned About Drug Babies, an Orange County Group is Offering Moms Cash if They Opt for Contraception or Even Sterilization. But is Such an Approach Moral? Critics Ask," *Los Angeles Times*, 3 April 1998, E1; Suzanne Herel, "Who Pays Addicts Not to Conceive Is Welcomed; 366 have been sterilized or given birth control," *San Francisco Chronicle*, 1 February 2001, A13; Mary A. Mitchell, "Sterilization plan beats alternative, activist says," *Chicago Sun–Times*, 1 August 1999, 16; Tatsha Robertson, "3 N.H. addicts give up fertility; Pick controversial program offering $200," *Boston Globe*, 28 August 1999, B1.

2. Smith.

3. Ibid.

4. Ibid.

5. For a discussion of coercion and choice, see Rosalind Petchesky, "Reproductive Choice in the Contemporary United States: A Social Analysis of Female Sterilization," in *And the Poor Get Children: Radical Perspectives on Population Dynamics*, edited by Karen L. Michaelson, 50–88 (New York: Monthly Review Press, 1981); Rashmi Luthra, "Toward a Reconceptualization of 'Choice': Challenges by Women at the Margins," *Feminist Issues* 13, no.1 (Spring 93): 41–55; Rickie Solinger, *Beggars and Choosers: How the Politics of Choice Shapes Adoption, Abortion, and Welfare in the United States* (New York: Hill and Wang, 2001).

6. Dorothy Roberts, "Punishing Drug Addicts with Babies: Women of Color, Equality, and the Right of Privacy," in *Abortion Wars: A Half Century of Struggle, 1950–2000*, edited by Rickie Solinger, 127–129 (Berkeley: University of California Press, 1998); Dorothy Roberts, "Symposium: Representing Race: Unshackling Black Motherhood," *Michigan Law Review* 95, no.4 (February 1997): 938–965; Dorothy Roberts, "Creating and Solving the Problem of Drug Use during Pregnancy," *Journal of Criminal Law & Criminology* 90, no.4 (Summer 2000): 1353–1371. The South Carolina Supreme Court decision that upheld prosecution for fetal abuse opens the door for further prosecutions in South Carolina and other states.

7. Roberts, "Punishing Drug Addicts with Babies," 135–136; Lawrence O. Gostin, "The Rights of Pregnant Women: The Supreme Court and Drug Testing," *The Hastings Center Report* 31, no.5 (Sept./Oct. 2001): 8–9.

8. Roberts, "Unshackling Black Motherhood," 946–948; Roberts, "Creating and Solving the Problem of Drug Use during Pregnancy," 1364; Roberts, "Punishing Drug Addicts with Babies," 132; Ira J. Chasnoff, Harvey J. Landress, and Mark E. Barrett, "The Prevalence of Illicit–Drug or Alcohol Use during Preg-

nancy and Discrepancies in Mandatory Reporting in Pinellas County, Florida," *New England Journal of Medicine* 322 (1990): 1202–1206.

9. Roberts, "Unshackling Black Motherhood," 953

10. It is impossible to estimate the exact number of coerced and forced sterilizations that occurred in this era. The vast majority of involuntary sterilizations went unreported. Many women were far too ashamed that they could no longer become pregnant to come forward about their sterilizations. Many other women did not know that anything could be done.

11. Roberts, "Creating and Solving the Problem of Drug Use during Pregnancy," 1365–1369.

12. Mary Ann Jimenez, "A Feminist Analysis of Welfare Reform: The Personal Responsibility Act of 1996," *Journal of Women & Social Work* 14, no.3 (Fall 1999): 278–294.

13. Ms. Foundation for Women's Reproductive Rights Coalition and Organizing Fund, REQUEST FOR PROPOSALS FOR (1) Reproductive Rights AND (2) Reproductive Rights & Welfare Reform, 2001, 1–2, 5; Jerido, Patricia. Interview by author. New York, NY. 25 June 2002.

14. Fried, Marlene Gerber. Interview by author. New York, NY. 26 June 2002. "Family caps" deny increased funds for additional children born to women receiving welfare. Both pro–choice and anti–choice activists oppose "family caps" because there is evidence that they cause an increase in abortion among poor women in states that have imposed them.

15. Loretta J. Ross, Sarah L. Brownlee, Dazon Dixon Diallo, Luz Rodriquez, and SisterSong Women of Color Reproductive Health Project, "Just Choices: Women of Color, Reproductive Health and Human Rights," in *Policing the National Body: Race, Gender, and Criminalization*, edited by Jael Silliman and Anannya Bhattacharjee, 147–174 (Cambridge: South End Press, 2002).

Index

About the Author

Jennifer Nelson is Director of the Sarah Isom Center for Women at the University of Mississippi. She completed her Ph.D. in U.S. and women's history at Rutgers University in 1999. Her undergraduate degree in semiotics is from Brown University.